## *The Writing Process*

1. Name the system scope and boundaries.
   *Track changes to this initial context diagram with th*

2. Brainstorm and list the primary actors.
   *Find every human and non-human primary actor, over the life of the system.*

3. Brainstorm and exhaustively list user goals for the system.
   *The initial Actor-Goal List is now available.*

4. Capture the outermost summary use cases to see who really cares.
   *Check for an outermost use case for each primary actor.*

5. Reconsider and revise the summary use cases. Add, subtract, or merge goals.
   *Double-check for time-based triggers and other events at the system boundary.*

6. Select one use case to expand.
   *Consider writing a narrative to learn the material.*

7. Capture stakeholders and interests, preconditions and guarantees.
   *The system will ensure the preconditions and guarantee the interests.*

8. Write the main success scenario (MSS).
   *Use 3 to 9 steps to meet all interests and guarantees.*

9. Brainstorm and exhaustively list the extension conditions.
   *Include all that the system can detect and must handle.*

10. Write the extension-handling steps.
    *Each will end back in the MSS, at a separate success exit, or in failure.*

11. Extract complex flows to sub use cases; merge trivial sub use cases.
    *Extracting a sub use case is easy, but it adds cost to the project.*

12. Readjust the set: add, subtract, merge, as needed.
    *Check for readability, completeness, and meeting stakeholders' interests.*

# The Agile Software Development Series

Alistair Cockburn and Jim Highsmith, Series Editors

Agile software development centers on four values identified in the Agile Alliance's Manifesto:

- Individuals and interactions over processes and tools

- Working software over comprehensive documentation

- Customer collaboration over contract negotiation

- Responding to change over following a plan

The development of Agile software requires innovation and responsiveness, based on generating and sharing knowledge within a development team and with the customer. Agile software developers draw on the strengths of customers, users, and developers, finding just enough process to balance quality and agility.

The books in The Agile Software Development Series focus on sharing the experiences of such Agile developers. Individual books address individual techniques (such as Use Cases), group techniques (such as collaborative decision making), and proven solutions to different problems from a variety of organizational cultures. The result is a core of Agile best practices that will enrich your experience and improve your work.

**Titles in the Series:**

Alistair Cockburn, *Surviving Object-Oriented Projects*, ISBN 0-201-49834-0

Alistair Cockburn, *Writing Effective Use Cases*, ISBN 0-201-70225-8

Lars Mathiassen, Jan Pries-Heje, and Ojelanki Ngwenyama, *Improving Software Organizations: From Principles to Practice*, ISBN 0-201-75820-2

Alistair Cockburn, *Agile Software Development*, ISBN 0-201-69969-9

Jim Highsmith, *Agile Software Development Ecosystems*, ISBN 0-201-76043-6

Steve Adolph, Paul Bramble, Alistair Cockburn, and Andy Pols, *Patterns for Effective Use Cases*, ISBN 0-201-72184-8

Anne Mette Jonassen Hass, *Configuration Management Principles and Practice*, ISBN 0-321-11766-2

DSDM Consortium and Jennifer Stapleton, *DSDM, Second Edition: Business Focused Development*, ISBN 0-321-11224-5

Mary Poppendieck and Tom Poppendieck, *Lean Software Development: An Agile Toolkit*, ISBN 0-321-15078-3

Craig Larman, *Agile and Iterative Development: A Manager's Guide*, ISBN 0-131-11155-8

Jim Highsmith, *Agile Project Management: Creating Innovative Products*, ISBN 0-321-21977-5

For more information visit www.awprofessional.com/series/agile

# Writing Effective Use Cases

## Custom Edition for ASPE Technology

Taken from:
*Writing Effective Use Cases*
by Alistair Cockburn

Teaching Individuals to Achieve...
Helping Companies Succeed

ISBN 0-536-25876-7

2006160407

SB

Please visit our web site at *www.pearsoncustom.com*

PEARSON CUSTOM PUBLISHING
75 Arlington Street, Suite 300, Boston, MA 02116
A Pearson Education Company

# Contents

## *Part 2*  *Frequently Discussed Topics*  **139**

## **Part 3**  *Reminders for the Busy*                          **203**

# *Appendices*

## *Appendix C*   *Glossary*     **253**

## *Appendix D*   *Readings*     **257**

## *Index*     **259**

*Thank You for Your Purchase!*

Welcome to American Society of Professional Education (ASPE) training! ASPE is a dynamic organization that is committed to the ongoing education of technology professionals. It is our goal to ensure that your experience with us has been enjoyable, engaging, educational and unique, so we ask that you provide your feedback on the course evaluation form provided to you. We are always seeking course feedback and new topic ideas, so tell us what courses you would like to see in your area.

ASPE is committed to assisting you in not only meeting your training goals, but exceeding them. We make every effort to ensure that you have educational options available to you that will complement your individual learning style and accommodate your busy schedule. If you are unable to attend one of our training programs, you can contact our office and discuss our flexible onsite training options for your organization or team.

Thank you again and enjoy the course!

Kindest Regards,

David Mantica
President

# About ASPE Technology

ASPE Technology is an IT training firm dedicated to providing tools, techniques, skills, and knowledge that enable professionals to successfully harness IT and transform it from a complex challenge into a strategic resource. From software development and testing training to unique project management issues, business analysis, and requirements development, ASPE Technology has the training solutions you need on today's critical topics. We maintain a full US public course schedule as well as a highly regarded customized on-site training practice.

## The methodology we use to integrate our customers' IT processes and business goals

Often, the most frequent organizational skills gaps are found within a company's software development life cycle (SDLC). Crippling disconnects are common between the technical and business sides of an organization's operations. ASPE Technology is building the "Skills Bridge" which allows organizations to cross the chasm between IT and Business. Only after these vital areas have been brought into a cooperative relationship with each other can your organization truly harness IT for business success. Using real-world training, ASPE Technology can help you implement tools, techniques, skills, and knowledge which will allow your organization to function at its maximum potential.

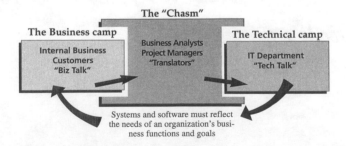

**Toll free: 877-800-5221**                     **www.aspetech.com**

# ASPE Technology provides "Need-to-Know" training.

**Why you should choose ASPE Technology**

ASPE is a multi-faceted training provider. We offer you a top-quality educational experience! What distinguishes ASPE from other training companies?

**1. Topical, Relevant Course Subjects** — Our multi-disciplined curricula bring years of research and development expertise to every training program we create. Known for our integrated solutions, ASPE provides in-depth training on …

**2. State-of-the-Art Material** — Our product managers, research staff and faculty continually update the content of every ASPE course. Built on a foundation of established practices, every ASPE course contains information on the latest research, practices and procedures.

**3. Thought-Leader Instructors** — All of our faculty members and instructors are recognized industry leaders with hands-on, real-world experience. We combine our proven adult educational training methods with leading edge industry expertise and practices to provide you with the best training experience possible.

**4. Maximum Flexibility for YOU** — To ensure that you are able to train when you want and how you want (allowing for maximum flexibility in your schedule) ASPE is able to offer a number of training options to match your specific educational needs. We offer self-paced learning, nationwide instructor-led training sessions, and customized onsite-training opportunities.

**5. 100% Satisfaction Guarantee** — Every ASPE course carries our 100% quality and satisfaction guarantee.

# How to get more information:

**1. Explore our website** — View our website www.aspetech.com for the latest course schedules and outlines or to request a brochure.

**2. Join our Mailing List** — To ensure that you are always in the know regarding the latest hot topics in your field, join our mailing list or enroll in our special offers program and we'll contact you periodically to share the latest trends and articles of interest along with the current course schedule. You may enroll by phone or web.

**Call us** — You can phone ASPE's friendly and knowledgeable customer service team toll free at: (877) 800-5221.

# You get free tools when you visit our website!

It's ASPE Technology's goal to provide our customers with tools, resources, and "toys" that make it easier to be a technology professional. It's fundamental: the world of technology continues to get more complex, from planning and design to administration and operations. It's the nature of technology itself. But that complexity breeds opportunities as well as challenges, and that's one of the pillars of our business. Visit www.aspetech.com to receive:

- *Free tools*
- *Reference material*
- *Useful templates*
- *Case documentation*

**Toll free: 877-800-5221**                    **www.aspetech.com**

# Private On-Site Training

An on-site allows you to address your issues head-on. You receive the benefit of working with confidentiality on project areas of immediate concern. Your training solution will meet your specific business needs, deal with your most pressing problems, and map to your operational procedures. On-site pricing starts at 8 students. **We offer the following classes as onsite training for your organization:**

### Business Analysis Curriculum:

- Business Analyst Fundamentals (PMI-approved for 13.5 PDUs)
- Developing & Confirming Effective Business Requirements (PMI-approved for 13 PDUs)
- Developing Requirements with Use Cases (PMI-approved for 13.5 PDUs)
- Planning and Facilitating Requirements Workshops (PMI-Approved for 13 PDUs)
- Business Process Analysis & Design (PMI-Approved for 14 PDUs)
- Business process Modeling (PMI-approved for 14 PDUs)
- Defining Business Systems with UML

### Software Testing and Quality Assurance Curriculum:

- Software Testing & Quality Assurance Techniques (PMI-approved for 14 PDUs)
- Mastering Test Plan Development & Design (PMI-approved for 13 PDUs)
- Web Application Testing
- Automated Software Testing
- Verification and Validation for Product Assurance
- Hands-On Software Security Testing Fundamentals

### Application Development Methodologies Curriculum

- Hands-on Fundamentals of Secure Coding
- Software Project Management (PMI-approved for 13 PDUs)

### Project Management Curriculum

- Developing & Implementing IT Project Management Techniques (PMI-approved for 13 PDUs)
- Hands-On IT Project Management (PMI-approved for 13.5 PDUs)
- Software project management (PMI-approved for 13.5 PDUs)
- Planning for & Managing Outsourced Service Providers (PMI-approved for 13 PDUs)
- Soliciting, Negotiating & Managing Outsourced Projects
- Deploying Enterprise Software Solutions
- Advanced Project Management Techniques
- The Project Management Professional (PMP) Boot Camp (PMI-approved for 35 PDUs)

### Professional Skills Curriculum

- Effective Meeting Design and Facilitation
- The project, Business & Management Professional's Toolkit

### Security Curriculum

- Voice over IP security (2-day training)
- Hands-on Wireless Network Defense
- Hands-on Network Security Administration
- Hands-On Fundamentals of Secure Coding
- Hands-On Software Security Testing Fundamentals
- Assessing IT Infrastructure Vulnerabilities
- Hands-on Patch Management
- Deploying Instant Messaging & Collaboration in the Enterprise
- Certified HIPAA Security Professional (CHSP)

### Telephony and Network Convergence Curriculum

- Hands-On Internetworking with SIP in Converged Networks
- Converging Voice & Data Networks
- Telecommunication Fundamentals
- Integrating IP Telephony in the Enterprise Networking Curriculum
- Hands-on WiFi Tuning & Troubleshooting
- Plan, Design, and Secure WiMAX Networks
- Hands-On MPLS (3-day workshop)
- Hands-on Networking Fundamentals
- Building & Managing a LAN
- Deploying Instant Messaging & Collaboration in the Enterprises
- Harnessing IT for Business Success
- Cisco Authorized Training (various courses)

### Operating System Curriculum

- Mainstream Linux: the "How to" Linux Bootcamp
- Hands-on Unix, Level 1: Fundamentals for Power Users
- Windows Server 2003

---

# *Preface*

More and more people are writing use cases, for behavioral requirements, for software systems or to describe business processes. It all seems easy enough—just write about using the system. But, faced with writing, one suddenly confronts the question, "Exactly what am I supposed to write—how much, how little, what details?" That turns out to be a difficult question to answer. The problem is that writing use cases is fundamentally an exercise in writing prose essays, with all the difficulties in articulating *good* that comes with prose writing in general. It is hard enough to say what a good use case looks like, but we really want to know something harder: how to write them so they will come out being good.

These pages contain the guidelines I use in my use case writing and in coaching: how a person might think, what he or she might observe, to end up with a better use case and use case set.

I include examples of good and bad use cases, plausible ways of writing differently, and, best of all, the good news that a use case need not be the *best* to be *useful*. Even mediocre use cases are useful, more so than are many of the competing requirements files being written. So relax, write something readable, and you will have done your organization a service.

## *Audience*

This book is predominantly aimed at industry professionals who read and study alone, and is therefore organized as a self-study guide. It contains introductory through advanced material: concepts, examples, reminders, and exercises (some with answers, some without).

Writing coaches should find suitable explanations and samples to show their teams. Course designers should be able to build course material around the book, issuing reading assignments as needed. (However, as I include answers to many exercises, they will have to construct their own exam material. :-) )

## Organization

The book is organized as a general introduction to use cases followed by a close description of the use case body parts, frequently asked questions, reminders for the busy, and end notes.

The **Introduction** contains an initial presentation of key notions, to get the discussion rolling: "What does a use case look like?," "When do I write one?," and "What variations are legal?" The brief answer is that they look different depending on when, where, with whom, and why you are writing them. That discussion begins in this early chapter, and continues throughout the book

**Part 1, The Use Case Body Parts,** contains chapters for each of the major concepts that need to mastered, and parts of the template that should be written. These include "The Use Case as a Contract for Behavior," "Scope," "Stakeholders and Actors," "Three Named Goal Levels," "Preconditions, Triggers, and Guarantees," "Scenarios and Steps," "Extensions," "Technology and Data Variations," "Linking Use Cases," and "Use Case Formats."

**Part 2, Frequently Discussed Topics,** addresses particular topics that come up repeatedly: "When Are We Done?," "Scaling Up to Many Use Cases," "CRUD and Parameterized Use Cases," "Business Process Modeling," "The Missing Requirements," "Use Cases in the Overall Process," "Use Case Briefs and eXtreme Programming," and "Mistakes Fixed."

**Part 3, Reminders for the Busy,** contains a set of reminders for those who have finished reading the book, or already know this material and want to refer back to key ideas. The chapters are organized as "Reminders for Each Use Case," "Reminders for the Use Case Set," and "Reminders for Working on the Use Cases."

There are four appendices: Appendix A discusses "Use Cases in UML" and Appendix B contains "Answers to (Some) Exercises." The book concludes with Appendix C, Glossary; and a list of materials used while writing, Appendix D, Readings.

## Heritage of the Ideas

In the late 1960s, Ivar Jacobson invented what later became known as use cases while working on telephony systems at Ericsson. In the late 1980s, he introduced them to the object-oriented programming community, where they were recognized as filling a significant gap in the requirements process. I took Jacobson's course in the early 1990s. While neither he nor his team used my phrases *goal* and *goal failure*, it eventually became clear to me that they had been using these notions. In several comparisons, he and I have found no significant contradictions between his and my models. I have slowly extended his model to accommodate recent insights.

I constructed the Actors and Goals conceptual model in 1994 while writing use case guides for the IBM Consulting Group. It explained away much of the mystery of use cases and provided guidance as to how to structure and write them. The Actors and Goals model has circulated informally since 1995 at *http://members.aol.com/ acockburn* and later at *www.usecases.org*, and finally appeared in the *Journal of Object-Oriented Programming* in 1997, in an article I authored entitled "Structuring Use Cases with Goals."

From 1994 to 1999, the ideas stayed stable, even though there were a few loose ends in the theory. Finally, while teaching and coaching, I saw why people were having such a hard time with such a simple idea (never mind that I made many of the same mistakes in my first tries!). These insights, plus a few objections to the Actors and Goals model, led to the explanations in this book and to the Stakeholders and Interests model, which is a new idea presented here.

The Unified Modeling Language (UML) has had little impact on these ideas—and vice versa. Gunnar Overgaard, a former colleague of Jacobson's, wrote most of the UML use case material and kept Jacobson's heritage. However, the UML standards group has a strong drawing-tools influence, with the effect that the textual nature of use cases has been lost in the standard. Gunnar Overgaard and Ivar Jacobson discussed my ideas and assured me that most of what I have to say about a use case fits *within* one of the UML ellipses, and hence neither affects nor is affected by what the UML standard has to say. That means that you can use the ideas in this book quite compatibly with the UML 1.3 use case standard. On the other hand, if you only read the UML standard, which does not discuss the content or writing of a use case, you will not understand what a use case is or how to use it, and you will be led in the dangerous direction of thinking that use cases are a graphical, as opposed to a textual, construction. Since the goal of this book is to show you how to write effective use cases and the standard has little to say in that regard, I have isolated my remarks about UML to Appendix A.

## Samples Used

The writing samples in this book were taken from live projects as much as possible, and they may seem slightly imperfect in some instances. I intend to show that they were sufficient to the needs of the project teams that wrote them, and that those imperfections are within the variations and economics permissible in use case writing.

The Addison-Wesley editing crew convinced me to tidy them up more than I originally intended, to emphasize correct appearance over the actual and adequate appearance. I hope you will find it useful to see these examples and recognize the writing that happens on projects. You may apply some of my rules to these samples and find ways to improve them. That sort of thing happens all the time. Since improving one's writing is a never-ending task, I accept the challenge and any criticism.

## Use Cases in The Crystal Collection

This is just one in a collection of books, The Crystal Collection for Software Professionals, that highlights lightweight, human-powered software development techniques. Some books discuss a single technique, some discuss a single role on a project, and some discuss team collaboration issues.

*Crystal* works from two basic principles:

◆ Software development is a cooperative game of invention and communication. It improves as we develop people's personal skills and increase the team's collaboration effectiveness.

◆ Different projects have different needs. Systems have different characteristics and are built by teams of differing sizes, with members having differing values and priorities. It is impossible to name one, best way of producing software.

The foundation book for the Crystal Collection, *Software Development as a Cooperative Game*, elaborates the ideas of software development as a cooperative game, of methodology as a coordination of culture, and of methodology families. That book separates the different aspects of methodologies, techniques and activities, work products and standards. The essence of the discussion, as needed for use cases, appears in this book in Section 1.2, Your Use Case Is Not My Use Case on page 7.

*Writing Effective Use Cases* is a technique guide, describing the nuts-and-bolts of use case writing. Although you can use the techniques on almost any project, the templates and writing standards must be selected according to each project's needs.

# *Acknowledgments*

Thanks to lots of people. Thanks to the people who reviewed this book in draft form and asked for clarification on topics that were causing their clients, colleagues, and students confusion. Special thanks to Russell Walters, a practiced person with a sharp eye for the direct and practical needs of the team, for his encouragement and very specific feedback. Thanks to FirePond and Fireman's Fund Insurance Company for the live use case samples. Pete McBreen, the first to try out the Stakeholders and Interests model, added his usual common sense, practiced eye, and suggestions for improvement. Thanks to the Silicon Valley Patterns Group for their careful reading of early drafts and their educated commentary on various papers and ideas. Mike Jones at the Fort Union Beans & Brew thought up the bolt icon for subsystem use cases.

Susan Lilly deserves special mention for the exact reading she did, correcting everything imaginable: sequencing, content, formatting, and even use case samples. The huge amount of work she contributed is reflected in the much improved final copy.

Other reviewers who contributed detailed comments and encouragement include Paul Ramney, Andy Pols, Martin Fowler, Karl Waclawek, Alan Williams, Brian Henderson-Sellers, Larry Constantine, and Russell Gold. The editors at Addison-Wesley did a good job of cleaning up my usual ungainly sentences and frequent typos.

Thanks to the people in my classes for helping me debug the ideas in the book.

Thanks again to my family, Deanna, Cameron, Sean, and Kieran, and to the people at the Fort Union Beans & Brew who once again provided lots of caffeine and a convivial atmosphere.

More on use cases is at the web sites I maintain: *members.aol.com/acockburn* and *www.usecases.org*. Just to save us some future embarassment, my name is pronounced Cō-burn, with a long o.

# Chapter 1

# *Introduction*

What do use cases look like?
Why do different project teams need different writing styles?
Where do use cases fit into the requirements gathering work?
How do we warm up for writing use cases?

It will be useful to have some answers to these questions before getting into the details of use cases themselves.

## 1.1 WHAT IS A USE CASE (MORE OR LESS)?

A use case captures a contract between the stakeholders of a system about its behavior. The use case describes the system's behavior under various conditions as the system responds to a request from one of the stakeholders, called the *primary actor*. The primary actor initiates an interaction with the system to accomplish some goal. The system responds, protecting the interests of all the stakeholders. Different sequences of behavior, or scenarios, can unfold, depending on the particular requests made and the conditions surrounding the requests. The use case gathers those different scenarios together.

Use cases are fundamentally a text form, although they can be written using flow charts, sequence charts, Petri nets, or programming languages. Under normal circumstances, they serve as a means of communication from one person to another, often among people with no special training. Simple text is, therefore, usually the best choice.

The use case, as a form of writing, can stimulate discussion within a team about an upcoming system. The team might or might not document the actual requirements with use cases. Another team might document their final design with use cases. All of the above might be done for a system as large as an entire company or as small as a piece of a software application program. What is interesting is that the same basic rules of writing apply to all of these situations, even though the teams will write with different amounts of rigor and at different levels of technical detail.

When use cases document an organization's business processes, the *system under discussion* (SuD) is the organization itself. The stakeholders are the company shareholders, customers, vendors, and government regulatory agencies. The primary actors include the company's customers and perhaps their suppliers.

When use cases record behavioral requirements for a piece of software, the SuD is the computer program. The stakeholders are the people who use the program, the company that owns it, government regulatory agencies, and other computer programs. The primary actor is the user sitting at the computer screen or another computer system.

A well-written use case is easy to read. It consists of sentences written in only one grammatical form—a simple action step—in which an actor achieves a result or passes information to another actor. Learning to read a use case should not take more than a few minutes.

Learning to write a good use case is harder. The writer has to master three concepts that apply to every sentence in the use case and to the use case as a whole. Odd though it may seem at first glance, keeping these three concepts straight is not easy. The difficulty shows up as soon as you start to write your first use case. The three concepts are

+ *Scope:* What is really the system under discussion?
+ *Primary actor:* Who has the goal?
+ *Level:* How high- or low-level is that goal?

Several examples of use cases follow. The parts of a use case are described in the next chapter. For now, remember these summary definitions:

+ *Actor:* anyone or anything with behavior.
+ *Stakeholder:* someone or something with a vested interest in the behavior of the system under discussion (SuD).
+ *Primary actor:* the stakeholder who or which initiates an interaction with the SuD to achieve a goal.
+ *Use case:* a contract for the behavior of the SuD.
+ *Scope:* identifies the system that we are discussing.
+ *Preconditions and guarantees:* what must be true before and after the use case runs.

- *Main success scenario:* a case in which nothing goes wrong.
- *Extensions:* what can happen differently during that scenario.
- Numbers in the extensions refer to the step numbers in the main success scenario at which each different situation is detected (for instance, steps 4a and 4b indicate two different conditions that can show up at step 4).
- When a use case references another use case, the referenced use case is <u>underlined</u>.

The first use case describes a person about to buy some stocks over the web. To signify that we are dealing with a goal to be achieved in a single sitting, I mark the use case as being at the *user-goal level*, and tag it with the *sea-level* symbol, ⋌⋌. The second use case describes a person trying to get paid for a car accident, a goal that takes longer than a single sitting. To show this, I mark the use case as being at the *summary level*, and tag it with the *above-sea-level* symbol, ⌂. These symbols are explained in Chapter 5, and summarized inside the front cover.

The first use case describes the person's interactions with a program ("PAF") running on a workstation connected to the Web. The black-box symbol, ▱, indicates that the system being discussed is a computer system. The second use case describes a person's interaction with a company, which I indicate with a building symbol, ⌂. The use of symbols is completely optional. Labeling the scope and level is not.

Here are Use Cases 1 and 2.

## Use Case 1  ▢ Buy Stocks over the Web ⌇⌇

**Primary Actor:** Purchaser

**Scope:** Personal Advisors / Finance package (PAF)

**Level:** User goal

**Stakeholders and Interests:**

> Purchaser—wants to buy stocks and get them added to the PAF portfolio automatically.

> Stock agency—wants full purchase information.

**Precondition:** User already has PAF open.

**Minimal Guarantee:** Sufficient logging information will exist so that PAF can detect that something went wrong and ask the user to provide details.

**Success Guarantee:** Remote web site has acknowledged the purchase; the logs and the user's portfolio are updated.

**Main Success Scenario:**

1. Purchaser selects to buy stocks over the web.
2. PAF gets name of web site to use (E*Trade, Schwab, etc.) from user.
3. PAF opens web connection to the site, retaining control.
4. Purchaser browses and buys stock from the web site.
5. PAF intercepts responses from the web site and updates the purchaser's portfolio.
6. PAF shows the user the new portfolio standing.

**Extensions:**

2a. Purchaser wants a web site PAF does not support:

> 2a1. System gets new suggestion from purchaser, with option to cancel use case.

3a. Web failure of any sort during setup:

> 3a1. System reports failure to purchaser with advice, backs up to previous step.

> 3a2. Purchaser either backs out of this use case or tries again.

4a. Computer crashes or is switched off during purchase transaction:

> 4a1. (What do we do here?)

4b. Web site does not acknowledge purchase, but puts it on delay:

> 4b1. PAF logs the delay, sets a timer to ask the purchaser about the outcome.

5a. Web site does not return the needed information from the purchase:

> 5a1. PAF logs the lack of information, has the purchaser update questioned purchase.

## Use Case 2  🏠 Get Paid for Car Accident 🔍

**Primary Actor:** Claimant
**Scope:** Insurance company ("MyInsCo")
**Level:** Summary
**Stakeholders and Interests:**
  Claimant—to get paid the most possible.
  MyInsCo—to pay the smallest appropriate amount.
  Department of Insurance—to see that all guidelines are followed.
**Precondition:** None.
**Minimal Guarantees:** MyInsCo logs the claim and all activities.
**Success Guarantees:** Claimant and MyInsCo agree on amount to be paid; claimant gets paid that.
**Trigger:** Claimant submits a claim.
**Main Success Scenario:**
1. Claimant submits claim with substantiating data.
2. Insurance company verifies claimant owns a valid policy.
3. Insurance company assigns agent to examine case.
4. Insurance company verifies all details are within policy guidelines.
5. Insurance company pays claimant and closes file.
**Extensions:**
1a. Submitted data is incomplete:
  1a1. Insurance company requests missing information.
  1a2. Claimant supplies missing information.
2a. Claimant does not own a valid policy:
  2a1. Insurance company denies claim, notifies claimant, records all this, terminates proceedings.
3a. No agents are available at this time.
  3a1. (What does the insurance company do here?)
4a. Accident violates basic policy guidelines:
  4a1. Insurance company denies claim, notifies claimant, records all this, terminates proceedings.
4b. Accident violates some minor policy guidelines:
  4b1. Insurance company begins negotiation with claimant as to amount of payment to be made.

Most of the use cases in this book come from live projects, and I have been careful not to touch them up (except to add the scope and level tags if they weren't there). I want you to see samples of what works in practice, not just what is attractive in the classroom. People rarely have time to make the use cases formal, complete, and pretty. They usually only have time to make them "sufficient," which is all that is necessary. I show these real samples because you rarely will be able to generate perfect use cases yourself, despite my coaching. Even I can't write perfect use cases most of the time.

Use Case 3 was written by Torfinn Aas of Central Bank of Norway for his colleague, his user representative, and himself. It shows how the form can be modified without losing value. The writer added additional business context to the story, illustrating how the computer application operates in the course of a working day. This was practical, as it saved having to write a separate document describing the business process. It confused no one and was informative to the people involved.

## Use Case 3 ⬜ Register Arrival of a Box 〰️

RA—"Receiving Agent"
RO—"Registration Operator"
**Primary Actor:** RA
**Scope:** Nightime Receiving Registry Software
**Level:** User goal
**Main Success Scenario:**
1. RA receives and opens box (box ID, bags with bag IDs) from Transport Company (TC)
2. RA validates box ID with TC registered IDs.
3. RA maybe signs paper form for delivery person.
4. RA registers box's arrival into system, which stores:
   RA ID
   Date, time
   Box ID
   Transport Company
   <Person name?>
   # bags (With bag IDs?)
   <Estimated value?>
5. RA removes bags from box, puts on cart, takes to RO.
**Extensions:**
2a. Box ID does not match transport company ID.
4a. Fire alarm goes off and interrupts registration.
4b. Computer goes down.
     Leave money on desk and wait for computer to come back up.
**Variations:**
4'.  With and without Person ID.
4''. With and without estimated value.
5'.  RA leaves bags in box.

## 1.2  *YOUR USE CASE IS NOT MY USE CASE*

Use cases are a form of writing that can be put to work in different situations, including the following:

- ◆ To describe a business's work process.
- ◆ To focus discussion *about* upcoming software system requirements, but not to be the requirements description.
- ◆ To be the functional requirements for a system.
- ◆ To document the design of the system.
- ◆ To be written in a small, close-knit group, or in a large or distributed group.

Each situation calls for a slightly different writing style. Here are the major subforms of use cases, driven by their *purpose*.

- ◆ A close-knit group gathering requirements, or a larger group discussing upcoming requirements, will write *casual* as opposed to *fully dressed* use cases, which are written by larger, geographically distributed, or formally inclined teams. The casual form "short-circuits" the use case template, making the use cases faster to write (see more on this later). Use Cases 1 through 3 are fully dressed, using the full use case template and step-numbering scheme. An example of casual form is shown in Use Case 4.

- ◆ Business process people write *business* use cases to describe the operations of their business, while a hardware or software development team writes *system* use cases for their requirements. The design team may write other *system* use cases to document their design or to break down the requirements for small subsystems.

- ◆ Depending on the level of view needed at the time, the writer will choose to describe a multi-sitting, or *summary*, goal; a single-sitting, or *user* goal; or a part of a user goal, or *subfunction*. Communicating which of these is being described is so important that my students have come up with two different gradients to describe them: by height relative to sea level (above sea level, at sea level, underwater), and by color (white, blue, indigo).

- ◆ Anyone writing requirements for a new system to be designed, whether business process or computer system, will write *black-box* use cases—those that do not discuss the innards of the system. Business process designers will write *white-box* use cases, showing how the company or organization runs its internal processes. The technical development team might do the same to document the operational context for the system they are about to design, and they might write white-box use cases to document the workings of the system they just designed.

It is wonderful that the use case writing form can be used in such varied situations, but it is confusing. Several of you sitting together are likely to find yourselves disagreeing on some matter of writing, just because your use cases are for different purposes. And you are likely to encounter several combinations of those characteristics over time.

Finding a general way to talk about use cases, while allowing all those variations, will plague us throughout the book. The best I can do is outline the issue now and let the examples speak for themselves.

You may want to test yourself on the use cases in this chapter. Use Cases 1, 3, and 5 were written for system requirements purposes, so they are the fully dressed, black-box, system type, at the user-goal level. Use Case 4 is the same, but casual, not fully dressed. Use Case 2, written as the context-setting use case for business process documentation, is fully dressed, black-box, and at the summary level.

The largest difference between use case formats is how "dressed up" they are. Consider these quite different situations:

- A team is working on software for a large, mission-critical project. They decide that the extra ceremony is worth the extra cost, so (a) the use case template needs to be longer and more detailed, (b) the writing team should write in the same style to reduce ambiguity and misunderstanding, and (c) the reviews should be tighter to more closely scrutinize the use cases for omissions and ambiguities. Having little tolerance for mistakes, they decide to reduce tolerances (variation between people) in the use case writing as well.

- A team of three to five people is building a system whose worst damage is the loss of comfort, easily remedied with a phone call. They consider all the ceremony a waste of time, energy, and money. They therefore choose (a) a simpler template, (b) to tolerate more variation in writing style, and (c) fewer and more forgiving reviews. The errors and omissions in the writing are to be caught by other project mechanisms, probably conversations among teammates and with users. They can tolerate more errors in their written communication and so more casual writing and more variation between people.

Neither is wrong. Such choices must be made on a project-by-project basis. This is the most important lesson that I, as a methodologist, have learned in the last five years. Of course we have been saying, "One size doesn't fit all" for years, but just how to translate that into concrete advice has remained a mystery.

The mistake is getting too caught up in precision and rigor when they are not needed, which will cost your project a lot in time and energy. As Jim Sawyer wrote in an email discussion, ". . . as long as the templates don't feel so formal that you get lost in a recursive descent that worm-holes its way into design space. If that starts to occur, I say strip the little buggers naked and start telling stories and scrawling on napkins."

I have come to the conclusion that just one use case template isn't enough. There must be at least two: a casual one for low-ceremony projects and a fully dressed one for higher-ceremony projects. Any one project will adapt one of the two forms for its situation. The next two use cases are the same but written in the two styles.

## Use Case 4 ⌂ Buy Something (Casual Version) ✎

The Requestor initiates a request and sends it to her or his Approver. The Approver checks that there is money in the budget, checks the price of the goods, completes the request for submission, and sends it to the Buyer. The Buyer checks the contents of storage, finding the best vendor for goods. The Authorizer validates Approver's signature. The Buyer completes request for ordering, initiates PO with Vendor. The Vendor delivers goods to Receiving, gets receipt for delivery (out of scope of system under design). The Receiver registers delivery, sends goods to Requestor. The Requestor marks request delivered.

At any time prior to receiving goods, the Requestor can change or cancel the request. Canceling it removes it from any active processing (deletes it from system?). Reducing the price leaves it intact in processing. Raising the price sends it back to the Approver.

## Use Case 5 ⌂ Buy Something (Fully Dressed Version) ✎

**Primary Actor:** Requestor

**Goal in Context:** Requestor buys something through the system, gets it. Does not include paying for it

**Scope:** Business—the overall purchasing mechanism, electronic and nonelectronic, as seen by the people in the company

**Level:** Summary

**Stakeholders and Interests:**

Requestor: Wants what he/she ordered, easy way to do that.

Company: Wants to control spending but allow needed purchases.

Vendor: Wants to get paid for any goods delivered.

**Precondition:** none

**Minimal Guarantees:** Every order sent out has been approved by a valid authorizer. Order was tracked so that company can be billed only for valid goods received.

**Success Guarantees:** Requestor has goods, correct budget ready to be debited.

**Trigger:** Requestor decides to buy something.

**Main Success Scenario:**

1. *Requestor:* initiate a request.
2. *Approver:* check money in budget, check price of goods, complete request for submission.

3. *Buyer:* check contents of storage, find best vendor for goods.
4. *Authorizer:* validate Approver's signature.
5. *Buyer:* complete request for ordering, initiate PO with Vendor.
6. *Vendor:* deliver goods to Receiving, get receipt for delivery (out of scope of system under design).
7. *Receiver:* register delivery; send goods to Requestor.
8. *Requestor:* mark request delivered.

**Extensions:**

1a. Requestor does not know vendor or price: Leave those parts blank and continue.

1b. At any time prior to receiving goods, Requestor can change or cancel request:
> Canceling it removes it from active processing (Delete from system?).
> Reducing price leaves it intact in processing.
> Raising price sends it back to Approver.

2a. Approver does not know vendor or price: Leave blank and let Buyer fill in or callback.

2b. Approver is not Requestor's manager: Still OK as long as Approver signs.

2c. Approver declines: Send back to Requestor for change or deletion.

3a. Buyer finds goods in storage: Send those up, reduce request by that amount, and carry on.

3b. Buyer fills in Vendor and price, which were missing: Request gets resent to Approver.

4a. Authorizer declines Approver: Send back to Requestor and remove from active processing. (What does this mean?)

5a. Request involves multiple Vendors: Buyer generates multiple POs.

5b. Buyer merges multiple requests: Same process, but mark PO with the requests being merged.

6a. Vendor does not deliver on time: System does alert of non-delivery.

7a. Partial delivery: Receiver marks partial delivery on PO and continues.

7b. Partial delivery of multiple-request PO: Receiver assigns quantities to requests and continues.

8a. Goods are incorrect or improper quality: Requestor refuses delivered goods. (What does this mean?)

8b. Requestor has quit the company: Buyer checks with Requestor's manager: either reassign Requestor or return goods and cancel request.

**Technology and Data Variations List:** None.

**Priority:** Various

**Releases:** Several

**Response Time:** Various

**Frequency of Use:** 3/day

**Channel to Primary Actor:** Internet browser, mail system, or equivalent

**Secondary Actors:** Vendor

**Channels to Secondary Actors:** Fax, phone, car
**Open Issues:**
>   When is a canceled request deleted from the system?
>   What authorization is needed to cancel a request?
>   Who can alter a request's contents?
>   What change history must be maintained on requests?
>   What happens when Requestor refuses delivered goods?
>   How does a requisition work differently from an order?
>   How does ordering reference and make use of the internal storage?

I hope it is clear that simply saying, "We write use cases on this project" does not say very much, and that any recommendation or process definition that simply says, "Write use cases" is incomplete. A use case valid on one project is not valid on another project. More must be said about whether fully dressed or casual use cases are being used, which template parts and formats are mandatory, and how much tolerance across writers is permitted.

The full discussion of tolerance and variation across projects is described in *Software Development as a Cooperative Game* (Cockburn, 2001). We don't need the full discussion to learn how to write use cases. We do need to separate the *writing technique* from *use case quality* and *project standards*.

"Techniques" are the moment-to-moment thinking or actions people use while constructing use cases. This book is largely concerned with technique: how to think, how to phrase sentences, in what sequence to work. The fortunate thing about techniques is that they are largely independent of the size of the project. A person skilled in a technique can apply it on projects both large and small.

"Quality" says how to tell whether the use cases that have been written are acceptable for their purpose. In this book, I describe the best way of writing I have seen for each use case part, across use cases, and for different purposes. In the end, though, the way you evaluate the quality of your use cases depends on the purpose, tolerance, and amount of ceremony you choose.

"Standards" say what the people on the project agree to when writing their use cases. In this book, I discuss alternative reasonable standards, showing different templates and different sentence and heading styles. I come out with a few specific recommendations, but ultimately it is for the organization or project to set or adapt the standards and to decide how strongly to enforce them.

In most of this book, I deal with the most demanding problem—writing precise requirements. In the following eyewitness account, Steve Adolph, a consultant, describes using use cases to *discover* requirements rather than to document them.

## ◆ Steve Adolph: "Discovering" Requirements in New Territory

Use cases are typically offered as a way to capture and model known functional requirements. People find the storylike format easier to comprehend than long shopping lists of traditional requirements. They actually understand what the system is supposed to do.

But what if no one knows what the system is supposed to do? The automation of a process usually changes the process. The printing industry was recently hit with one of the biggest changes since the invention of offset printing—the development of direct-to-plate/direct-to-press technology. Formerly, setting up a printing press was a labor-intensive, multi-step process. Direct-to-plate and direct-to-press made industrial scale printing as simple as submitting a word processor document for printing.

How would you, as the analyst responsible for workflow management for that direct-to-plate system, gather requirements for something so totally new? You could first find the use cases of the existing system and identify the system's actors and services. However, that only gives you the existing system. No one has done the new work yet, so all the domain experts are learning the system along with you. You are designing a new process and new software at the same time. Lucky you. How do you find the tracks on this fresh snow? Take the existing model and ask the question, "What changes?" The answer could well be "Everything."

When you write use cases to *document* requirements, someone has already created a vision of the system.

You are simply expressing that vision so everyone clearly understands it. In *discovering* the requirements, however, you are creating the vision.

Use the use cases as a brainstorming tool. Ask the question, "Given the new technology, which steps in the use case no longer add value to the use case goal?" Create a new story for how the actors reach their goals. The goals are still the same, but some of the supporting actors are gone or have changed.

Use a *dive-and-surface* approach. Create a broad, high-level model of how you think the new system may work. Keep things simple, since this is new territory. Discover what the main success scenario might look like. Walk it through with the former domain experts.

Then dive down into the details of one use case. Consider the alternatives. Take advantage of the fact that people find it easy to comprehend stories, to flush out missing requirements. Read a step in a use case and ask the question, "Well, what happens if the client wants a hard-copy rather than a digital-copy proof?" This is easier than trying to assemble a full mental model of how the system works.

Finally, come back to the surface. What has changed now that you have submerged yourself in the details? Adjust the model, then repeat the dive with another use case.

My experience has been that using use cases to *discover* requirements leads to higher-quality functional requirements. They are better organized and more complete.

## 1.3 REQUIREMENTS AND USE CASES

If you are writing use cases as requirements, keep two things in mind:

* *They really are requirements*. You shouldn't have to convert them into some other form of behavioral requirements. Properly written, they accurately detail what the system must do.

* *They are not all of the requirements*. They don't detail external interfaces, data formats, business rules, and complex formulae. They constitute only a fraction (perhaps a third) of all the requirements you need to collect—a very important fraction but a fraction nonetheless.

Every organization collects requirements to suit its needs. There are even standards available for requirements descriptions. In any of them, use cases occupy only one part of the total requirements documented.

The following requirements outline is one that I find useful. I adapted it from the template that Suzanne Robertson and the Atlantic Systems Guild published on their Web site and in the book *Managing Requirements* (Robertson and Robertson, 1999). Their template is intimidating in its completeness, so I've cut it down to the form shown in the outline that follows, which I use as a guideline. This is still too large for most projects I encounter, and so I tend to cut it down further as needed. Whatever its size, it asks many interesting questions that otherwise would not be asked, such as "What is the human backup to system failure?" and "What political considerations drive any of the requirements?"

While it is not the role of this book to standardize your requirements deliverable, I have run into many people who have never seen a requirements outline. I pass along this one for your consideration. Its main purpose is to illustrate the place of use cases in the overall requirements and to make the point that use cases will not hold all the requirements, but only describe the behavioral portion, the required function.

**A Plausible Requirements Outline**

Chapter 1. Purpose and Scope
    1a. What is the overall scope and goal?
    1b. Stakeholders (Who cares?)
    1c. What is in scope, what is out of scope?

Chapter 2. Terms Used / Glossary

Chapter 3. The Use Cases
    2a. The primary actors and their general goals
    2b. The business use cases (operations concepts)
    2c. The system use cases

Chapter 4. The Technology Used
   4a. What technology requirements are there for this system?
   4b. What systems will this system interface with, with what requirements?
Chapter 5. Other Requirements
   5a. Development process
      Q1. Who are the project participants?
      Q2. What values will be reflected (simple, soon, fast, or flexible)?
      Q3. What feedback or project visibility do the users and sponsors want?
      Q4. What can we buy, what must we build, what is our competition?
      Q5. What other process requirements are there (testing, installation, etc.)?
      Q6. What dependencies does the project operate under?
   5b. Business rules
   5c. Performance
   5d. Operations, security, documentation
   5e. Use and usability
   5f. Maintenance and portability
   5g. Unresolved or deferred
Chapter 6. Human Backup, Legal, Political, Organizational Issues
   Q1. What is the human backup to system operation?
   Q2. What legal and what political requirements are there?
   Q3. What are the human consequences of completing this system?
   Q4. What are the training requirements?
   Q5. What assumptions, dependencies are there on the human environment?

The thing to note is that use cases occupy only Chapter 3 of the requirements. They are not all of the requirements—they are *only* the behavioral requirements but they are *all of* the behavioral requirements. Business rules, glossary, performance targets, process requirements, and many other things do not fall into the category of behavior. They need their own chapters (see Figure 1.1).

## Use Cases as Project-Linking Structure

Use cases connect many other requirements details. They provide a scaffolding that connects information in different parts of the requirements and they help crosslink user profile information, business rules, and data format requirements.

Outside the requirements document, use cases help structure project planning information such as release dates, teams, priorities, and development status. Also, they help the design team track certain results, particularly the design of the user interface and system tests.

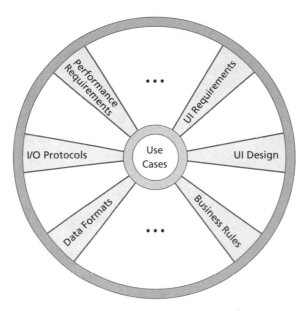

**Figure 1.1** *The "Hub-and-Spoke" model of requirements*

While not in the use cases, all these requirements are connected to them. The use cases act as the hub of a wheel, as in Figure 1.1, and the other information acts as spokes leading in different directions. It is for this reason that people seem to consider use cases to be the central element of the requirements or even the central element of the project's development process.

## 1.4 WHEN USE CASES ADD VALUE

Use cases are popular largely because they tell coherent stories about how the system will behave in use. The users of the system get to see just what this new system will be. They get to react early to fine-tune or reject the stories ("You mean we'll have to do *what*?"). That is, however, only one of the ways use cases contribute value and possibly not the most significant.

The first moment at which use cases create value is when they are named as user goals that the system will support, and are collected into a list. This list announces what the system will do, revealing the scope of the system, its purpose in life. It becomes a communication device between the different stakeholders on the project.

The list of goals will be examined by user representatives, executives, expert developers, and project managers, who will estimate the cost and complexity of the system starting from it. They will negotiate which functions get built first and how the teams are to be set up. The list is a framework to which to attach complexity, cost, timing, and status measures. It collects diverse information over the life of the project.

The second particularly valuable moment is when the use case writers brainstorm all the things that could go wrong in the successful scenario, list them, and begin documenting how the system should respond. At that moment, the team is likely to uncover something surprising, something that they or their requirements givers had not thought about.

When I get bored writing a use case, I hold out until I get to the failure conditions. There I regularly discover a new stakeholder, system, goal, or business rule while documenting the failure handling. As we work out how to deal with one of these conditions, I often see the business experts huddled together or making phone calls to resolve what the system should be doing here.

Without discrete use case steps and failure brainstorming, many error conditions go undetected until some programmer discovers them while typing a code fragment. That is very late to be discovering new functions and business rules. The business experts usually are gone and time is pressing, and so the programmers type whatever they think up at the moment instead of researching the desired behavior.

People who write one-paragraph use cases save a lot of time by writing so little and already reap one of the benefits of use cases. People who perservere through failure handling save a lot of time by finding subtle requirements early.

## 1.5 MANAGE YOUR ENERGY

Save your energy. Or at least manage it. If you start writing all the details at the first sitting, you won't move from topic to topic in a timely way. If you write down just an outline to start with and then write just the essence of each use case, you can

- Give your stakeholders a chance to offer correction and insight about priorities early.
- Permit the work to be split across multiple groups, increasing parallelism and productivity.

People often say, "Give me the 50,000-foot view," "Give me just a *sketch*," or "We'll add *details* later." They mean "Work at low precision for the moment; we can add more later."

*Precision* is how much you care to say. When you state, "A 'Customer' will want to rent a video," you are not using very many words, but you are actually communicating a great deal to your readers. When you show a list of all the goals that your proposed system will support, you have given your stakeholders an enormous amount of information from a small set of words.

Precision is not the same as accuracy. If someone tells you, "$\pi$ is 4.141592," they are using a lot of precision. They are, however, quite far off or inaccurate. If they say, "$\pi$ is about 3," they are not using much precision (there aren't very many digits), but they are accurate for as much as they said. The same ideas hold for use cases.

You will eventually add details to each use case, increasing precision. If you happen to be wrong (*inaccurate*) with your original, low-precision statement of goals, then the energy put into the high-precision description is wasted. Better to get the goal list correct before expending the dozens of work-months of energy required for a fully elaborated set of use cases.

I divide the energy of writing use cases into four stages of precision, according to the amount of energy required and the value of pausing after each stage:

1. *Actors and goals*. List what actors and which of their goals the system will support. Review this list for accuracy and completeness. Prioritize and assign goals to teams and releases. You now have the functional requirements to the first level of precision.

2. *Use case brief or main success scenario*. For the use cases you have selected to pursue, sketch the main success scenario. Review these in draft form to make sure that the system really is delivering the interests of the stakeholders you care about. This is the second level of precision on the functional requirements. It is fairly easy material to draft, unlike the next two levels.

3. *Failure conditions*. Complete the main success scenario and brainstorm all the failures that could occur. Draft this list completely before working out how the system must handle them. Filling in the failure handling takes much more energy than listing the failures. People who start writing the failure handling immediately often run out of energy before listing all the failure conditions.

4. *Failure handling*. Write how the system is supposed to respond to each failure. This is often tricky, tiring, and surprising work. It is surprising because quite often a question about an obscure business rule will surface during this writing, or the failure handling will suddenly reveal a new actor or new goal that needs to be supported.

Most projects are short on time and energy. Managing the precision level to which you work should therefore be a project priority. I strongly recommend working in the order given here.

## 1.6 WARM UP WITH A USAGE NARRATIVE

A usage *narrative* is a situated example of the use case in operation—a single, highly specific example of an actor using the system. It is not a use case, and in most projects it does not survive into the official requirements document. However, it is a very useful device that is worth my describing and your writing.

On starting a new project, you or the business experts may have little experience with use case writing or may not have thought through the system's detailed operation. To become comfortable with the material, sketch out a *vignette*, that is, a few moments in the day of the life of one of the actors.

In this narrative, invent a fictional but specific actor and briefly capture the mental state of that person—why he wants what he wants or what conditions drive him to act as he does. As with all use case writing, you needn't write much. It is astonishing how much information can be conveyed with just a few words. Capture how the world works, in this particular case, from the start of the situation to the end.

Brevity is important so the reader can get the story at a glance. Details and motives, or emotional content, are important so that every reader, from the requirements validator to the software designer, test writer, and training materials writer, can see how the system should be optimized to add value to the user.

A usage narrative takes little energy to write and little space, and leads the reader into the use case itself easily and gently. Here is an example.

**Usage Narrative: Getting "Fast Cash"**

> Mary, taking her two daughters to the day care center on the way to work, drives up to the ATM, runs her card across the card reader, enters her PIN code, selects FAST CASH, and enters $35 as the amount. The ATM issues a $20 and three $5 bills, plus a receipt showing her account balance after the $35 is debited. The ATM resets its screens after each transaction with FAST CASH, so Mary can drive away and not worry that the next driver will have access to her account. Mary likes FAST CASH because it avoids the many questions that slow down the interaction. She comes to this particular ATM because it issues $5 bills, which she uses to pay the day care provider, and she doesn't have to get out of her car to use it.

People write usage narratives to help them envision the system in use. They also use it to warm up before writing a use case, to work through the details. Occasionally, a team publishes the narratives at the beginning of all the use cases or just before the specific use cases they illustrate. One group wrote that they get a user, an analyst, and a requirements writer together and animate the narrative to help scope the system and create a shared vision of it in use.

The narrative is not the requirements; rather, it sets the stage for more detailed and generalized descriptions of the requirements. The narrative anchors the use case. The use case itself is a dried-out form of the narrative—a formula—with a generic actor name instead of the actual name used in the usage narrative.

## 1.7  EXERCISES

### Requirements File

**1.1.** Which sections of the requirements file outline are sensitive to use cases, and which are not? Discuss this with another person and think about why you come up with different responses.

**1.2.** Design another plausible requirements outline that can be put on an HTML-linked intranet. Pay attention to your subdirectory structure and date-stamping conventions (why will you need date-stamping conventions?).

### Usage Narrative

**1.3.** Write two usage narratives for the ATM you use. How and why do they differ from the narrative example? How significant are those differences for the designers about to design the system?

**1.4.** Write a usage narrative for a person going into a brand new video rental store, interested in renting the original version of *The Parent Trap*.

**1.5.** Write a usage narrative for your current project. Get another person to write a usage narrative for the same situation. Compare notes and discuss. Why are they different, what do you care to do about those differences—is that tolerance in action or is the difference significant?

# Part 1

# *The Use Case Body Parts*

# Chapter 2

# The Use Case as a Contract for Behavior

The system under discussion is a mechanism to carry out a contract between various stakeholders. Use cases provide the behavioral part of that contract. Every sentence in a use case is there because it describes an action that protects or furthers some interest of some stakeholder. A sentence might describe an interaction between two actors or what the system must do internally to protect the stakeholders' interests.

Let's first look at a use case purely in the way it captures interactions between actors with goals. Once we have that, we can broaden the discussion to cover the use case as a contract between stakeholders with interests. I refer to the first part as the **Actors and Goals** conceptual model and the second as the **Stakeholders and Interests** conceptual model.

## 2.1 INTERACTIONS BETWEEN ACTORS WITH GOALS

### Actors Have Goals

Imagine a clerk responsible for taking service requests over the phone (the clerk is the primary actor in Figure 2.1). When a call comes in, the clerk has a goal: to have the computer register and initiate the request.

The system also has a responsibility: to register and initiate the service request in our example. (It actually has the responsibility to protect the interests of *all* the stakeholders, with the clerk—the primary actor—being just one of them. For now, however, let's just focus on the system's responsibility to provide a service to the primary actor.)

To carry out its responsibility, the system formulates subgoals. It can carry out some subgoals internally, but needs the help of a *supporting actor* to carry out others. This supporting actor may be a printing subsystem or it may be another organization, such as a partner company or government agency.

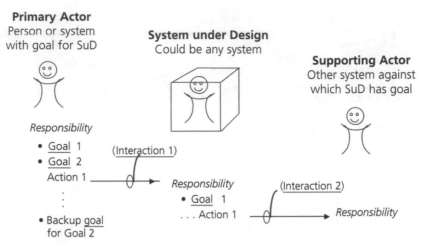

**Figure 2.1**   *An actor with a goal calls on the responsibilities of another*

The supporting actor usually carries out its promise and delivers the subgoal to the system under discussion (SuD). The SuD interacts with external actors. It achieves its subgoals in some sequence until it finally delivers its responsibility, that is, its service promise.

Delivering a service promise is a topmost goal, achieved through subgoals. The subgoals can be broken down into sub-subgoals indefinitely. There is potentially no end to listing sub-sub-(. . . sub) goals if we want to break down the actions of the actors finely enough. As the Irish satirist and poet Jonathan Swift wrote (not about use cases) in *On Poetry, A Rhapsody,*

> So, naturalists observe, a flea
> Hath smaller fleas that on him prey
> And these have smaller still to bite 'em
> And so proceed *ad infinitum.*

Probably the most difficult part of writing good use cases is controlling the fleas on the fleas—the sub-subgoals in the writing. Read more on this in Chapter 5, Three Named Goal Levels; Guideline 6, Have the Use Case Contain a "Reasonable" Set of Actions, in Chapter 7; and Reminder 6, Get the Goal Level Right, in Chapter 20.

The Actors and Goals conceptual model is handy, since it applies equally to businesses and computer systems. The actors can be individual people, organizations, or computers. We can describe mixed systems, consisting of people, companies, and computers. We can describe a software system driven by another computer system calling on a human supporting actor, or an organization calling on a computer system or an individual. It is a useful and general model.

## Goals Can Fail

What is the clerk with a customer on the phone supposed to do if the computer goes down in the middle of taking down the request? If the system cannot deliver its service promise, the clerk must invent a *backup* goal—in this case, probably using pencil and paper. The clerk still has a main job responsibility and must have a plan in case the system fails to perform its part.

Similarly, the system might encounter a failure in one of its subgoals. Perhaps the primary actor sent in bad data, perhaps there is an internal failure, or perhaps the supporting actor failed to deliver its promised service. How is the system supposed to behave? *That* is a really interesting part of the SuD's behavioral requirements.

In some cases, the system can repair the failure and resume the normal sequence of behavior. In some cases it must simply give up on the goal. If you go to your ATM and try to withdraw more money than you have access to, your goal to withdraw cash will simply fail. It will also fail if the ATM has lost its connection with the network computer. If you merely mistype your personal code, the system will give you a second chance to type it in correctly.

This focus on goal failures and failure responses is one reason use cases make good behavioral descriptions of systems and excellent functional requirements in general. People who have done functional decomposition and dataflow decompositions mention this as the most significant benefit that use cases offer them.

## Interactions Are Compound

The simplest interaction is sending a message. "Hi, Jean," I say, as we pass in the hall—that is a simple interaction. In procedural programming, the corresponding simple interaction is a function call, such as print(value). In object-oriented programming, it is one object sending a message to another, such as objectA->print(value).

A *sequence of messages,* or *scenario,* is a compound interaction. Suppose I go to the soda machine, put in a dollar bill for an 80-cent drink, and am told I need exact change. My interaction with the machine is this:

1. I insert a dollar bill.
2. I press "cola."
3. The machine says "Exact change required."
4. I curse, push the Coin Return.
5. The machine returns a dollar's worth of coins.
6. I take the coins (and walk away mumbling).

We can compact a sequence as though it were a single step ("I tried to buy a cola from the machine, but it needed exact change.") and put that compacted step into a larger sequence:

1. I went to the company bank and got some money.
2. I tried to buy a cola from the machine, but it needed exact change.
3. I walked down to the cafeteria and bought one there.

Thus, interactions can be rolled up or broken down as needed, just as goals can. Each step in a scenario captures a goal, and so each step can be unfolded into its own use case. It seems interactions have fleas with fleas, just as goals do.

The good news is that we can present the system's behavior at a very high level, with rolled-up goals and interactions. Unrolling them bit by bit, we can specify the system's behavior as precisely as we need to. I often refer to the set of use cases as an *ever-unfolding story*. It is our job to write this story in such a way that the reader can move around in it comfortably.

The astute reader will spot that I have used the word *sequence* rather loosely. In many cases, the interactions don't have to occur in any particular sequence. To buy that 80-cent drink, I could put in eight dimes, three quarters and a nickel, or . . . (you can fill in the list). It doesn't matter which coin goes in first.

Officially, *sequence* is not the right word. The correct phrase from mathematics is *partial ordering*. However, *sequence* is shorter, close to the point, and more easily understood by people writing use cases. If someone asks you about messages that can happen in parallel, say, "Fine, write a little about that," and see what they come up with. My experience is that people write wonderfully clear descriptions with very little coaching. I therefore continue to say *sequence*. See Use Case 22, Register a Loss, on page 75 for a sample with complex sequencing.

If you are interested in creating a formal language for use cases, it is easy to get into difficulty at this point. Most language designers either force the writer to list all possible orders or invent complex notations to permit the arbitrary ordering of events. Since we are writing use cases for another person to read, not a computer, we are more fortunate. We simply write, "Buyer puts in 80 cents, in nickels, dimes, or quarters, in any order."

Sequences are good for describing interactions in the past because the past is fully determined. To describe interactions in the future, we need *sets of possible sequences*, one for each possible future condition of the world. If I tell you about my asking for raise yesterday, I say,

"I had a serious interaction with the boss today: I said, '. . .' She said, '. . .' I said, '. . .', etcetera."

But speaking into the future, I will have to say,

> "I am really nervous about this next interaction with the boss."
> "Why?"
> "I'm going to ask for a raise."
> "How?"
> "Well, first I'm going to say, " . . . " Then if she says, " . . . ," I'll respond with " . . . "
> But if she says, " . . . ," then I'll try, " . . . " and so forth.

Similarly, if we tell another person how to buy a soda, we say,

> "First get your money ready."
> "If you have exact change, put it in and press the cola button."
> "If you don't, put in your money and see whether it can give change. If it can . . . "

To describe an interaction in the future, we have to deal with different conditions, creating sets of sequences. For each one, we say what the condition is, what the sequence will be, and what the outcome will be.

We can fold a set of sequences into a single statement. "First go and buy a drink from the machine" or "Then you ask your boss for a raise." As with sequences, we can fold these statements into brief, high-level descriptions or unfold them into detailed descriptions to suit our needs.

So far, we have seen that a use case contains the set of possible scenarios for achieving a goal. To be more complete, we need to add that

- All the interactions relate to the same goal of the same primary actor.
- The use case starts at the triggering event and continues until the goal is delivered or abandoned, *and* the system completes its responsibilities with respect to the interaction.

## A Use Case Collects Scenarios

The primary actor has a goal; the system should help the primary actor reach that goal. Some scenarios show the goal being achieved; some end with it being abandoned. Each scenario contains a sequence of steps showing how the actions and interactions unfold. A use case collects all the scenarios together, showing all the ways that the goal can succeed or fail.

A useful metaphor for this is illustrated in the *striped trousers* image (Figure 2.2). The belt on the trousers names the goal that holds all the scenarios together. Of the two legs, one is for the scenarios that end in success and one is for the scenarios

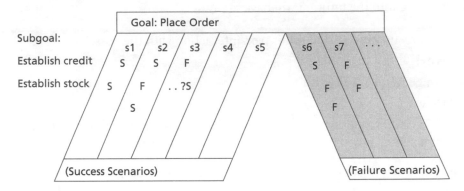

**Figure 2.2**  *Striped trousers: Scenarios succeed or fail*

that end in failure. Each stripe corresponds to a scenario, any one being on the success leg or the failure leg. We'll call the first stripe on the success leg the *main success scenario*. The other stripes are other scenarios that ultimately end in success—some through alternate success paths and some after recovering from an intermediate failure. All of the stripes on the failure leg run through failures, possibly recovering and then failing in the end.

We won't actually write every scenario separately from top to bottom. That is a poor writing strategy because it is tedious, redundant, and hard to maintain. The striped trousers image is useful for keeping in mind that every use case has two exits, that the primary actor's goal binds all the scenarios, and that every scenario is a simple description of the goal succeeding or failing.

In Figure 2.3, I add to the striped trousers image to show a sub use case fitting into the use case that names it. A customer wants to *Place an Order*. One of the customer's subgoals is to *Establish Credit*. That subgoal is complex and might succeed or fail: It is a use case we have rolled up into a single step. The step **Customer establishes credit** is the belt on another set of trousers. In the stripe or scenario containing that step, the subgoal succeeds or doesn't. In scenarios 1 and 2 in the figure, the subgoal works. In scenarios 3 and 7, it fails. In scenario 3, however, the next subgoal for establishing credit succeeds, and the scenario ends with success. In scenario 7, the second attempt also fails, and the entire use case ends with the failure to place an order.

The point of showing the little stripes on the sub use case in Figure 2.3 is to illustrate that the outer use case doesn't care what the sub use case went through to get to its end state. It either succeeded or didn't. The outer, or calling, use case simply builds on the success or failure of the step naming the sub use case.

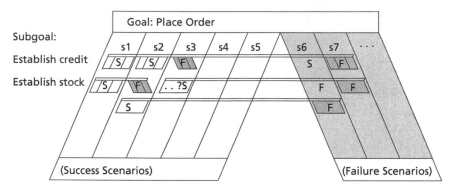

**Figure 2.3** *The striped trousers showing subgoals.*

The principles we see from the trousers image are that

♦ Some scenarios end with success; some end with failure.

♦ A use case collects together all the scenarios, success and failure.

♦ Each scenario is a straight description for one set of circumstances with one outcome.

♦ Use cases contain scenarios (stripes on the trousers), and a scenario contains sub use cases as its steps.

♦ A step in a scenario does not care which stripe in the sub use case was used but only whether it ended with success or failure.

We will make use of these principles throughout our writing.

## 2.2 CONTRACT BETWEEN STAKEHOLDERS WITH INTERESTS

The Actors and Goals model explains how to write sentences in the use case, but it does not cover the need to describe the internal behavior of the system under discussion. For that reason the Actors and Goals model needs to be extended with the idea of a use case as a contract between stakeholders with interests, which I will refer to as the *Stakeholders and Interests* conceptual model. The Stakeholders and Interests portion of the model identifies what to include in the use case and what to exclude.

The SuD operates a contract between stakeholders, with the use cases detailing the behavioral part of that contract. Not all of the stakeholders are present while the system is running. The primary actor is usually present, but not always. The other stakeholders are not present, and so we might call them *offstage actors*. The system acts to satisfy the interests of these offstage actors, including gathering information, running validation checks, and updating logs (see Figure 2.4).

The ATM must keep a log of all interactions to protect the stakeholders in case of a dispute. It logs other information so they can find out how far a failed transaction got before it failed. The ATM and banking system verify that the account holder has adequate funds before giving out cash to make sure that the ATM gives out no more than the amount of money that customers actually have in the bank.

The use case, as the contract for behavior, captures *all and only* the behaviors related to satisfying the stakeholders' interests.

To carefully complete a use case, we list all the stakeholders, name their interests with respect to the operation of the use case, and state what it means to each stakeholder that the use case completes successfully and what guarantees they want from the system. Having those, we write the use case steps, ensuring that all the various interests are satisfied from the moment the use case is triggered until it completes. That is how we know when to start and stop writing and what to include and exclude from the use case.

Most people do not write use cases this carefully, and often they happily get away with it. Good writers do this exercise in their heads when writing casual use cases. They probably leave some things out, but have ways of catching those omissions during software development. That is fine on many projects. However, sometimes there is a large cost involved. See the story about forgetting some interests in Section 4.1, Stakeholders, on page 53.

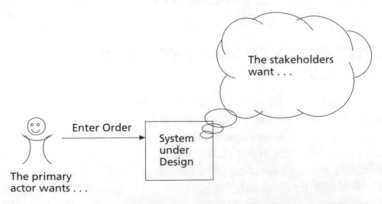

**Figure 2.4**   *The SuD serves the primary actor, protecting offstage stakeholders*

To satisfy the interests of the stakeholders, we need to describe three sorts of actions:

◆ An interaction between two actors (to further a goal)
◆ A validation (to protect a stakeholder)
◆ An internal state change (on behalf of a stakeholder)

The Stakeholders and Interests model makes only a small change in the overall procedure for writing a use case: List the stakeholders and their interests and use that list as a double check to make sure that none was omitted in the use case body. That small change makes a big change in the quality of the use case.

## 2.3 THE GRAPHICAL MODEL

This section is intended only for people who like to build abstract models. Feel free to skip this section if you are not one of them.

As noted, a use case describes the behavioral contract between stakeholders with interests. We organize the behavior by the operational goals of a selected set of the stakeholders—those who will ask the system to *do* something for them—which we call *primary actors*. The use case's name is the primary actor's goal. It contains all the behavior needed to describe that part of the contract.

The system has the responsibility to satisfy the agreed-upon interests of the agreed-upon stakeholders with its actions. An action is of one of three types:

◆ An interaction between two actors, in which information may be passed back or forth.
◆ A validation to protect the interests of one of the stakeholders.
◆ An internal state change, also to protect or further an interest of a stakeholder.

A scenario consists of action steps. In a *success scenario*, all of the (agreed-upon) interests of the stakeholders are satisfied for the service it has the responsibility to perform. In a *failure scenario*, all those interests are protected according to the system's guarantees. The scenario ends when all of the interests of the stakeholders are satisfied or protected.

The three triggers that request a goal's delivery are the primary actor initiating an interaction with the system, the primary actor using an intermediary to initiate that interaction, or a time- or state-based initiation.

The model of use cases described in this chapter is shown in Figures 2.5 through 2.8 using the Unified Modeling Language (UML).

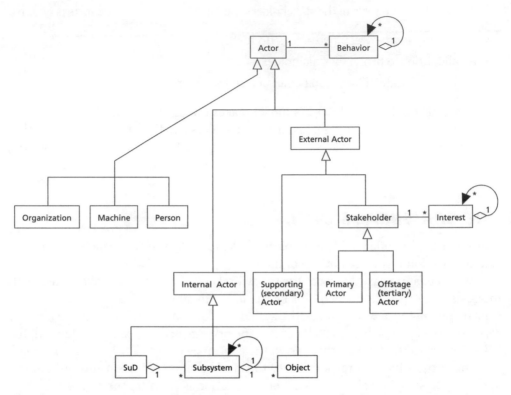

**Figure 2.5 Actors and stakeholders.** *A stakeholder has interests. An actor has behaviors. The primary actor is also a stakeholder.*

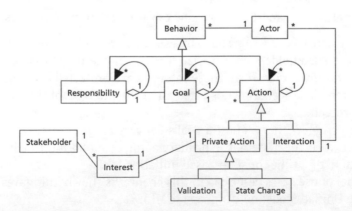

**Figure 2.6 Behavior.** *Goal-oriented behavior consists of responsibilities, goals, and actions. The private actions we write are those that forward or protect the interests of stakeholders. Interactions connect the actions of one actor with another.*

**Figure 2.7  Use Case as responsibility invocation.** *The use case captures the primary actor's goal, calling on the responsibility of the SuD.*

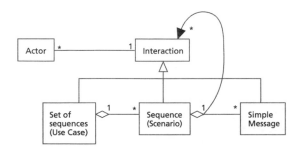

**Figure 2.8  Interactions as composite.** *N actors participate in an interaction. Interactions decompose into use cases, scenarios, and simple messages. Once again, the term sequence is used as a convenience.*

Here is a bit of truth in advertising. I don't know how to debug this model without several years of testing it on projects using a model-based tool. In other words, it probably contains some subtle errors. I include it for those who wish to experiment, perhaps to create such a model-based tool.

# Chapter 3

# *Scope*

*Scope* is the word we use for the extent of what we design as opposed to someone else's design job or an already existing design.

Keeping track of the scope of a project, or even just the scope of a discussion, can be difficult. The consultant Rob Thomsett introduced me to a wonderful little tool for tracking and managing scope discussions—the *in/out list*. Absurdly simple and remarkably effective, it can be used to control scope discussions for ordinary meetings as well as project requirements.

Simply construct a table with three columns. The left column contains any topic; the next two columns are labeled "In" and "Out." Whenever there might confusion as to whether a topic is within the scope of the discussion, add it to the table and ask people whether it is in or out. The amazing result, as Rob described and I have seen, is that while is it completely clear to each person in the room whether the topic is in or out, the views are often opposing. Rob relates that sometimes it requires an appeal to the project's steering committee to settle whether a particular topic really is within the scope of work or not. In or out can make a difference of many work-months. Try this technique on your next project or perhaps your next meeting.

Table 3.1 is a sample in/out list we produced for our purchase request tracking system.

Use the in/out list right at the beginning of the requirements or use case writing activity, to separate the things that are within the scope of work from those that are out of scope. Refer to it whenever the discussion seems to be going off track or some requirement is creeping into the discussion that might not belong. Update the chart as you go.

Use the in/out list for topics relating to both the functional scope and the design scope of the system under discussion.

**Table 3.1.**   *A Sample In/Out List*

| Topic | In | Out |
|---|---|---|
| Invoicing in any form | | Out |
| Producing reports about requests (e.g., by vendor, by part, by person) | In | |
| Merging requests into one PO | In | |
| Partial deliveries, late deliveries, wrong deliveries | In | |
| All new system services, software | In | |
| Any nonsoftware parts of the system | | Out |
| Identification of any preexisting software that can be used | In | |
| Requisitions | In | |

## 3.1  FUNCTIONAL SCOPE

Functional scope refers to the services your system offers and that will eventually be captured by the use cases. As you start your project, however, it is quite likely that you won't know it precisely. You are deciding the functional scope at the same time you are identifying the use cases—the two tasks are intertwined. The in/out list helps with this, since it allows you to draw a boundary between what is in and what is out of scope. The other two tools are the *actor-goal list* and the *use case briefs*.

### The Actor-Goal List

The actor-goal list names all the user goals that the system supports, showing the system's functional content. Unlike the in/out list, which shows items that are both in and out of scope, the actor-goal list includes only the services that will actually be supported by the system. Table 3.2 is one project's actor-goal list for the purchase request tracking system.

To make this list, construct a table of three columns. Put the names of the primary actors—the actors having the goals—in the left column; put each actor's goals with respect to the system in the middle column; and put the priority, or an initial guess as to the release in which the system will support that goal, in the third column. Update this list continually over the course of the project so that it always reflects the status of the system's functional boundary.

Some people add additional columns—*trigger*, to identify the use cases that will get triggered by time instead of by a person, and *business priority, development complexity,*

**Table 3.2.** *A Sample Actor-Goal List*

| Actor | Task-level Goal | Priority |
|---|---|---|
| Any | Check on requests | 1 |
| Authorizor | Change authorizations | 2 |
| Buyer | Change vendor contacts | 3 |
| Requestor | Initiate a request | 1 |
| | Change a request | 1 |
| | Cancel a request | 4 |
| | Mark request delivered | 4 |
| | Refuse delivered goods | 4 |
| Approver | Complete request for submission | 2 |
| Buyer | Complete request for ordering | 1 |
| | Initiate PO with vendor | 1 |
| | Alert of nondelivery | 4 |
| Authorizer | Validate Approver's signature | 3 |
| Receiver | Register delivery | 1 |

and *development priority*, so they can separate the business needs from the development costs to derive the development priority.

The actor-goal list is the initial negotiating point between the user representative, the financial sponsor, and the development group. It focuses the layout and content of the project.

## The Use Case Briefs

I will keep repeating the importance of managing your energy and working at low levels of precision wherever possible. The actor-goal list is the lowest level of precision in describing system behavior, and it is very useful for working with the total picture of the system. The next level of precision will either be the main success scenario or a *use case brief*.

The use case brief is a two-to-six sentence description of use case behavior, mentioning only the most significant activity and failures. It reminds people of what is going on in the use case. It is useful for estimating work complexity. Teams constructing

**Table 3.3.** *Sample Use Case Briefs*

| Actor | Goal | Brief |
|---|---|---|
| Production Staff | Modify the administrative area lattice | Production staff adds administrative area metadata (administrative hierarchy, currency, language code, street types, etc.) to the reference database. Contact information for source data is cataloged. This is a special case of updating reference data. |
| Production Staff | Prepare digital cartographic source data | Production staffs convert external digital data to a standard format and validate and correct it in preparation for merging with an operational database. The data is cataloged and stored in a digital source library. |
| Production and Field Staff | Commit update transactions of a shared checkout to an operational database | Staff applies accumulated update transactions to an operational database. Nonconflicting transactions are committed to the operational database. The application context is synchronized with the operational database. Committed transactions are cleared from the application context, leaving the operational database consistent, with conflicting transactions available for manual/interactive resolution. |

from commercial, off-the-shelf components (COTS) use this description in selecting the components. Some project teams, such as those having extremely good internal communications and continual discussion with their users, never write more than these use case briefs for their requirements; they keep the rest of the requirements in the continual discussions, prototypes, and frequently delivered increments.

You can prepare the use case brief as a table, as an extension to the actor-goal list, or directly as part of the use case body in its first draft. Table 3.3 is a sample of briefs, thanks to Paul Ford, Steve Young, and Paul Bouzide of Navigation Technologies.

## 3.2 DESIGN SCOPE

Design scope is the extent of the system—I would say "spatial extent" if software took up space. It is the set of systems, hardware and software, that we are charged with designing or discussing; it is that boundary. If we are to design an ATM, we are to produce hardware and software that sits in a box—the box and everything in it is ours to design. The computer network that the box will talk to is not ours to design—it is out of the design scope.

From now on, when I write *scope* alone, I mean *design scope*. This is because the functional scope is adequately defined by the actor-goal list and the use cases, while the design scope is a topic of concern in every use case.

As the following story illustrates, it is very important that the writer and reader are in agreement about the design scope for a use case—and correct. The price of being wrong can be a factor of two or more in cost, with disastrous results for the outcome of a contract. The readers of a use case must quickly see what you intend to be inside the system boundary. That will not be obvious just from the name of the use case or the primary actor. Systems of different sizes show up even within the same use case set.

Typically, writers consider the scope of the system to be so obvious that they don't mention it. However, once there are multiple writers and multiple readers, the design scope of a use case is not obvious at all. One writer is thinking of the entire corporation as the scope (see Figure 3.1), one is thinking of all of the company's software systems, one is thinking of the new, client–server system, and one is thinking of only the client or only the server. Readers, having no clue as to what is meant, get lost or misunderstand the document.

What can we do to clear up the misunderstanding?

The only answer I have found is to *label each and every use case with its design scope*, using specific names for the most significant scopes. To be concrete, let us suppose

---

### ◆ A Short, True Story

To help with constructing a fixed-time, fixed-cost bid of a large system, we were walking through some sample designs. I picked up the printer and spoke its function. The IS expert laughed. "You personal computer people crack me up, "he said," You think we just use a little laser printer to print our invoices? We have a huge printing system, with a chain printer, batch I/O, and everything. We produce invoices by the boxful!"

I was shocked. "You mean the printer is not in the scope of the system?"

"Of course not! We'll use the printing system we already have."

Indeed, we found that there was a complicated interface to the printing system. Our system was to prepare a magnetic tape with things to be printed. Overnight, the printing system would read the tape and print what it could. It would prepare a reply tape describing the results of the printing job, with error records for anything it couldn't print. The following day, our system would read back the results and note what had not been printed correctly. The design job for interfacing to that tape was significant, and completely different from what we had been expecting.

The printing system was not for us to design, but was for us to use. It was out of our design scope. (It was, as described in Section 3.3, a *supporting actor*.) Had we not detected this mistake, we would have written the use case to include it in our scope and turned in a bid to build more system than was needed.

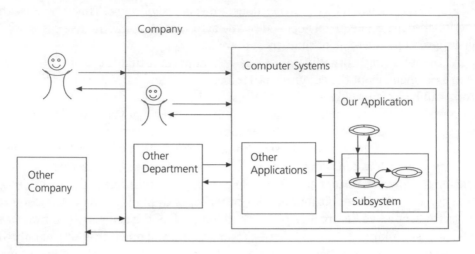

**Figure 3.1** *Design scope can be any size*

that MyTelCo is designing a NewApp system, which includes a Searcher subsystem. The design scope names are these:

◆ *Enterprise* (i.e., *MyTelCo*) 🏠. You are discussing the behavior of the entire organization or enterprise in delivering the goal of the primary actor. Label the *Scope* field of the use case with the name of the organization—*MyTelCo*—rather than just "the company." If discussing a department, use the department name. Business use cases are written at the enterprise scope.

◆ *System* (i.e., *NewApp*) ▱. This is the piece of hardware or software you are charged with building. Outside the system are all the pieces of hardware, software, and humanity that the system is to interface with.

◆ *Subsystem* (i.e., *Searcher*) 〰. You have opened up the main system and are about to talk about how a piece of it works.

## Using Graphical Icons to Highlight the Design Scope

Consider attaching a graphic to the left of the use case title to signal the design scope to readers before they start reading. There are no tools at this time to manage the icons, but I find that drawing them reduces confusion. In this book I label each use case with its appropriate icon to make it easier for you to note its scope.

As you read the following list, remember that a *black-box* use case does not discuss the internal structure of the system under discussion while a *white-box* use case does.

- A *business* use case has the enterprise as its scope. Its graphic is a building. Color it grey (🏠) if you treat the whole enterprise as a black box. Color it white (🏠) if you talk about the departments and staff within the organization.

- A *system* use case has a computer system as its scope. Its graphic is a box. Color it grey (▱) if you treat it as a black box, white (▱) if you reveal how its componentry works.

- A *component* use case is about a subsystem or component of the system under design. Its graphic is a bolt 〔▥▥▥. See Use Cases 13 through 17 for an example.

## Design Scope Examples

I offer three examples to illustrate systems at different scopes.

### (1)   Enterprise-to-System Scope

Suppose that we work for telephone company, *MyTelCo*, which is designing a new system, *Acura*, to take orders for services and upgrades. Acura consists of a workstation connected to a server. The server will be connected to a mainframe running the old system, *BSSO*. BSSO is just a terminal attached to the mainframe. We are not allowed to make any changes to it; we can only use its existing interfaces.

The primary actors for Acura include the customer, the clerk, various managers, and BSSO (we are clear that BSSO is not within our scope).

Let's find a few of the goals the system should support. The most obvious is "Add a new service." We decide that the primary actor for that is the company clerk, acting on behalf of the customer. We sit down to write a few use cases.

The immediate question is "What is the system under discussion?" It turns out that there are two that interest us:

- *MyTelCo*. We are interested in the question, "What does MyTelCo's service look like to the customer, showing the new service implementation in its complete form, from initial request to implementation and delivery?" This question is of double interest. The company managers will want to see how the new system appears to the outside world, and the implementation team will want to see the context in which the new system will sit.

  This use case will be written at the enterprise scope (🏠), with the Scope field labeled MyTelCo and the use case written without mention of company-internal players (no clerks, no departments, no computers). This sort of use case is often referred to as a *business use case*, since it is about the business.

- *Acura*. We are interested in the question, "How does Acura's service appear, at its interface to the clerk or customer on one side and to the BSSO system on the other side?" This is the use case the designers care most about, since it states exactly what they are to build. The use case will be written at the system scope ( ▢ ), with the Scope field labeled "Acura." It will freely mention clerks and departments and other computer systems, but not the workstation and the server subsystems.

We produce two use cases. To avoid having to repeat the same information twice, we write the enterprise use case at a higher level (the kite symbol), showing MyTelCo responding to the request, delivering it, and perhaps even charging for it and getting paid. The purpose of the enterprise use case is to show the context around the new system. Then we describe in detail the 5- to 20-minute handling of the request in the user-goal use case having Acura as its scope.

### Use Case 6  🏠 Add New Service (Enterprise) ◇

**Primary Actor:** Customer
**Scope:** MyTelCo
**Level:** Summary
1. Customer calls MyTelCo, requests new service . . .
2. MyTelCo delivers . . . etc. . . .

### Use Case 7  ▢ Add New Service (Acura) 〜〜

**Primary Actor:** Clerk for external customer
**Scope:** Acura
**Level:** User goal
1. Customer calls in, clerk discusses request with customer.
2. Clerk finds customer in Acura.
3. Acura presents customer's current service package . . . etc. . . .

No use case will be written with a scope of Acura workstation or Acura server, as these are not of interest to us. Later, someone in the design team may choose to document Acura's subsystem design using use cases. At that time, they will write two use cases, one with a scope of Acura workstation, the other with a scope of Acura server. My experience is that these use cases are never written, since there are other adequate techniques for documenting subsystem architecture.

### (2)   Many Computers to One Application

The following is a less common situation, but one that is very difficult. Let us build onto the MyTelCo situation.

> Acura will slowly replace BSSO. New service requests will be put into Acura and then modified using BSSO. Over time, Acura will take on more function. The two systems must co-exist and synchronize with each other. Thus, use cases have to be written for both systems: Acura being entirely new and BSSO being modified to synchronize with it.

The difficulty in this situation is that there are four use cases, two for Acura and two for BSSO. There is one use case for each system having the clerk as primary actor and one having the other computer system as the primary actor. There is no way to avoid these four use cases, but people looking at them get confused because they look redundant.

To document this situation, I first write a summary-level use case whose scope is both computer systems. This gives me a chance to document their interactions over time. In that use case, I reference the specific use cases that comprise each system's requirements. This first use case will be of the white-box type (note the white-box symbol).

The situation is complicated enough that I also include diagrams of each use case's scope.

### Use Case 8   ⬚ Enter and Update Requests (Joint System) ✎

**Primary Actor:** Clerk for external customer
**Scope:** Computer systems, including Acura and BSSO (see diagram)
**Level:** Summary

**Main Success Scenario:**
1. Clerk <u>adds new service</u> into Acura.
2. Acura <u>notes new service request</u> in BSSO.
3. Some time later, Clerk <u>updates service request</u> in BSSO.
4. BSSO <u>notes the updated request</u> in Acura.

The four sub use cases are all user-goal use cases and get marked with the sea-level symbol. Although they are all system use cases, they are for different systems—hence the diagrams. In each diagram, I circle the primary actor and shade the SuD. The use cases are black-box this time, since they are requirements for new work. In addition, I give them slightly different verb names, using the verb "note" to indicate one system synchronizing with the other.

### Use Case 9   &#x1F5D7; Add New Service (into Acura)

**Primary Actor:** Clerk for external customer
**Scope:** Acura
**Level:** User goal
. . . use case body follows. . .

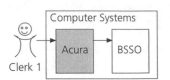

### Use Case 10   &#x1F5D7; Note New Service Request (in BSSO)

**Primary Actor:** Acura
**Scope:** BSSO
**Level:** User goal
. . . use case body follows. . .

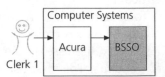

### Use Case 11   &#x1F5D7; Update Service Request (in BSSO)

**Primary Actor:** Clerk for external customer
**Scope:** BSSO
**Level:** User goal
. . . use case body follows. . .

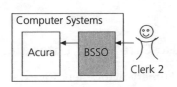

### Use Case 12   &#x1F5D7; Note Updated Request (in Acura)

**Primary Actor:** BSSO
**Scope:** Acura
**Level:** User Goal
. . . use case body follows. . .

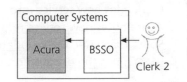

If you are using UML use case diagrams, you might draw the summary-level use case instead of writing it. That still does not reduce the confusion within the four user-goal use cases, so you should still carefully mark their primary actor, scope, and level, and possibly still draw the scope diagrams within the use cases.

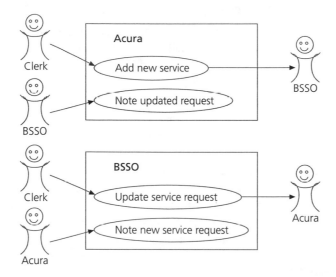

**Figure 3.2** **Use case diagrams for Acura–BSSO**. *This is the UML style of denoting the interactions between the two systems. The upper section shows that BSSO is a supporting actor to one use case of Acura and a primary actor to another use case. In the lower diagram, the roles are reversed.*

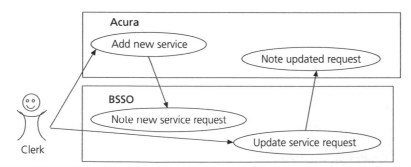

**Figure 3.3** **A combined use case diagram for Acura-BSSO**. *This drawing shows the relationships of the four use cases most clearly, but is nonstandard, since it shows one system's use case triggering another system's use case.*

Personally, I do not find that this eliminates much confusion. I would consider drawing the nonstandard use case diagram in Figure 3.3 to show the connection between the two systems. This diagram is clearer but harder to maintain over time. Draw whichever you and your readers find communicates best for you.

### (3) Nuts and Bolts Use Cases

At the far end of the scale, let's look at the way one group documented their design framework with use cases. They started with an 18-page, diagram-loaded description of the rules for their framework. They decided it was too hard to read and experimented with use cases as the descriptive technique.

The group spent one week on the task. First they drafted 40 use cases to make sure they had captured all the requests their framework would handle. Using extensions and the data variations list, they revised those down to just six.

Most readers will find these use cases incomprehensible because they are not in that business. However, I expect some readers to be technical programmers looking for ways to document their designs, so I include these use cases to show how this group documented an internal architecture and how they made use of the variations list. I find them fairly easy to read, given the complexity of their problem. Notice that sub use cases are underlined. Thanks to Dale Margel in Calgary for the writing.

**General Description:**

The overall architecture must be able to handle concurrent tasks. To do this, it must support Process Threads and Resource Locking. These services are handled by the Concurrency Service Framework (CSF). CSF is used by client objects to protect critical sections of code from unsafe access by multiple processes.

## Use Case 13    Serialize Access to a Resource

**Primary Actor:** Service Client object
**Scope:** Concurrency Service Framework (CSF)
**Level:** User goal
**Main Success Scenario:**
1. Service Client asks a Resource Lock to give it specified access.
2. The Resource Lock returns control to the Service Client so that it may use the Resource.
3. Service Client uses the Resource.
4. Service Client informs the Resource Lock that it is finished with the Resource.
5. Resource Lock cleans up after the Service Client.
**Extensions:**
2a. Resource Lock finds that Service Client already has access to the resource:
    2a1. Resource Lock applies a lock conversion policy (Use Case 14) to the request.
2b. Resource Lock finds that the resource is already in use:
    2b1. The Resource Lock applies a compatibility policy (Use Case 15) to grant access to the Service Client.
2c. Resource Locking Holding time limit is nonzero:
    2c1. Resource Lock starts the holding timer.

3a. Holding Timer expires before the Client informs the Resource Lock that it is finished:

   3a1. Resource Lock sends an Exception to the Client's process.

   3a2. Fail!

4a.  Resource Lock finds nonzero lock count on Service Client:

   4a1. Resource Lock decrements the reference count of the request.

   4a2. Success!

5a.  Resource Lock finds that the resource is currently not in use:

   5a1. Resource Lock <u>applies an access selection policy</u> (Use Case 16) to grant access to any suspended service clients.

5b.  Holding Timer is still running:

   5b1. Resource Lock cancels Holding Timer.

**Technology and Data Variations List:**

1. The specified requested access can be:

  ◆ For exclusive access

  ◆ For shared access

2c. The lock holding time-out can be specified by:

  ◆ The Service Client

  ◆ A Resource Locking policy

  ◆ A global default value

## Use Case 14   Apply a Lock Conversion Policy

**Primary Actor:** Client object

**Scope:** Concurrency Service Framework (CSF)

**Level:** Subfunction

**Main Success Scenario:**

1. Resource Lock verifies that request is for exclusive access.

2. Resource Lock verifies that Service Client already has shared access.

3. Resource Lock verifies that there is no Service Client waiting to upgrade access.

4 Resource Lock verifies that there are no other Service Clients sharing the resource.

5. Resource Lock grants Service Client exclusive access to the resource.

6. Resource Lock increments Service Client lock count.

**Extensions:**

1a.  Resource Lock finds that the request is for shared access:

   1a1.  Resource Lock increments lock count on Service Client.

   1a2.  Success!

2a.  Resource Lock finds that the Service Client already has exclusive access:

   2a1.  Resource Lock increments lock count on Service Client.

   2a2.  Success!

3a.   Resource Lock finds that there is another Service Client waiting to upgrade access:

    3a1.   Signal Service Client that requested access could not be granted.

    3a2.   Fail!

4a.   Resource Lock finds that there are other Service Clients using the resource:

    4a1.   Resource Lock <u>makes Service Client wait for resource access</u> (Use Case 17).

## Use Case 15   〰 **Apply an Access Compatibility Policy** ⋊⟳

**Primary Actor:** Service Client object

**Scope:** Concurrency Service Framework (CSF)

**Level:** Subfunction

**Main Success Scenario:**

1.   Resource Lock verifies that request is for shared access.

2.   Resource Lock verifies that all current usage of resource is for shared access.

**Extensions:**

2a.   Resource Lock finds that the request is for exclusive access:

    2a1.   Resource Lock <u>makes Service Client wait for resource access</u> (Use Case 17)
        (the process is resumed later by the Lock serving strategy).

2b.   Resource Lock finds that the resource is being exclusively used:

    2b1.   Resource Lock <u>makes Service Client wait for resource access</u> (Use Case 17)

**Variations:**

1.   The compatibility criterion may be changed.

## Use Case 16   〰 **Apply an Access Selection Policy** ⋊⟳

**Primary Actor:** Client object

**Scope:** Concurrency Service Framework (CSF)

**Level:** Subfunction

**Main Success Scenario:**

**Goal in Context:** Resource Lock must determine which (if any) waiting requests should be served.

**Note:** This strategy is a point of variability.

1.   Resource Lock selects oldest waiting request.

2.   Resource Lock grants access to selected request(s) by making its process runnable.

**Extensions:**

1a.   Resource Lock finds no waiting requests:

    1a1.   Success!

1b.   Resource Lock finds a request waiting to be upgraded from a shared to an exclusive access:

    1b1.   Resource Lock selects the upgrading request.

1c. Resource Lock selects a request that is for shared access:

    1c1.  Resource repeats [Step 1] until the next one is for exclusive access.

**Variations:**

1. The selection ordering criterion may be changed.

## Use Case 17   &#x2500;  **Make Service Client Wait for Resource Access**  &#x2500;&#x25CB;

**Primary Actor:** Client object

**Scope:** Concurrency Service Framework (CSF)

**Level:** Subfunction

**Main Success Scenario:**

**Used By:** CC 2,4 Resource Locking:

1. Resource Lock suspends Service Client process.
2. Service Client waits until resumed.
3. Service Client process is resumed.

**Extensions:**

1a. Resource Lock finds that a waiting time-out has been specified:

    1a1. Resource Lock starts timer.

2a. Waiting Timer expires:

    2a1. Signal Service Client that requested access could not be granted.

    2a2. Fail!

**Technology and Data Variations List:**

1a1. The Lock waiting time-out can be specified by:

    &#x25C6; The Service Client

    &#x25C6; A Resource Locking policy

    &#x25C6; A global default value

## 3.3 *THE OUTERMOST USE CASES*

In the Enterprise-to-System Scope subsection on page 41, I recommend writing two use cases, one for the system under design and one at an outer scope. Now we can get more specific about that: For each use case, find the outermost design scope at which it still applies and write a summary-level use case at that scope.

    The use case is written to a design scope. Usually, you can find a wider design scope that still has the primary actor outside it. If you keep widening the scope, you reach the point at which widening it farther would bring the primary actor inside. That is the *outermost scope*. Sometimes the outermost scope is the enterprise, sometime the department, and sometimes just the computer. Often, the computer department is the primary actor on computer security use cases, the marketing department is the primary actor on advertising use cases, and the customer is the primary actor on the main system function use cases.

Typically, there are only two to five outermost use cases for the entire system, so not every use case gets written twice. There are so few of them because each one merges the primary actors having similar goals on the same design scope, and pulls together all the lower-level use cases for those actors.

I highly recommend writing the outermost use cases because it takes very little time and provides excellent context for the use case set. The outermost use cases show how the system ultimately benefits the most external users of the system; they also provide a table of contents for browsing through the system's behavior.

Let's visit the outermost use cases for MyTelCo and its Acura system.

> MyTelCo decides to let web-based customers access Acura directly to reduce the load on the clerks. Acura will also report on the clerks' sales performance. Someone will have to set security access levels for customers and clerks. We have four use cases: *Add Service (by Customer)*, *Add Service (by Clerk)*, *Report Sales Performance*, and *Manage Security Access*.

We know we will have to write all four use cases with Acura as the scope of the SuD. We need to find the outermost scope for each of them.

The customer is clearly outside MyTelCo, so there is one outermost use case with the customer as primary actor and MyTelCo as scope. This use case will be at the summary level, showing MyTelCo as a black box, responding to the customer's request, delivering the service, and so on. In fact, the use case is outlined in Use Case 6, *Add New Service (Enterprise),* on page 42.

The clerk is inside MyTelCo. The outermost scope for *Add Feature (by Staff)* is All Computer Systems. This use case will gather all the interactions the clerks have with the computer systems. I would expect all the clerks' user-goal use cases to be in this outermost use case, along with a few subfunction use cases, such as *Log In* and *Log Out*.

*Report Sales Performance* has the Marketing Department as the ultimate primary actor. The outermost use case is at scope Service Department and shows the Marketing Department interacting with All Computer Systems and the Service Department for setting up performance bonuses, reporting sales performance, and so on.

*Manage Security Access* has the Security or IT Department as its ultimate primary actor and either the IT Department or All Computer Systems as the outermost design scope. The use case references all the ways the Security Department uses All Computer Systems to set and track security issues.

Notice that these four outermost use cases cover security, marketing, service, and customers, using Acura in all the ways that it operates. It is unlikely that more than these four need to be written for the Acura system, even if there are a hundred lower-level use cases to write.

## 3.4 USING THE SCOPE-DEFINING WORK PRODUCTS

You are defining the functional scope for your upcoming system, brainstorming, and moving between several work products on the whiteboard. On one part of the whiteboard, you have the in/out list to keep track of your scoping decisions ("No, Bob, we decided that a new printing system is out of scope—or do we need to revisit that entry in the in/out list?"). You have the actors and their goals in a list. You have a drawing of the design scope, showing the people, organizations, and systems that will interact with the system under discussion.

You find that you are evolving them all as you move between them, working out what you want your new system to do. You think you know what the design scope is, but a change in the in/out list moves the boundary. Now you have a new primary actor, and the goal list changes.

Sooner or later, you will probably find that you need a fourth item: a *vision statement* for the new system. The vision statement holds together the overall discussion. It helps you decide whether something should be in scope or out of scope in the first place.

When you are done, you have the four work products that bind the system's scope:

◆ Vision statement
◆ Design scope drawing
◆ In/out list
◆ Actor-goal list

What I want you to take from this short discussion is that the four work products are intertwined and that you are likely to change them all while establishing the scope of the work to be done.

## 3.5 EXERCISES

### Design Scope

**3.1.** Name at least five system design scopes that the following user story fragment could be about: "... *Jenny is standing in front of her bank's ATM. It is dark. She has entered her PIN and is looking for the Enter button* ..."

**3.2.** Draw a picture of the multiple scopes for an ATM, including hardware and software.

**3.3.** What system are you, personally, writing requirements for? What is its extent? What is inside it? What is outside it that it must communicate with? What is the system that encloses it, and what is outside that containing system that *it* must communicate with? Give the enclosing system a name.

**3.4.** Draw a picture of the multiple scopes for the Personal Advisors/Finance (PAF) system. (See Excercise 4.4.)

**3.5.** Draw a picture of the multiple scopes for a web application in which a user's workstation is connected through the web to your company's web server, which is attached to a legacy mainframe system.

**3.6.** Describe the difference between *enterprise-scope white-box business use cases* and *enterprise-scope black-box business use cases*.

# Chapter 4

# *Stakeholders and Actors*

A stakeholder is someone who participates in the contract. An actor is anything having behavior—as one student said, "It must be able to execute an *if* statement." An actor might be a person, a company or organization, a computer program, or a computer system—hardware, software, or both.

Look for actors in

- The *stakeholders* of the system
- The *primary actor* of a use case
- The *system under design* (*SuD*) itself
- The *supporting actors* of a use case
- The *internal actors*—the components within the SuD

## 4.1 STAKEHOLDERS

A stakeholder is someone or something that has a vested interest in the behavior of the use case.

Every primary actor is, of course, a stakeholder, but some stakeholders never interact directly with the system, even though they have a right to care how the system behaves. Examples are the owner of the system, the company's board of directors, and regulatory bodies such as the Internal Revenue Service and the Department of Insurance.

Students have nicknamed stakeholders that never appear directly in the action steps of the use case *offstage, tertiary,* or *silent* actors.

Paying attention to these silent actors significantly improves the quality of a use case. Their interests show up in the checks and validations the system performs, the logs it creates, and the actions it performs. The business rules are documented because the system must enforce them on behalf of the stakeholders. The use cases need to show how the system protects these stakeholders' interests. Here is a story that illustrates the cost of forgetting them.

---

◆ **A Short, True Story**

In the first year of operation after selling several copies of its new system, a company received some system change requests. That all seemed natural enough, until they took a use case course and were asked to brainstorm the stakeholders and interests in their recently delivered system.

Much to their surprise, they found they were naming their recent change request items during their brainstorming. Evidently, while developing the system, they had completely overlooked some of the interests of some of the stakeholders. It didn't take those stakeholders long to notice that the system wasn't serving them properly, and hence the change requests had started coming in.

The leader has since become adamant about naming stakeholders and interests early on, to avoid a repeat of this expensive mistake.

---

My colleagues and I find that we identify significant and otherwise unmentioned requirements early by asking about the stakeholders and their interests. It doesn't take much time to do this, and it saves a great deal of effort later on.

## 4.2 THE PRIMARY ACTOR

The primary actor of a use case is the stakeholder that calls on the system to deliver one of its services. It has a goal with respect to the system—one that can be satisfied by its operation. The primary actor is often, but not always, the actor who triggers the use case.

Usually, the use case starts because the primary actor sends a message, pushes a button, enters a keystroke, or in some other way initiates the story. However, there are two common situations in which the initiator of the use case is not the primary actor. The first is when a company clerk or phone operator initiates the use case on behalf of someone else; the second is when the use case is triggered by time.

A company clerk or phone operator is often a technological convenience for the *ultimate primary actor,* the person who actually cares. With technology shifting, it becomes more likely that the ultimate primary actor will initiate, or trigger, the use case directly, using the web or an automated phone system. An example is the customer who currently phones in with a request. In a web redesign of the system, she may enter her request directly (as with *Amazon.com*).

Similarly, the marketing or auditing division might insist on use cases that are to be operated by a clerk. It is not the clerk's goal to have the use case run; the use case is a technological convenience for the marketing managers. Under slightly different circumstances, the marketing managers would run the use cases themselves.

These days I write, "sales rep for the customer" or "clerk for the marketing department" to capture that the user of the system is acting for someone else. This lets us know that the user interface and security clearances need to be designed for a clerk, but that the customer or marketing department is the one who cares about the outcome.

Time is the other example of a nonoperator trigger. There is no clerk triggering the use cases that run every midnight or at the end of the month. In this case, it is easy to see that the primary actor is whichever stakeholder cares that the use case runs at that time.

We could get into long arguments on the topic of users versus ultimate primary actors. I suggest you don't spend too much time on it or else argue in a pub. When the team starts investigating the user interface design, they will—or should—put a good deal of effort into studying the real users' characteristics. When they review the requirements, they will find it useful to know the ultimate primary actor for each use case, that is, who it is that really cares.

As one student astutely asked, "How much damage is there if we get the primary actor wrong at this point?" The answer is "Not much," as the following section illustrates.

## Why Primary Actors Are Unimportant (and Important)

Primary actors are important at the beginning of requirements gathering and just before system delivery. Between those two points, they are remarkably unimportant.

### At the Beginning of Use Case Production

Listing primary actors helps us get our minds around the entire system for one brief moment (it will escape us soon enough). We brainstorm to name all the actors in order to brainstorm to name all the goals. It is the goals that really interest us, but if we brainstorm them directly, we will miss too many. Brainstorming the primary actors sets up a work structure. We can then traverse that structure to get a better goal list.

Creating a slightly larger number of primary actors does not hurt, since at the worst we will generate the same goal twice. When we go over the actors and goals to prioritize the work, we will find and remove the duplicates.

Even with this careful double brainstorming, however, it is unlikely that we will name all of the goals our system needs to support. New ones have a tendency to show up while writing the failure-handling steps of a use case, but that is something we can't change at this early stage. We do our best to capture all the goals by listing all the primary actors first.

A rich list of primary actors confers three other advantages:

- It focuses our minds on the people who will use the system. In the requirements document, we write down who we expect the primary actors to be, their job descriptions, and their typical background and skills. We do this so that the user interface and system designers can match the system to that expertise.
- It sets up the structure for the actor-goal list, which will be used to prioritize and partition the development work.
- It will be used to partition a large set of use cases into packages that can be given to different design teams.

## During Use Case Writing and during Design

Once we start developing the use cases in detail, the primary actors become almost unimportant, which is surprising. What happens is that over time, use case writers discover that a use case can be used by many sorts of actors. For example, anyone higher than *Clerk* might answer the phone and talk to a customer. Thus, the writers often start naming the primary actor in an increasingly generic way, using role names such as *Loss Taker*, *Order Taker*, or *Invoice Producer*. This leads to use cases that say, The invoice producer produces the invoice..., or The order taker takes the order..., (which is not terribly enlightening).

You can handle this fragmentation of roles in several ways, each with a small advantage and disadvantage. No strategy is clearly superior, so you just have to choose one.

*ALTERNATIVE 1.* Break down the primary actors according to the roles they play. Create an actor-to-role table that lists all the different people and systems that are the primary actor in any use case and all the roles they play. Use role names in the Primary Actor field. Use the actor-role table to get from the use cases to the people and systems in the world.

This strategy allows writers to ignore the intricacies of job titles and simply get on with their writing. Someone, perhaps the user interface designer or the software packager, will use the actor-to-role table to match up the use cases with their eventual users. The trouble with alternative 1 is that there is a separate list to maintain and read.

*ALTERNATIVE 2.* Somewhere in the front of the use case section, write, "The Manager can do any use case the Clerk can, plus more. The Regional Manager can do any use case the Manager can, plus more. Therefore, wherever we write that the primary actor is (e.g.) the Clerk, it is to be understood that any person with more seniority—the Manager and Regional Manager in this case—can also do the use case."

This writing is easier to maintain than the actor-to-role table, as it is unlikely to change. Its disadvantage is that people will spend more time reminding each other that when *Clerk* is written as the primary actor, *Manager* also can run the use case.

People achieve adequate results with both alternatives. For what it's worth, I use the second one because I like having one less work product to write, review, and maintain.

The point is, the *Primary Actor* field of the use case template becomes devalued over time. This is normal, and you shouldn't worry about it.

### After Design, Preparing to Deploy the System

Just before delivering the system, the primary actors become important again. We need the list of all the *people* and which use cases they will run. We need these:

+ To package the system into units that get loaded onto the various users' machines
+ To set security levels for each use case (web users, internal, supervisor, etc.)
+ To create training for the various user groups

## *Actors versus Roles*

The word *actor* implies an *individual* in action. Sometimes, in a use case, it means an individual. Sometimes, though, it indicates the general category of individuals who can play a given role.

Suppose that Kim is a customer of MyTelCo, Chris is a clerk, and Pat is a sales manager. Any one of them can *Place an Order*. Using the language of *actors*, we say that Kim, Chris, and Pat can be primary actors for the *Place an Order* use case. We also say that *Customer, Clerk*, and *Sales Manager* are the allowed primary actors for *Place an Order*. We might say that "A sales manager can perform any use case a clerk can." These are all fine ways of speaking.

Using the language of *roles*, we say that Kim, Chris, and Pat are individual actors. Any one of them can play the role of *Customer*, but only Chris and Pat can play the role of *Clerk*, and only Pat can play the role of *Sales Manager*. Then we say that the role that drives the *Place an Order* use case is *Order Taker* and that *Customer, Clerk*, or *Sales Manager* can play the *Order Taker* role. This way of speaking is more precise than the previous way, and some people prefer it. It is, however, nonstandard in the use case world.

The point is that you should use whichever terms your team prefers. In the earlier subsection, Why Primary Actors Are Unimportant (and Important), I showed why the matter should not cause you too much stress and how to deal with some of the situations that arise. In the meantime, *actor* is the term the industry has accepted. It works quite adequately, which is why I use it in this book.

### Unified Modeling Language Diagrams and Actor/Role Specialization

UML provides a hollow-headed arrow to indicate that one actor *specializes* another (see Figure A.6, Correctly closing a big deal, on page 241).

The good part about this arrow is that it allows you to express succinctly that a manager can do anything a clerk can do: simply draw the arrow with its head at *Clerk* and its tail at *Manager*.

The bad part is that to many people, the resulting drawing appears backwards. They don't think of a manager as *a special kind of* clerk or a clerk as *a special kind of* customer, which is what the drawing seems to assert (it actually asserts that the one *can do anything the other can do*). They think of a manager as *more than a* clerk. This reaction is not a big thing, but you will have to deal with it.

The specialization arrow does not help at all with the main part of the actor–role question. A *Sales Clerk* and an *Auditing Clerk* have overlapping use case sets, but you cannot use the specialization arrow between them, since neither can do all that the other can do. Thus, you are back in the middle of the actor–role controversy.

## *Characterizing the Primary Actors*

Just having a list of actors is not of much help to designers, who should know what skills the users will have so they can design the system behavior and the user interface to match. Teams that create an *actor profile table* say they keep a better view of how their software will suit the needs of the end users, because they have the skills of their end users in front of them during development.

The simplest actor profile table has just two columns, as shown in the Table 4.1. Some also list other names, or *aliases*, the actors are known by. Variations of the actor profile table are discussed in *Software for Use* (Constantine and Lockwood, 1999).

**Table 4.1.** *A Sample Actor Profile Table*

| Name | Profile: Background and Skills |
| --- | --- |
| Customer | Person off the street, able to use a touch-screen display, but not expected to operate a GUI with subtlety or ease. May have difficulty reading, be shortsighted, colorblind, etc. |
| Returned Goods Clerk | Person working with this software continuously. Touch-types and is a sophisticated user. May want to customize the UI. |
| Manager | Occasional user, used to GUIs but not familiar with any particular software function. Impatient. |

## 4.3 SUPPORTING ACTORS

A supporting actor in a use case is an external actor that provides a service to the system under design. It might be a high-speed printer, a web service, or humans who have to do some research and get back to us (for example, the coroner's office, which provides the insurance company with confirmation of a person's death). We used to call this a *secondary* actor, but people found the term confusing. More people are now using *supporting* actor, which is the more natural term.

We identify supporting actors in order to identify the external interfaces the system will use and the protocols that cross those interfaces. This feeds the other requirements, such as the data formats and external interfaces (see Figure 1.1 on page 15).

An actor can be primary in one use case and supporting in another.

## 4.4 THE SYSTEM UNDER DISCUSSION

The system under discussion is itself an actor—a special one. We usually refer to it by its name, for example, *Acura*, or we say *the system,* the *system under discussion,* the *system under design,* or *SuD*. It is named or described in the Design Scope field of the use case.

The SuD is not a primary or supporting actor for any use case, although it is an actor. It was discussed at length in the *Design Scope* subsection on page 38.

## 4.5 INTERNAL ACTORS AND WHITE-BOX USE CASES

Most of the time, we treat the system under discussion as a *black box*, which we cannot see inside. Internal actors are purposely not mentioned, which makes good sense when we use the use cases to name requirements for a system that has not yet been designed.

Occasionally we want to use the use-case form to document how the parts of the system cooperate to deliver the correct behavior. We do this when documenting business processes, as in Use Case 5, *Buy Something (Fully Dressed Version),* on page 9, and Use Case 19, *Handle a Claim (Business)* on page 70. We might do this when showing the larger design for a multi-computer system, as in Use Case 8, *Enter and Update Requests (Joint System),* on page 43. In such circumstances, components of the system show up as actors.

When we look inside the system and name the components and their behavior, we treat the system as a *white box*. Everything about writing use cases still works; it is just that we discuss the behaviors of both the internal and the external actors. There are more than just two actors in a white-box use case, since the components of the system as well as the external actors are being shown.

It is extremely rare, and usually a mistake, to write white-box use cases as behavioral requirements for a computer system to be designed.

## 4.6 EXERCISES

### Actors and Stakeholders

**4.1.** Identify a use case for a vending machine in which the owner is the primary actor.

**4.2.** You have been hired to create the requirements document for a new ATM. Decide whether each item in the following list is a stakeholder, a primary actor, a supporting actor, the system under design, or not an actor at all (or a multiple of the above).

> The ATM
> The customer
> The ATM card
> The bank
> The front panel
> The bank owner
> The serviceman
> The printer
> The main bank computer system
> The bank teller
> The bank robber

**4.3.** The ATM is a component in a larger system. In fact, it is part of several larger systems. Repeat the previous exercise for one such containing system.

**4.4.** Personal Advisors, Inc. (a hypothetical company) is coming out with a new product that will allow people to review their financial investment strategies, such as retirement, education funds, land, and stock. The product Personal Advisor/Finance (PAF) comes on a CD. The user installs it and then runs various financial scenarios to learn how to optimize his financial future. PAF can also interrogate various tax packages, such as Kiplinger Tax Cut, for tax laws. Personal Advisors is setting up an agreement with Kiplinger to allow direct exchange. They are also setting up an agreement with various mutual fund and web stock services, such as Vanguard and E*Trade, to directly buy and sell funds and stocks over the web. The company thinks it would also be a great idea to have a version of PAF that is web active, on a pay-per-use basis.

Name and identify PAF's actors, primary actors, supporting actors, system under design, and containing system (a system having PAF as a component).

# Chapter 5

# *Three Named Goal Levels*

We have seen that both the goals and the interactions in a scenario can be unfolded into finer- and finer-grained goals and interactions. This is normal, and we handle it well in everyday life. The following two paragraphs illustrate how our goals contain sub- and sub-subgoals.

I want this sales contract. To do that I have to take this manager out to lunch. To do that I have to get some cash. To do that I have to withdraw money from this ATM. To do that I have to get it to accept my identity. To do that I have to get it to read my ATM card. To do that I have to find the card slot.

I want to find the tab key so I can get the cursor into the Address field, so I can put in my address, so I can get my personal information into this quote software, so I can get a quote, so I can buy a car insurance policy, so I can get my car licensed, so I can drive.

However normal this is in everyday life, it causes confusion when writing a use case. A writer is faced with the question "What level of goal should I describe?" at every sentence.

Giving names to goal levels helps. The following sections describe the goal-level names and icons I have found useful and how to find the goal level you need at the moment. Figure 5.1 illustrates the names and visual metaphors I use.

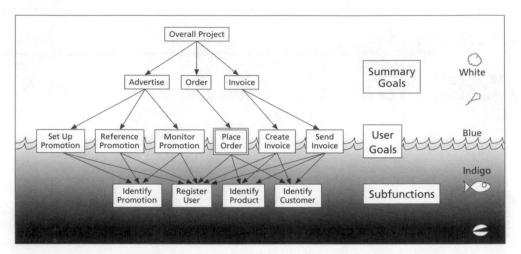

**Figure 5.1  *Use case levels.*** *The use case set reveals a hierarchy of goals—the* ever-unfolding story.

## 5.1 USER GOALS (BLUE, SEA-LEVEL ◡◡ )

The *user goal* is of the greatest interest. It is the goal the primary actor has in trying to get work done or the one the user has in using the system. It corresponds to "elementary business process" in business process engineering.

A user goal addresses the question "Can the primary actor go away happy after having done this?" For a clerk, it is "Does your job performance depend on how many of these you do today?," or the *coffee break test*: "After I get done with this, I can take a coffee break." In most circumstances, it passes the one person, one sitting test (2–20 minutes).

Neither "Complete an online auction purchase" nor "Log on" generally counts as a user goal. Online auctions take several days and so fail the single-sitting test. Logging on 42 times in a row does not (usually) satisfy the person's job responsibilities or purpose in using the system.

"Register a new customer" and "Buy a book" are likely to be user goals. Registering 42 new customers has some significance to a sales agent. A book purchase can be completed in a single sitting.

So far it should all look easy. However, faced with a slew of phrases on a whiteboard, or a use case that doesn't look right for some reason, it is easy to become uncertain. I find that most people can get their bearings when expressing goal levels either in *colors* or *altitudes*.

The color gradient runs from white to blue to indigo to black (shown as shades of grey in this book). The user goal is blue. Longer-range, higher-level goals, such as

"Complete an online auction" and "Get paid for a car accident," are white. Shorter-range, lower-level goals are indigo. Black indicates that a goal is at so low a level that it would be a mistake to write a use case for it. "Hit tab key" is a good example.

The idea with the sea-level metaphor is this: The sky goes upwards for a long distance above sea level, and the water goes down for a long distance below sea level, but there is only one level where sky and sea meet: *at* sea level. The same holds for goals. There are many goal levels above the user goal and many below, but the user goals are the important ones to write. Therefore, sea level (waves) corresponds to them. A cloud or a kite indicates higher than sea level; a fish or a clam indicates lower than sea level.

The system is justified by its support of sea-level goals. Here is one such goal:

> You are a clerk sitting at your station. The phone rings, you pick it up. The person on the other end says, ". . . " You turn to your computer. On your mind at that moment is that you need to accomplish G. You work with the computer and the customer for a while and finally accomplish G. You turn away from computer, say, "Good-bye," and hang up the phone.

G is the blue, or sea-level, user goal. In accomplishing G, you accomplish a number of lower-level (indigo) goals. The person on the phone probably has a higher-level goal in mind, and accomplishing G is only one step in that. That person's higher-level goals are white.

The sea-level/blue user goals are incredibly important, so it is worth a large amount of effort to understand and internalize them. The shortest summary of a system's function is the list of user goals it supports—this is the basis for prioritization, delivery, team division, estimation, and development.

Use cases will be written at levels above and below sea level. It is handy to think of the enormous number of lower-level goals and use cases as being "underwater," as that implies that we don't really want to write them or read them.

---

### ◆ A Short, True Story

I was once sent over a hundred pages of use cases, all indigo, or underwater. That requirements document was so long and boring that it did not serve either its writers or readers. The sender later sent me the six sea-level use cases that had replaced them and said that everyone found them easier to understand and work with.

---

## *Two Levels of Blue*

Usually, a blue use case has one white use case above it and several indigo use cases below it. However, it occasionally refers to another blue use case. I have seen this occur only in one situation, but that situation shows up repeatedly.

Suppose I walk past the video rental store, doing some errands. I think, "I might as well register now, while I'm here." So I walk in and ask to *Set up a Membership*. That is my user goal, the blue use case. The next week, I go in with my membership card and *Rent a Video*. I execute the two user goals on different days.

However, you rent differently. You walk into the video store to *Rent a Video*. The clerk asks, "Are you a member?" You say, "No," and so the clerk has you *Set up a Membership* within the process of renting your first video. *Set up a Membership* is a step inside *Rent a Video*, even though both are blue goals.

This "Register a person in passing" is the only situation in which I recall seeing one blue use case inside another one. When asked about this, I say, a bit tongue-in-cheek, that both are at sea level, but *Rent a Video* sits at the top of a wave shown in Figure 5.1, and *Set up a Membership* sits in its trough.

## 5.2  SUMMARY LEVEL (WHITE, CLOUD ◌ /KITE ◿)

*Summary-level* goals[*] involve multiple user goals. They serve three purposes in describing the system:

◆ They show the context in which the user goals operate.

◆ They show life-cycle sequencing of related goals.

◆ They provide a table of contents for the lower-level use cases, both white and blue.

Summary use cases are white on the color gradient. White use cases have steps that are white, blue, or occasionally even indigo ("Log in" is an indigo goal likely to be found in a white use case). I don't find it useful to distinguish between various levels of white, but occasionally a speaker will say something like "That use case is *really* white, 'way-up-in-the-clouds' white." In terms of the sea-level metaphor, we say that most summary use cases are "like a kite, just above sea level" and that others are "way up in the clouds."

Summary use cases typically execute over hours, days, weeks, months, or years. Here is the main scenario from a long-running use case, whose purpose is to tie together blue use cases scattered over years. You should be able to see that the graphics highlight that the use case deals with the company as a black box and that the goal level is very white (up in the clouds). The underlined phrases are lower-level use cases. Note the plus sign at the end of the name. Putting a suffix of '+' is an alternate way to indicate summary-level use cases, and is further described in Section 5.4.

---

[*] In previous writing, I used both "strategic" and "summary." I recently decided "summary" causes the least confusion and so chose that word for this book.

## Use Case 18  🏠 Operate an Insurance Policy+ ☁

**Primary Actor:** The customer
**Scope:** The insurance company ("MyInsCo")
**Level:** Summary ("white")
**Steps:**
1. Customer gets a quote for a policy.
2. Customer buys a policy.
3. Customer makes a claim against the policy.
4. Customer closes the policy.

Other white use cases in this chapter are

- Use Case 19, *Handle a Claim (Business),* on page 70
- Use Case 20, *Evaluate Work Comp Claim,* on page 72
- Use Case 21, *Handle a Claim (Systems)*, on page 73

## *The Outermost Use Cases Revisited*

Earlier, I recommended that you write a few outermost use cases for the system you are designing. Here is the more precise process for finding those use cases:

1. Start with a user goal.
2. Ask, "What (preferably outside the organization) primary actor, AA, does this goal serve?" Actor AA is the *ultimate primary actor* of the use cases we are about to collect.
3. Find the outermost design scope S such that AA is still outside S. Name the scope S. I typically find three such outermost design scopes:
   - The company.
   - The software systems combined.
   - The specific software system being designed.
4. Find all the user goals having ultimate primary actor AA and design scope S.
5. Work out the summary goal, GG, that actor AA has for system S.
6. Write the summary use case for goal GG of actor AA against system S. This use case ties together a number of sea-level use cases.

There are usually only about four or five of these topmost use cases (GG) even in the largest systems. They summarize the interests of the three or four ultimate primary actors (AA):

- The customer, to the company
- The marketing department, to the software systems combined
- The security department, to the software system itself

These outermost use cases are very useful in holding the work together, and I highly recommend writing them for the reasons given earlier. They will not, however, provide your team with the functional requirements for the system to be built—those reside in the user-goal (blue) use cases.

## 5.3  SUBFUNCTIONS (INDIGO/BLACK, UNDERWATER ⋈/CLAM ⊜)

*Subfunction-level* goals are those required to carry out user goals. Include them only as you have to—they are needed on occasion for readability or because many other goals use them. Examples of subfunction use cases are *Find a Product, Find a Customer,* and *Save as a File*. See, in particular, the unusual indigo use case, Use Case 23, *Find a Whatever (Problem Statement),* on page 78.

Subfunction use cases are underwater, indigo. Some are so far underwater that they sit on the bottom. Those we color black to mean "This is so low level, please don't even expand it into a use case" ("It doesn't even swim . . . it's a clam!"). It is handy to have a special name for these ultra-low-level use cases, so that when someone writes one you can indicate that it shouldn't be written, that its contents ought to be rolled into another use case.

Blue use cases have indigo steps, and indigo use cases have deeper indigo steps, as shown later in Figure 5.2. The figure also shows that to find a higher goal level for your goal phrase, you answer the question, "Why is the actor doing this?" This "how/why" technique is discussed more in Section 5.5.

Note that even the farthest underwater, lowest subfunction use case has a primary actor that is outside the system. I wouldn't bother to mention this, except that people occasionally talk about subfunctions as though they were somehow internal design discussions or lacking a primary actor. A subfunction use case follows all the rules for use cases. It is probable that a subfunction has the same primary actor as that of the higher-level use case that refers to it.

### Summarizing Goal Levels

For now, three points about goal levels are important:

- Put a lot of energy into detecting the sea-level use cases. These are the important ones.
- Write a few outermost use cases to provide context for the others.

- Don't make a big fuss over whether your favorite phrase among the system requirements sentences "makes it" as a use case title.

Making it as a use case title doesn't mean "most important requirement," and not making it doesn't mean "unimportant." I see people upset because their favorite requirement was *merely* a step in a use case that did not get promoted to a use case that is tracked on its own.

Don't worry about this. One of the points of the goal model is that it is a relatively small change to move a complex chunk of text into its own use case or to fold a trivial use case back into a higher-level one. Every sentence is written as a goal, and every goal can be unfolded into its own use case. We cannot tell by looking at the writing which sentences have been unfolded and which have not (except by following the links). This is good, since it preserves the integrity of the writing across minor changes. The only goals that are guaranteed to have their own use cases are the blue ones.

## 5.4  USING GRAPHICAL ICONS TO HIGHLIGHT GOAL LEVELS

In the Using Graphic Icons to Highlight the Design Scope subsection on page 40, I showed some icons that are usefully put to the left of the use case title. Because goal levels are at least as confusing as titles, I put a goal-level icon at the top right of the title. This is in addition to filling the fields in the template. My experience is that readers (and writers) can use all the help they can get in knowing the level.

In keeping with the altitude nomenclature, I separate five altitudes. You will use only the middle three in most situations.

- Very summary (very white) use cases get a cloud, ☁. Use this on that rarest of occasions when you see that the steps in the use case are themselves white goals. If you cannot add icons, add a plus sign (+) to the end of the use case name, as in Use Case 18.

- Summary (white) use cases get a kite, ◊. This is for most summary use cases, whose steps are blue goals. Again, add a "+" to the use case name if you cannot use the icon.

- User-goal (blue, sea-level) use cases get waves, 〜. Add no suffix or an exclamation mark (!) to the name if you cannot use icons.

- Subfunction (indigo) use cases get a fish, ⋈. Use this for most indigo use cases. Add a minus sign (−) if you cannot use icons.

- Some subfunctions (black) should never be written. Use a clam, ⊖, to mark a use case that needs to be merged with its calling use case.

With these icons, you can mark the design scope and goal level even on UML use case diagrams as soon as the tool vendors support them. You can use the suffixes right away. If your template already contains Design Scope and Goal Level fields, you may use them as redundant markers. If your template does not contain those fields, add them.

## 5.5 FINDING THE RIGHT GOAL LEVEL

Finding the right goal level is the single hardest thing about use cases. Focus on these guidelines:

- Find the user's goal.
- Use 3 to 10 steps per use case.

### Finding the User's Goal

In all of the goal levels, only one stands out from the others:

> You are describing a system, whether a business or a computer. You care about someone using the system. That person wants something from your system *now*. After getting it, she can go on and do something else. What is it she wants from your system now?

> That level has many names. In business process modeling, it is called an *elementary business process*. In French, it is the system's *raison d'être*. In use cases, it is the *user's goal*.

> Ask the question "Is this what the primary actor really wants from the system now?" For most first drafts of use cases, the answer is "No." Most beginners draft underwater use cases, thinking they are at sea level. To find the higher-level goal, ask either of these two questions:

- What does the primary actor really want?
- Why is this actor doing this?

The answer might be the actor's real goal, but ask the question again, until you are sure. The interesting thing is that even though the tests for a user goal are subjective, people soon come to consensus on the matter. Experienced people have surprisingly similar answers for user goals. It seems to be a stable concept.

## *Raising and Lowering Goal Levels*

The steps in a use case describe how a process gets done; the name of the use case indicates why the process is of interest. You can draw on this how-why relationship when searching for the appropriate goal level to use in a step (see Figure 5.2).

To raise the goal level of one or several steps, ask "Why is the actor doing this?" The answer will be a goal one level higher.

A way to judge goal levels is to look at the use case length. Most well-written use cases have 3 to 8 steps. I have never seen one longer than 11 steps that didn't get better when shortened. I doubt there is anything magical about those numbers, but if I were to guess, I would say that people do not tolerate or think in terms of processes that take more than 10 intermediate steps. I keep waiting for a legitimate counter-example just to prove that the numbers have no deep significance.

Whatever the reason, use this observation to improve your writing. If you have more than 10 steps, you probably included user interface details or wrote action steps at too low a level.

◆ Remove the user interface details. Show the actor's intent, not his movement.

◆ Raise the goal level by asking the "why" question to find the next higher goal level.

◆ Merge steps.

◆ Compare your use cases with the writing samples in Section 5.6 and in Chapter 19, Mistakes Fixed.

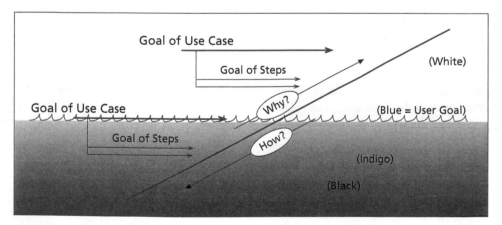

**Figure 5.2** *Ask "why" to shift levels*

## 5.6 A LONGER WRITING SAMPLE: "HANDLE A CLAIM" AT SEVERAL LEVELS

I would like to thank the people at Fireman's Fund Insurance Corporation in Novato, California, for allowing me to include Use Cases 19 through 23 as writing samples.[*] They were written by claims-handling professionals directly from the field, working with business analysts from the IT department and the technical development staff. The field staff had insights about the use of the system that the IT staff could not have guessed, and the IT staff helped the field staff make the writing precise. Between them, they combined field, corporate, and technical viewpoints.

The writing team included Kerry Bear, Eileen Curran, Brent Hupp, Paula Ivey, Susan Passini, Pamela Pratt, Steve Sampson, Jill Schicktanz, Nancy Jewell, Trisha Magdaleno, Marc Greenberg, Nicole Lazar, Dawn Coppolo, and Eric Evans. They demonstrate that usage experts with no software background can work with IT staff in writing requirements.

I include five use cases to illustrate the things we have discussed so far, particularly design scopes and goal levels. These use cases also illustrate good writing style for steps and extensions. I provide a commentary before each use case, indicating some points of interest or contention.

The set starts with a cloud-level, white-box business use case that shows the business processes involved in handling a claim. Watch how the goals go into lower levels and how the system scope shrinks from "company operations" to "all computer systems" to just "the system under design." The underlined phrases are references to other use cases. The template was modified a little so that the main success scenario is closer to the top and faster to read.

**COMMENTARY ON USE CASE 19.** The SuD is the operations of the company. Note that the computer system is not even mentioned. The use case will be used by the business to anchor its business procedures and to search for a way to use the computer to facilitate its operations. At the moment, this use case is only in its first stage of sketching. As usual, the main success scenario looks trivial, as it should. It shows how things work in the best success situation! The interesting bits will show up in the failure conditions and in how the company uses this information to make improvements to its IT support of operations. Note the stakeholders.

---

[*] Copyright © 1999 by the Fireman's Fund, Novato, CA. Used with permission.

## Use Case 19 ⌂ Handle a Claim (Business) ◯

**Scope:** Insurance company operations ⌂
**Level:** Business summary
**Release:** Future
**Status:** Draft
**Revision:** Current
**Context of Use:** Claims Adjuster handles claim.
**Preconditions:** A loss has occurred.
**Trigger:** A claim is reported to insurance company.
**Main Success Scenario:**
1. A reporting party who is aware of the event <u>registers a loss</u> to insurance company.
2. Clerk receives and <u>assigns the claim</u> to a claims adjuster.
3. The assigned Claims Adjuster
   <u>conducts an investigation</u>
   <u>evaluates damages</u>
   <u>sets reserves</u>
   <u>negotiates the claim</u>
   <u>resolves the claim</u> and <u>closes it</u>
**Extensions:**
   To be written.
**Success Guarantee:** Claim is resolved and closed.
**Minimal Guarantee:** None.
**Stakeholders and Interests:**
   Insurance company Divisions who sell insurance company policies
   Insurance company Customers who have purchased policies
   Department of Insurance, which sets market conduct
   Claimants who have a loss as a result of act of an insured
   Insurance company Claims Division
   Future Customers

**COMMENTARY ON USE CASE 20.** Here is another business use case, in which the SUD is still the operations of the company. However, the goal is at a lower level than in Use Case 19. It shows an adjuster's work that may take days, weeks, or months. It is a kite-level summary use case because it contains many single-sitting activities.

The writer does not mention the computer directly, but only names the goals of the adjuster. The team must take a leap of imagination to invent what in this process the computer can help with. This use case is the raw material for their act of invention.

Step 7 was added because of the interests of the Department of Insurance.

## Use Case 20 🏠 Evaluate Work Comp Claim 🔍

**Scope:** Insurance company Operations 🏠

**Level:** White (summary, above single user goal level)

**Context of Use:** Claims Adjuster completes thorough evaluation of the facts of a loss.

**Primary Actor:** Claims Adjuster

**Preconditions:** To be documented

**Trigger:** To be documented

**Main Success Scenario:**

**Please Note:** Investigation has ideally been completed prior to evaluation, although the depth of the investigation can vary from claim to claim.

1. Adjuster reviews and <u>evaluates the medical reports</u>, lien documents, benefits paid to date, and other supporting documents.
2. Adjuster <u>rates the permanent disability</u> by using a jurisdictional formula to determine % of disability.
3. Adjuster <u>sums the permanent disability owed</u>, taking credit for advances and payment of liens to arrive at the claim's full value.
4. Adjuster <u>determines the final settlement range</u>.
5. Adjuster <u>checks reserves</u> to make sure they are in line with settlement range.
6. Adjuster <u>seeks authorization for settlement and reserve increase</u> if above his/her authority level.
7. Adjuster <u>documents the file</u>.
8. Adjuster <u>sends any correspondence and/or documentation</u> to parties involved as necessary.
9. Adjuster continues to <u>document file</u> regarding all settlement activity.

**Extensions:** . . .

**Frequency of Occurrence:** Every claim is evaluated; this can happen several times a day.

**Success Guarantee:** Claim is evaluated and settlement range determined.

**Minimal Guarantee:** Additional investigation or medical evaluations are completed until claim is ready to be re-evaluated for settlement.

**Stakeholders and Interests:**

Claimant—wants maximum settlement.

Adjuster—wants lowest legitimate settlement.

Insurance company—same.

Attorney (defense and plaintiff) of Insureds.

Division of Insurance, and state governing offices (each state has a separate governing department that oversees the administration of benefits and fairness of settlements), wants fairness and adherence to procedures.

**Open Issues:** Jurisdictional issues will have to be addressed when writing the business rules.

**COMMENTARY ON USE CASE 21.** To many people on the project, this system use case seemed so vague as to be useless. However, it paid for its writing time in several ways.

First, it glues together a number of user-goal use cases, showing how they fit within the business guidelines. It describes closing, purging, and archiving a claim, which was a mystery to a number of people on the project. Although the last three steps do not generate work for the programmers, they are part of the story of handling a claim, useful contextual information for every reader.

Second, it put into the official files certain business rules that were unknown to some of the team. The team had spent three work-hours the day before trying to guess those rules. Once this use case was written, many more hours of discussion on the topic were saved.

This use case serves as an introduction and table of contents to new readers ranging from company executives to new hires. Executives can see that the key processes are included; newcomers can learn how the company works, and drill down into the user-goal use cases. Extension *a1 is interesting, since it calls out a failure-handling use case that couldn't be written by the claims adjustors but had to be written by the technical group.

## Use Case 21    🗇 Handle a Claim (Systems) + 🖉

**Scope:** "System" means all computer systems combined 🗇.
**Level:** Summary (white)
**Release:** 1st
**Status:** Ready for review
**Revision:** Current
**Context of Use:** Customer wants to get paid for an incident.
**Primary Actor:** Customer
**Preconditions:** None
**Trigger:** Customer reports a claim.
**Main Success Scenario:**
1. Customer reports a claim (paper, phone, or fax) to Clerk.
2. Clerk <u>finds the policy, registers loss</u> in System, and assigns an Adjuster.
3. Adjuster investigates the claim and <u>updates the claim</u> with additional information.
4. Adjuster <u>enters progress notes</u> over time.
5. Adjuster <u>corrects entries</u> and <u>sets monies aside</u> over time.
6. Adjuster receives documentation including bills throughout the life of the claim and <u>enters bills</u>.
7. Adjuster <u>evaluates damages</u> for claim and documents the negotiation process in System.

8. Adjuster settles and closes claim in System.

9. System purges claim 6 months after close.

10. System archives claim after time period.

**Extensions:**

*a. At any time, System goes down:

   *a1. System group <u>repairs system</u>.

1a. Submitted data is incomplete:

   1a1. Insurance company requests missing information.

   1a2. Claimant supplies missing information.

      1a2a.  Claimant does not supply information within time period:

         1a2a1.  Adjuster closes claim in System.

2a. Claimant does not own a valid policy:

   2a1. Insurance company declines claim, notifies claimant, updates claim, closes claim.

3a. No agents are available at this time:

   3a1. (What do we do here?)

8a. Claimant notifies adjuster of new claim activity:

   8a1. Clerk reopens claim. Reverts to step 3.

**Technology and Data Variations List:**

**Frequency of Occurrence:** To be documented.

**Success Guarantee:** Claim is closed, settled, and archived.

**Minimal Guarantee:** Claim closed but may be reopened later.

**Stakeholders and Interests:**

   The company—make smallest accurate settlement.

   Customer—get largest settlement.

   Department of Insurance—ensure correct procedures.

**Business Rules:**

**Data Descriptions:** Will be defined in other use cases.

**UI Links:** To be documented.

**Open Issues:** What are the time periods for archiving claims?

**COMMENTARY ON USE CASE 22.**  This is one of the most complex use cases I have seen. It shows why use cases should be written in natural-language prose.

The first source of complexity is the sequencing. A clerk on the phone talking to a distraught customer must be able to enter information in any order, while still attempting to follow a standard question sequence. Simultaneously, the computer uses this information as it is entered to do whatever processing can be done, such as pulling the customer's records and assigning a claim number and an adjuster. The writers wrote at least four complete versions of this use case, trying to be clear, to show the normal work path and to show the computer working asynchronously. Perhaps on the seventh or eighth revision they would have found something better, but they felt they had passed the point of diminishing returns and stopped with the version here.

This use case invokes the use case *Find a Whatever* several times, each time mentioning a different thing to find and different search criteria. The team came up with an ingenious solution to avoid rewriting the standard steps for searching for something: match lists, sorting criteria, resorting, researching, no items found, and so forth. I ask you to do the same in Exercise 5.4 at the end of the chapter.

The handling of extension *a. Power failure generated surprising new requirements questions. It introduced the notion of intermediate saves. Having an intermediate save suddenly implied that the clerk could search for one later. This was a surprise to the writers and introduced questions of storing and searching for temporarily saved losses—more surprises for the team. It all ended with the failure condition 6b, which dealt with time-out on a temporarily saved loss and confronted the writers with the very detailed question: "What are the business rules for an allegedly temporarily entered loss, which cannot be committed because it is missing key information but shouldn't be deleted because it passed the minimum entry criteria?" The team toyed with the unacceptable alternatives—not doing intermediate saves and deleting the loss—before settling on this solution.

Extension 1c shows failures within failures. The writers could have turned this into its own use case, but they decided that that would introduce too much complexity into the use case set: A new use case would have to be tracked, reviewed, and maintained. Instead, they made it an extension of the extension. Many people take use case extensions this far for that reason, although for most this is about as far as they feel comfortable going before making the extension its own use case.

Extension 2–5a shows how malleable the medium is. The condition can arise in any of steps 2 through 5. How should it be written—once for each time it could occur? That seemed a waste of energy. The solution was just to write 2–5a and 2–5b, which is clear to readers.

## Use Case 22  ▱ Register a Loss  〜

**Scope:** "System" means the claims-capturing computer system ▱.
**Level:** Blue (user goal) 〜
**Release:** 2
**Status:** Reviewed
**Revision:** Current
**Context of Use:** Capture loss fully.
**Primary Actor:** Clerk
**Preconditions:** Clerk has already logged in.

**Trigger:** Clerk has already started entering loss.

**Success Guarantee:** Loss information is captured and stored.

**Minimal Guarantee:** Nothing happens.

**Stakeholders and Interests:** As before

**Main Success Scenario:**

To speed up the clerk's work, the System should do its work asynchronously, as soon as the required data is captured. The Clerk can enter data in any order to match the needs of the moment. The following sequence is foreseen as the most likely.

1. Clerk enters insured's policy number or else name and date of incident. System populates available policy information and indicates that claim is matched to policy.
2. Clerk enters basic loss information. System confirms there are no existing, possibly competing claims and assigns a claim number.
3. Clerk continues entering loss information specific to claim line.
4. Clerk has System pull other coverage information from other computer systems.
5. Clerk selects and assigns an Adjuster.
6. Clerk confirms they are finished; System saves and triggers acknowledgment to be sent to Agent.

**Extensions:**

*a. Power failure during loss capture:

   *a1. System autosaves intermittently (possibly at certain transaction commit points, open issue).

*b. Claim is not for our company to handle:

   *b1. Clerk indicates to System that claim is entered "only for recording purposes" and either continues or ends loss.

1a. Found policy information does not match the insured's information:

   1a1. Clerk enters correct policy number or insured name and asks System to populate with new policy index information.

1b. Using search details, System could not find a policy:

   1b1. Clerk returns to loss and enters available data.

1c. Clerk changed policy number, date of loss, or claim line after initial policy match:

   1c1. System validates changes, populates loss with correct policy information, validates and indicates that claim is matched to policy.

      1c1a.  System cannot validate policy match:

         1c1a1.  System warns Clerk.

         1c1a2.  Clerk <u>finds the policy</u> using the search details for "policy."

   1c2. System warns Clerk to re-evaluate coverage.

1d. Clerk wants to restart a loss which has been interrupted, saved, or needs completion:

   1d1. Clerk <u>finds a loss</u> using search details for "loss."

   1d2. System opens it for editing.

2–5a. Clerk changes claim line previously entered and no line-specific data has been entered:

 2–5a1. System presents appropriate line-specific sections of loss based on Clerk entering a different claim line.

2–5b. Clerk changes claim line previously entered and there is data in some of the line-specific fields:

 2–5b1. System warns that data exists and asks Clerk to either cancel changes or proceed with new claim line.

  2–5b1a. Clerk cancels change: System continues with the loss.

  2–5b1b. Clerk insists on new claim line: System blanks out data which is line specific (it keeps all basic claim-level data).

2c. System detects possible duplicate claim:

 2c1. System displays a list of possible duplicate claims from within loss database.

 2c2. Clerk selects and views a claim from the list. This step may be repeated multiple times.

  2c2a. Clerk finds that the claim is a duplicate:

   Clerk opens duplicate claim from list of claims for editing if not yet marked completed (based on Clerk's security profile). Clerk may delete any data in previously saved file.

  2c2b. Clerk finds that the claim is not a duplicate: Clerk returns to loss and completes it.

2d. Preliminary loss information is changed after initial duplicate claim check is done:

 2d1. System performs duplicate claim check again.

2e. Clerk can save the loss any time before completion of steps 2 through 6. (Some reasons to save may be just a comfort level or that the Clerk must interrupt entry for some reason—e.g., claim must be handled by and immediately transferred to higher-level Adjuster).

 2e1. Clerk has System save the loss for completion at a later time.

4–5a. Either claim line or loss description (see business rules) is changed after coverage was reviewed by Clerk:

 4–5a1. System warns Clerk to re-evaluate coverage.

6a. Clerk confirms he/she is finished without completing minimum information:

 6a1. System warns Clerk it cannot accept the loss without date of loss, insured name or policy number, and handling Adjuster:

  6a1a. Clerk decides to continue entering loss or decides to save without marking complete.

  6a1b. Clerk insists on exiting without entering minimum information: System discards any intermediate saves and exits.

 6a2. System warns Clerk it cannot assign claim number without required fields (claim line, date of loss, policy number, or insured name): System directs Clerk to fields that require entry.

> 6b. Time-out: Clerk has saved the loss temporarily, intending to return; System de-
> cides it is time to commit and log the loss, but handling Adjuster has still not
> been entered:
>
>     6b1. System assigns default Adjuster (see Business Rules).
>
> **Frequency of Occurrence:** ??
>
> **Business Rules:**
>
> *. When does saved loss go to main system (timelines)?
>
> 1. Minimum fields needed for saving a loss (and be able to find it again) are: . . .
> 2. Claim number, once assigned by system, cannot be changed.
> 3. Business rules for manual entry of claim number—needed?
> 4. Loss description consists of two fields, one being free form, the other from
>    a pull-down menu.
> 5. System should know how to find coverage depending on policy prefix.
> 6. Required fields in order to confirm a loss is finished are: . . .
>
> 6b. Rules for default Adjuster are: . . .
>
> **Data descriptions used:**
>
> Search details for policy, policy index information, preliminary loss information,
> claim-line-specific loss information, additional information.
>
> Search details for loss, duplicate claim check criteria, list of possible duplicate claims,
> a claim from the list.
>
> **UI Links:** To be documented
>
> **Owner:** Susan and Nancy
>
> **Critical Reviewers:** Alistair, Eric . . .
>
> **Open Issues:**
>
> How often does it autosave?
>
> Agent acknowledgment cards—where and how do they print, etc.?

The project team decided it would be silly to write the almost identical use cases Find a Customer, Find a Policy, and so forth. Instead, they created a generic mechanism that every writing team used.

Any sentence of the form Find a. . . , such as Find a Customer or Find a Product, would mean that the use case Find a Whatever would be called, with an implicit substitution of the specific term for *"whatever."* Each use case would need its own searching, sorting, and display criteria, so the writer would put the data and search restrictions on a different, hyperlinked, sheet. A sample sentence would therefore read as <u>Find a customer</u> using <u>Customer search details</u>.

With this neat convention, the logistical details of *Find a Whatever* could be written just once and used in many similar, but different, contexts. This made the developers happy, since they knew that all the searches would use the same mechanism, and they could develop a common one.

I want you to try your hand at doing this, so I'll defer showing this team's solution. Work Exercise 5.4 before looking at the solution, which is discussed in Section 14.2, Parameterized Use Cases, on page 150.

---

**Use Case 23    ▱ Find a Whatever (Problem Statement)** ⋈⚲

To be filled in as an exercise.

## 5.7 EXERCISES

### Goal Levels

**5.1.** Jenny is standing in front of her bank's ATM. It is dark. She has entered her PIN and is looking for the Enter button. Name a white, blue, and indigo goal for Jenny.

**5.2.** List at least ten goals that the ATM's various primary actors will have with respect to the ATM and label their goal levels.

**5.3.** List the summary and user goals of all the primary actors for the PAF software package described in Exercise 4.4. Identify the highest-level, outermost actor-scope-goal combinations.

**5.4.** Find a Whatever. Write the use case for *Find a Whatever* whose trigger is the user's desire to locate something. The use case should allow the user to enter searching and sorting information. It should also deal with all the situations that might arise and, in the success case, end with a "whatever" being identified by the computer for whatever use the calling use case specifies next.

# Chapter 6

# *Preconditions, Triggers, and Guarantees*

## 6.1 PRECONDITIONS

The *precondition* of the use case announces what the system will ensure is true before letting the use case start. Since it is enforced by the system and known to be true, it will not be checked again during the use case execution. A common example is, The user has already logged on and has been validated.

Generally, a precondition indicates that some other use case has already run to set it up. Let's say that *Place an Order* relies on a precondition, being logged on. I immediately look to see which use case set it up (I would look for *Log On*). I, personally, usually create a higher-level use case that mentions *Place an Order* and *Log On*, so the reader can see the way the two fit together. In this example, it might be the summary use case, *Use the Application*. In this example, we get the following structure (I abbreviate the template to show just the relevant parts). Note the goal levels of the three use cases.

**Use Case: Use the Application**

**Level:** Summary (white)
**Precondition:** None
1. Clerk <u>logs on</u>.
2. Clerk <u>places an order</u>.

**Use Case: Log On**

**Level:** Subfunction (indigo)
**Precondition:** None
. . .

**Use Case: Place an Order**

**Level:** User goal (blue)
**Precondition:** Clerk is logged on.
. . .


Not everybody follows my habit of writing the higher level use case to glue together the lower-level ones. Thus, you are likely to pick up only *Log On* and *Place an Order* in the preceding example. You have to be able to deduce from the writing that the precondition is correct and will be enforced.

Let's continue this example to show a use case that sets a condition in one step and relies on that condition in a sub use case. Once again, the sub use case expects the condition to be true and will not check for mistakes.


**Use Case: Place an Order**

**Level:** User goal (blue)
**Precondition:** Clerk is logged on.
1. Clerk identifies customer, system pulls up customer record.
2. Clerk enters order information.
3. System <u>calculates charges</u>.
   . . .


**Use Case: Calculate Charges**

**Level:** Subfunction (indigo)
**Precondition:** Customer is established and known to system; order contents are known.
1. System calculates base charge for order.
2. System calculates discount for customer.
   . . .


This example illustrates how one use case relies upon information captured in a calling use case. The writer of *Calculate Charges* declared the information that is already available and can now go ahead and refer to the customer information.

The alert reader will be suspicious about the use case *Calculate Charges*. I declared it as being indigo, but so far in the writing there is little to justify it even being a use case on its own. If I, as the writer, don't uncover complicated interactions with the user, or interesting failure cases, I will reclassify it as black (clam, using the icons). That is the signal to merge the text back into *Place an Order* and eliminate *Calculate Charges* altogether.

Write a precondition as a simple assertion about the state of the world at the moment the use case opens. Suitable examples are

**Precondition:** The user is logged on.

**Precondition:** The customer has been validated.

**Precondition:** The system has already located the customer's policy information.

A common mistake is to write into the precondition something that is often, but not necessarily, true.

Suppose we are writing *Request Benefits Summary*, with primary actor Claimant. We might think that Claimant would have submitted at least one claim or bill before asking for the benefits summary. However, that is not always the case; the system cannot ensure it, and in fact it isn't essential. Claimants should be able to ask for their benefit summary at any time, so it is wrong to write Precondition: The Claimant has submitted a bill.

## 6.2 MINIMAL GUARANTEES

The *minimal guarantees* are the fewest promises the system makes to the stakeholders, particularly when the primary actor's goal cannot be delivered. They hold when the goal is delivered, of course, but they are of real interest when the main goal is abandoned. Most of the time, two or more stakeholders have to be addressed in the minimal guarantees, examples being the user, the company providing the system, and possibly a government regulatory body.

Do not bother listing in the Minimal Guarantees section all the ways the use case can fail. There are dozens of ways to fail and they have little in common. All of the failure conditions and handling show up in the extensions section, and it is both tiring and error prone to try to keep the two lists synchronized. The purpose of this section of the template is to announce what the system promises.

The most common minimal guarantee is The system logged how far it got. Logging transaction failures is neither obvious nor trivial. System logs are often forgotten in the requirements description and sometimes rediscovered by programmers. However, they are crucial to the system's owners as well as to its users. The system uses the log to continue a transaction once normal operating conditions resume; the stakeholders use it to settle disputes. The use case writer should discover the need for a log either by investigating the stakeholders' interests or when brainstorming failure conditions.

The minimal guarantees are written as a number of simple assertions that will be true at the end of any running of the use case. It shows the interests of each stakeholder being satisfied.

**Minimal Guarantee:** Order will be initiated only if payment received.

**Minimal Guarantee:** If the minimum information was not captured, the partial claim has been discarded and no log made of the call. If the minimum information was captured (see Business Rules), then the partial claim has been saved and logged.

The pass/fail test for a minimal guarantee is that the stakeholders agree that their interests are protected under failure conditions for this goal.

## 6.3 SUCCESS GUARANTEE

The *success guarantee* states what interests of the stakeholders are satisfied after a successful conclusion of the use case, either at the end of the main success scenario or at the end of a successful alternative path. It is generally written to be added to the minimal guarantees: The minimal guarantees are delivered, *and* some extra conditions are true; those additional conditions include at least the goal stated in the use case title.

Like the minimal guarantees, the success guarantee is written as a set of simple assertions that apply at the end of a successful running of the use case and that show the interests of each stakeholder being satisfied. Suitable examples are:

**Success Guarantee:** The claimant will be paid the agreed-upon amount, the claim closed, the settlement logged.

**Success Guarantee:** The file will be saved.

**Success Guarantee:** The System will initiate an order for the customer, will have received payment information, and logged the request for the order.

The pass/fail test for the success guarantee section is that the stakeholders agree that their interests have been satisfied.

The best way to uncover the success guarantee is to ask "What would make this stakeholder *unhappy* at the end of a successful run?" That question is usually easy to answer. Then write the negative of that. To see an example, do Exercise 6.4 and then read the discussion in Appendix B.

## 6.4 TRIGGERS

The *trigger* specifies the event that gets the use case started. Sometimes the trigger precedes the first step of the use case, sometimes it is the first step. To date, I have not seen a convincing argument that one form can be applied in all cases, nor have I noticed any confusion from choosing one way over the other. You will have to develop your personal or project style.

Consider that an ATM system wakes up only when a user inserts his or her card. Thus, it is not meaningful to say that the trigger is when someone decides to use the ATM. The trigger Customer inserts card is also the first step in the use case.

---

**Use Case: Use the ATM**

**Trigger:** Customer inserts card.
1. Customer inserts card with bank ID, bank account, and encrypted PIN.
2. System validates . . .

---

Now consider a clerk sitting all day at a workstation showing a number of graphical icons to run different application programs. The trigger is that a customer calls with a particular request, which can be written using either form. I'll write it the second way to illustrate.

---

**Use Case: Log a Complaint**

**Trigger:** Customer calls in a complaint.
1. Clerk calls up the application.
2. The system brings up the clerk's recent complaints list.
. . .

---

# 6.5 EXERCISES

## Minimal Guarantees

**6.1.** Write the minimal guarantee for withdrawing money from the ATM.
**6.2.** Write the minimal guarantee for the PAF system's main use case (PAF is described in Exercise 4.4).
**6.3.** Write the minimal guarantee for a sea-level use case for your current system. Show it to a colleague and have him analyze it with respect to the stakeholders' interests.

## Success Guarantees

**6.4.** Write the success guarantee for withdrawing money from the ATM.
**6.5.** Write the success guarantee for the PAF system's main use case.
**6.6.** Write the success guarantee for a sea-level use case for your current system. Show it to a colleague and have her analyze it with respect to the interests of the stakeholders.

# Chapter 7

# *Scenarios and Steps*

A set of use cases is an ever-unfolding story of primary actors pursuing goals. Each use case has a crisscrossing story line that shows the system delivering the goal or abandoning it. This story line is presented as a main scenario and a set of scenario fragments as extensions to it. Each scenario or fragment starts from a triggering condition that indicates when it runs and goes until it shows completion or abandonment of its goal. Goals come in all different sizes, as we have seen, so we use the same writing form to describe the pursuit of any size goal at any scenario level.

## 7.1 THE MAIN SUCCESS SCENARIO

We often explain things to other people by starting with an easy to understand description and then adding, "Well, actually, there is a little complication. When such-and-such occurs, what really happens is . . ."

People do very well with this style of explanation, and it is the way we write the crisscrossing story line that becomes the use case. We first write a top-to-bottom description of one easy-to-understand and fairly typical scenario in which the primary actor's goal is delivered and all stakeholders' interests are satisfied. This is the *main success scenario*. All other ways to succeed, and the handling of all failures, are described in the extensions to it.

### The Common Surrounding Structure

The main success scenario and all scenario extensions sit within a structure that consists of the following:

- ◆ *A condition under which the scenario runs.* For the main success scenario, this is the precondition plus the trigger. For an extension scenario, this is the extension condition (perhaps with the step number or place in the scenario where that condition applies).

- ◆ *A goal to achieve.* For the main success scenario, this is the use case name, satisfying, of course, the stakeholders' interests. For an extension scenario, the goal is either to complete the use case goal or to rejoin the main success scenario after handling the condition.

- ◆ *A set of action steps.* These form the body of the scenario and follow the same rules in every scenario or scenario fragment.

- ◆ *An end condition.* The goal is achieved at the end of the main success scenario. A scenario fragment may end with the goal being either achieved or abandoned.

- ◆ *A possible set of extensions written as scenario fragments.* Extensions to the main success scenario are placed in the *extensions* section of the use case template. Extensions to extensions are placed inline, inside, or just after the extension body.

Here are two extracts from Use Case 1, which I have stripped down to show just the similarities of their surrounding structures.

Here is a main success scenario:

**Use Case: Buy Stocks over the Web**

---

**Precondition:** User already has PAF open.
**Trigger:** User selects "buy stocks":
1. User selects to buy stocks over the web.
2. PAF gets name of web site to use (E*Trade, Schwab, etc.) from user.
3. PAF opens web connection to the site, retaining control.
4. User browses and buys stock from the web site.
5. PAF intercepts responses from the web site and updates the user's portfolio.
6. PAF shows the user the new portfolio standing.

Here is an extension to it:

3a. Web failure of any sort during setup:
   3a1. System reports failure to user with advice, backs up to previous step.
   3a2. User either backs out of this use case or tries again.

In this chapter, we look in detail at the body of the scenario, which consists of action steps.

## The Scenario Body

Every scenario or fragment is written as a sequence of goal-achieving actions by the various actors. I say *sequence* for convenience, but we are allowed to add notes to show that steps can go in parallel, can be taken in different orders, or can be repeated, or even that some are optional.

As noted in Section 2.2, Contract between Stakeholders with Interests, on page 29, any one step will describe

◆ An interaction between two actors ("Customer enters address")

◆ A validation step to protect an interest of a stakeholder ("System validates PIN code")

◆ An internal change to satisfy an interest of a stakeholder ("System deducts amount from balance").

Here is an example of a typical main success scenario, borrowed from Use Case 22, *Register a Loss,* on page 75. Notice that steps 1, 3, and 5 through 8 are interactions, step 4 is a validation, and steps 2 and 9 are internal changes.

1. Clerk enters insured's policy number or else name and date of incident.
2. System populates available policy information and indicates claim is matched to policy.
3. Clerk enters basic loss information.
4. System confirms there are no competing claims and assigns a claim number.
5. Clerk continues entering loss information specific to claim line.
6. Clerk has System pull other coverage information from other computer systems.
7. Clerk selects and assigns an Adjuster.
8. Clerk confirms he/she is finished.
9. System saves and triggers acknowledgment to be sent to Agent.

Each action step is written to show a simple, active action. I liken it to describing a soccer match: *Person 1 kicks ball to person 2; person 2 dribbles ball; person 2 kicks ball to person 3.*

Once you master writing the three kinds of action steps, you are pretty well set for your writing style. The same style is used for action steps in every part of any use case, whether main success scenario or extension or business or system, and every type of use case, high-level or low-level.

## 7.2  ACTION STEPS

The action steps that make up a well-written use case are in one grammatical form, a simple action in which one actor accomplishes a task or passes information to another actor.

> User enters name and address.
> At any time, user can request the money back.
> The system verifies that the name and account are current.
> The system updates the customer's balance to reflect the charge.

Usually the timing can be omitted, since steps generally follow one after the other.

There are many minor variations in writing the action steps, as you have already seen in the use case samples. However you choose to write, preserve the following characteristics in each step.

## Guidelines

### Guideline 1:  Use Simple Grammar

The sentence structure should be absurdly simple:

> Subject . . . verb . . . direct object . . . prepositional phrase.

For example:

> The system . . . deducts . . . the amount . . . from the account balance.

That's all there is to it. I mention this matter because many people accidently leave off the first noun, making it no longer clear who is controlling the action (who has the ball). If your sentence is badly formed, the story becomes hard to follow.

### Guideline 2:  Show Clearly "Who Has the Ball"

A useful visual image is that of friends kicking a soccer ball around. Sometimes person 1 kicks to person 2; person 2 dribbles a while and then kicks to person 3. Occasionally the ball gets muddy, and one of the players wipes the mud off.

A scenario has the same structure. At each step one actor "has the ball." That actor is going to be the subject of the sentence—the first actor named—probably as the first or second word in the sentence. The "ball" is the message and data that are passed from actor to actor.

The actor with the ball will do one of three things: kick it to himself, kick it to someone else, or clean off the mud. About half of the time, the step ends with another actor having the ball. Ask yourself, "At the end of the sentence, who has the ball?" The answer should always be clear in the writing.

### Guideline 3: Write from a Bird's Eye View

Beginning use case writers, particularly programmers who are writing the use case document, often write the scenario as seen by the system looking out at the world and talking to itself. Their sentences have the appearance "Get ATM card and PIN number. Deduct amount from account balance."

Instead, write the use case from a bird's eye view:

The customer puts in the ATM card and PIN.
The system deducts the amount from the account balance.

Some writers like to use another style that has the quality of a play, describing actors performing their parts.

Customer: Puts in the ATM card and PIN.
System: Deducts the amount from the account balance.

Note that the information is the same in both styles.

### Guideline 4: Show the Process Moving Forward

The amount of progress made in one step is related to how high or low the use case goal is. In a summary or white use case, the step probably moves forward an entire user goal. In a subfunction use case, it moves forward by a much smaller increment. If we see the step User hits the tab key, either we are looking at a deep indigo (or black) use case or the writer has simply chosen an action too small to describe.

The mistake of choosing very small steps shows up in the length of the use case. If a use case has 13 or 17 steps, it is quite likely that the sentences are not moving the goal forward very much. The use case is easier to read, clearer, and contains the same essential information when those small steps are merged. I rarely encounter a well-written use case with more than 9 steps in the main success scenario.

To find the slightly higher-level goal for a step, ask "Why is the actor doing that?" (as described in the subsection, Raising and Lowering Goal Levels on page 69). The answer to that question is probably the goal you need for the step, although you may have to ask the question several times to get the answer you want. Here is an example of raising the goal level by asking why:

User hits tab key.

Why is the user hitting the tab key? To get to the Address field.

Why is she trying to get to the Address field? Because she has to enter her name and address before the system will do anything.

Oh! She wants to get the system to do something (probably the use case itself), and to get it to do anything she has to enter her name and address.

Thus, the action sentence that moves the process distinctly forward is

User enters name and address.

### Guideline 5: Show the Actor's Intent, Not the Movements

Describing the user's movements in operating the system's user interface is one of the more common and severe mistakes in use case writing and is related to writing goals at too low a level. I call this an *interface detail description*. Interface detail descriptions make the requirements document worse in three ways: longer, brittle, and overconstrained.

- Longer documents are harder to read and more expensive to maintain.
- The dialog being described is probably not a requirement but just how the writer imagines the user interface design at that moment.
- The dialog is brittle in the sense that small changes in the system design will invalidate the writing.

It is the user interface designer's job to create a user interface that is effective and that permits the user to achieve the intent of the use case. The description of particular movements belongs in that design task, not in the functional requirements document.

In the requirements document, we are interested in the description of the *intention* of the interface—that is, the one that announces the user's intent, and summarizes the information passed from one actor to another. Larry Constantine and Lucy Lockwood devote a portion of their book, *Software for Use,* to just this topic, using the term *essential use cases* to designate sea-level system use cases describing interface intentions.

Typically, all the data that passes in one direction gets collected into just one action step. Here is a common piece of faulty writing and the way to fix it:

*Before:*

1. System asks for name.
2. User enters name.
3. System prompts for address.
4. User enters address.
5. User clicks "OK."
6. System presents user's profile.

*After:*

    1. User enters name and address.

    2. System presents user's profile.

If more than three data items are being passed, you may prefer to put each item on a separate line in a tabbed list. Either of the following will work well, but the first works better when you are first drafting the use cases since it is faster to write and read. The second works better if you want enhanced accuracy for traceability or testing.

*Acceptable Variant 1:*

    1. User enters name, address, phone number, secret information, emergency contact phone number.

*Acceptable Variant 2:*

    1. User enters
- Name
- Address
- Phone number
- Secret information
- Emergency contact phone number

## Guideline 6: Include a "Reasonable" Set of Actions

Ivar Jacobson has described a step in a use case as representing a *transaction*. With this phrasing, he captures four pieces of a compound interaction (see Figure 7.1.):

1. The primary actor sends request and data to the system.
2. The system validates the request and the data.
3. The system alters its internal state.
4. The system responds to the actor with the result.

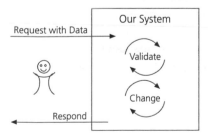

**Figure 7.1** *A transaction has four parts*

You can write each piece as a separate action step or combine the pieces in various ways, putting up to all four in a single action step. Which is best depends on how complicated each piece is and where the natural breaks occur in the processing.

Here are five variations for you to consider. None is wrong, although I consider version 1 too complicated to read easily. I like version 2 when the pieces are simple, but I find them a bit too long to work in this instance. Version 3 is my preference for this example, and version 4 is also good. I find the action steps in version 5 a bit too small, making the scenario too long and unwieldy, but this version does have the advantage of steps that are separately testable units, possibly suited for a more formal development situation.

*Version 1:*

1. The customer enters the order number. The system detects that it matches the winning number of the month, registers the user and order number as this month's winner, sends an e-mail to the sales manager, congratulates the customer, and gives them instructions on how to collect the prize.

*Version 2:*

1. The customer enters the order number.
2. The system detects that it matches the winning number of the month, registers the user and order number as this month's winner, sends an e-mail to the sales manager, congratulates the customer, and gives them instructions on how to collect the prize.

*Version 3:*

1. The customer enters the order number.
2. The system detects that it matches the winning number of the month.
3. The system registers the user and order number as this month's winner, sends an e-mail to the sales manager, congratulates the customer, and gives them instructions on how to collect the prize.

*Version 4:*

1. The customer enters the order number.
2. The system detects that it matches the winning number of the month.
3. The system registers the user and order number as this month's winner, and sends an e-mail to the sales manager.
4. The system congratulates the customer and gives them instructions on how to collect the prize.

*Version 5:*

1. The customer enters the order number.
2. The system detects that it matches the winning number of the month.

3. The system registers the user and order number as this month's winner.
4. The system sends an e-mail to the sales manager.
5. The system congratulates the customer and gives them instructions on how to collect the prize.

### Guideline 7: "Validate," Don't "Check Whether"

One of the three kinds of action steps is system verification that some business rule is satisfied. Often people write that the system *checks* the condition. This is not a good action verb. It does not move the process distinctly forward, it is not really the goal, and it leaves open what the result of the check is. You immediately have to write, "If the check passes . . ." and "If the check fails . . "

Let's use the ask why technique to find a better phrase. Why is the system *checking* the condition? Answer: It is *establishing* or *validating* or *ensuring* something. Those are good goal-achieving action verbs. Replace "The system checks whether the password is correct" with

> The system verifies that the password is correct.

Let the presence of the word *if* trigger you to recall this guideline. Any time you see If the (condition)... then..., look at the sentence before it. It is likely to say *checks*. Replace the first sentence with *validates*, and make the second sentence a simple action with no *if*. Here is a before and after example:

*Before:*
2. The system checks whether the password is correct.
3. If it is, the system presents the available actions for the user.

*After:*
2. The system validates that the password is correct.
3. The system presents the available actions for the user.

Notice that the writing in the second case describes the scenario as succeeding. It also triggers the reader to ask at step 2, "But what if the password is not valid?" He will turn to the extensions section and look for the extension starting with Password is not valid. This gives the use case a consistent rhythm that makes it easy to read and review.

### Guideline 8: Optionally Mention the Timing

Most steps follow directly from the previous one. Occasionally, you will need to say something like

> At any time between steps 3 and 5, the user will . . .

or

> As soon as the user has . . . , the system will . . .

Feel free to put in the timing, but only when you need to. Usually the timing is obvious and need not be mentioned.

### Guideline 9:  Idiom: "User Has System A Kick System B"

Here is a situation you might encounter. You want the system under design (A) to fetch information from system (B) or otherwise run an interaction with it. It should do so only when the primary actor indicates that the time is right. We cannot write, User hits Fetch button, at which time the system fetches the data from system B. That would have us describing the interface details.

We can use two steps:

> 4. User signals to the system to fetch data from system B.
> 5. The system fetches the background data from system B.

However, while acceptable, they are awkward and redundant. Better to write:

> 4. User has the system fetch the background data from system B.

With this small shift, we indicate that the user controls the timing and that the ball passes from the user to system A to system B, and show the responsibilities of all three systems. The details of how the user initiates the action are unspecified, as they should be.

### Guideline 10:  Idiom: "Do Steps x–y until Condition"

On occasion, we want to mark that some steps can be repeated. Here again, we are lucky that we are writing in plain prose rather than programming formalisms. Just write that the step or steps will be repeated.

If there is only one step being repeated, you can put the repetition right into the step:

> The user selects one or more products.
> The user searches through various product catalogs until he finds the one he wants to use.

If several steps are being repeated, you can write the repetition before or after the repeating steps. I write the repetition after the steps to make the scenario a little easier to read, but either way will work.

> 1. Customer supplies either account identifier or name and address.
> 2. System brings up the customer's preference information.

3. User selects an item to buy, marks it for purchase.
4. System adds the item to the customer's "shopping cart."
   Customer repeats steps 3–4 until indicating that he/she is done.
5. Customer <u>purchases the items in the shopping cart</u>.

Notice that we need not number the statement about repetition, and need not have a statement that opens the repetition. Both of those clutter up the writing, making the scenario harder, not easier, to read.

A variant of Do steps x–y until condition is Steps x–y can happen in any order. I find it works well to put this before the steps affected.

1. Customer logs on.
2. System presents available products and services.
   Steps 3–5 can happen in any order.
3. User selects products to buy.
4. User specifies preferred form of payment.
5. User gives destination address.
6. User indicates shopping spree is complete.
7. System initiates order, with selected products to be charged against the form of payment and to be sent to the destination address.

## To Number or Not to Number

Step numbers clarify the steps and give places to refer to in the extensions section. They are, however, harder to maintain. Without good tools to automatically renumber when we insert or delete steps, it becomes tedious renumbering steps *yet again* for the same use case. You can write good use cases with or without numbering the steps, so it comes down to preference, to be settled on a project-wide basis.

The teams I have visited who have tried both methods consistently select numbered sentences over paragraphs, and so numbered sentences have become my standard way of writing. Other people are simply happy writing in simple paragraph form and have no interest in switching.

I include templates for both casual and fully dressed use cases, to emphasize the equivalence and personal nature of this choice.

Paragraphs are the default suggestion in both the casual template and the Rational Unified Process template (used in Use Case 32, *Manage Reports* on page 146). You can still number the steps if you wish, as that one does. I almost always use numbers, even if everything else about the use case is casual, because I just find they make it easier to examine the behavior.

The fully dressed form requires the numbers.

## *7.3 EXERCISES*

### *Action Steps*

**7.1.** Write a scenario for one of your use cases in two ways: using interface detail description and using intention description. Discuss the differences between the two.

**7.2.** Write the main success scenario for the task-level use case *Withdraw Money Using Fast Cash Option*.

**7.3.** Write the main success scenario for one strategic use case and one task use case for the PAF system.

**7.4.** Your junior colleague sends you the following. Using the reminders you have learned so far, send back a critique and corrections.

**Use Case: Login**

This use case describes the process by which users log in to the order-processing system. It also sets up access permissions for various categories of users.

**Flow of Events:**

**Basic Path:**

1. The use case starts when the user starts the application.
2. The system will display the Login screen.
3. The user enters a username and password.
4. The system will verify the information.
5. The system will set access permissions.
6. The system will display the Main screen.
7. The user will select a function.
8. While the user does not select Exit loop
9. If the user selects Place Order, Use Place Order.
10. If the user selects Return Product, Use Return Product.
11. If the user selects Cancel Order, Use Cancel Order.
12. If the user selects Get Status on Order, Use Get Status.
13. If the user selects Send Catalog, Use Send Catalog.
14. If the user selects Register Complaint, Use Register Complaint.
15. If the user selects Run Sales Report, Use Run Sales Report.
end if
16. The user will select a function.
end loop
17. The use case ends.

# Chapter 8

# *Extensions*

We know that a use case should contain all of the scenarios, both success and failure, and we know how to write the main success scenario. Now we need a way to add all the others.

We could write every scenario individually. That would fit the striped trousers metaphor, as illustrated in Figure 2.2 on page 28. This approach is advocated from time to time, and some tools force the writer to work this way. However, as described in Chapter 2, it is a maintenance nightmare. Each change to a scenario has to be copied to all the other scenarios that contain the same text.

A second alternative is to write *if* statements throughout the text: If the password is good, the system does . . . , otherwise the system does . . . . This is perfectly legal, and some people write use cases this way. However, readers have a hard time with the *if* conditions, especially when one *if* is inside another *if*. They lose track of the behavior after just two *if* branches, and most use cases contain many branching points.

A third way to arrange the text is to write the main success scenario as a simple sequence running from trigger to completion, and then write a scenario *extension* for each branch point. This seems to be the best of the three choices.

## 8.1  EXTENSION BASICS

Extensions work this way. Below the main success scenario, for every point where the behavior can branch because of a particular condition, write down the condition and then write the steps that handle it. Many extensions end by simply remerging with the main success scenario.

The extension is really a stripped down use case. It starts with a condition—the one that makes it relevant. It contains a sequence of action steps describing what happens under that condition, and ends with delivery or abandonment of the extension goal. Extensions to the extensions to handle the *if*s and *but*s might be encountered along the way.

These extensions are where the most interesting system requirements reside. The main success scenario often is known to the people on the team. Failure handling often uses business rules that the developers do not know. The requirements writers frequently have to research the correct system response, and quite often that research introduces a new actor, a new use case, or a new extension condition.

Here is a fairly typical discussion that illustrates my point.

"Suppose there is a sudden network failure. What do we do?"

"System logs it."

"Got it. Hey, if the network goes down, what's supposed to happen when it comes up again?"

"Oh, I guess we have to add a new use case for *System Restarts after Network Failure*. The system will come back up, get the log, and either complete or abort the transaction."

"Yes, but what if the log is corrupt? Then what's the system supposed to do?"

"I don't know. Let's write it as an Open Issue and continue."

This conversation uncovered both a new use case and the need to research a business policy. Don't be fooled into thinking that discussing these extensions is unnecessary. Some programmer on the project will run into the same conditions while programming, and that is an expensive time to discover new business rules that need researching. Requirements gathering is the best time for that.

I recommend working in three phases:

1. Brainstorm and include every possibility you and your colleagues can conjure up.
2. Evaluate, eliminate, and merge the ideas according to the guidelines in Section 8.2.
3. Sit down and work your way through the system's handling of each of these conditions.

## 8.2 THE EXTENSION CONDITIONS

*Extension conditions* are the conditions under which the system takes a different behavior. We say *extension* as opposed to *failure* or *exception* so that we can include alternative success as well as failure conditions.

Here are two snippets that illustrate success and failure paths in extensions.

*Example 1:*

> . . .
>
> 4. User has the system save the work so far.
>
> . . .

**Extensions:**

4a. System autodetects the need for an intermediate save:

> 4a1. . . .

4b. Save fails:

> 4b1. . . .

The way to read the above is "Instead of the user saving the work so far, the system might have autodetected the need for an intermediate save. In this case . . . (do something). The save (coming from the user's request or from the autosave) may fail during execution. In this case . . . (do something else)."

*Example 2:*

> . . .
>
> 3. The system goes through the document, checking every word against its spelling dictionary.
> 4. The system detects a spelling mistake, highlights the word, and presents a choice of alternatives to the user.
> 5. The user selects one of the choices for replacement. The system replaces the highlighted word with the user's replacement choice.
>
> . . .

**Extensions:**

4a. The system detects no more misspellings through the end of the document:

> 4a1. The system notifies the user, terminates the use case.

5a. User elects to keep the original spelling:

> 5a1. The system leaves the word alone and continues.

5b. User types in a new spelling not on the list:

> 5b1. The system revalidates the new spelling, returns to step 3.

> . . .

## Brainstorm All Conceivable Failures and Alternative Courses

It is important to brainstorm and get good coverage of the extension conditions before writing how to handle them. This brainstorming is tiring, and so is documenting the extension handling. Thinking up just one extension and correctly working out how the system deals with it costs a lot of energy, and working your way through three or four extensions is draining. This means that you will not think up the next set of extension conditions that you should.

If, on the other hand, you brainstorm all the alternative success and failure situations, you will have a list that acts as the scaffolding for your work for the next several hours or days. You can walk away from it at lunchtime or overnight, come back, and take up where you left off.

Brainstorm all the possible ways in which the scenario can fail or alternate ways it can succeed. Be sure to consider all of these:

◆ An alternate success path (Clerk uses a shortcut code).

◆ The primary actor behaving incorrectly (Invalid password).

◆ Inaction by the primary actor (Time-out waiting for password).

◆ Every occurrence of the phase "the system validates," implying that there will be an extension to handle validation failure (Invalid account number).

◆ Inappropriate or lack of response from a supporting actor (Time-out waiting for response).

◆ Internal failure within the system under design, which must be detected and handled as part of normal business (Cash dispenser jams).

◆ Unexpected and abnormal internal failure, which must be handled and will have an externally visible consequence (Corrupt transaction log discovered).

◆ Critical performance failures of the system that you must detect. (Response not calculated within 5 seconds).

Many people brainstorm the steps from the beginning of the scenario to the end, to ensure the best coverage of the conditions. When you do this, you will be amazed at the number of things you can think of that can go wrong. Exercise 8.1 is your chance to try brainstorming a set of failures. The answer, found in Appendix B, can serve as a check on your thoroughness. Two students in my course, John Colaizzi and Allen Maxwell, named almost three times as many failures as I did in my answer to the exercise. How well can you do?

### Guideline 11: Make the Condition Say What Was Detected

Write down *what the system detects*, not just what *happened*. Don't write, Customer forgets PIN. The system can't detect this. Perhaps the customer walked away, had a heart attack, or is busy quieting a crying baby. What does the system detect in this case? Inaction, which means it detects that a time limit was exceeded. Write, Time limit exceeded waiting for PIN to be entered or PIN entry time-out.

The condition is often just a phrase describing what was detected. Sometimes a sentence is appropriate. I like to put a colon (:) after the condition to make sure the reader doesn't think it is an action step. This little convention saves many mistakes. Here are a few examples:

Invalid PIN:
Network is down:
The customer does not respond (time-out):
Cash did not eject properly:

If you are using numbered steps, give the number of the step where the condition would be detected, and put a letter after it (e.g., 4a). There is no sequence associated with the letters, so there is no implication that 4b follows 4a. This allows us to attach as many extension conditions as we like to any one action step.

2a. Insufficient funds:
2b. Network down:

If the condition can occur at several steps and you feel it important to indicate that, simply list those steps:

2–5a. User quit suddenly:

If the condition can occur at any time, use an asterisk (*) instead of the step number. List the asterisk conditions before the numbered conditions.

*a. Network goes down:
*b. User walked away without notice (time-out):
2a. Insufficient funds:
2b. Network down:

Don't fuss about whether the failure occurs at the step where the user enters some data or at the step after, where the system validates the data. One could argue that the error happens at either place, but the argument is not worth the time. I usually put it with the validation step if there is one.

When writing in straight paragraphs with no step numbers, you cannot refer to the specific step where the condition occurs. Therefore, make the condition sufficiently descriptive for the reader to know when the condition might occur. Put a blank line or a space before each condition, and put the condition in some emphasis, such as *italics,* so that it stands out. See Use Case 32, *Manage Reports,* on page 146 for a sample.

◆ **A Short, True, Sad Story**

The opposite of good extension brainstorming happened on an important, large project I worked on.

Like many developers, we didn't want to consider what would happen in case the program encountered bad data in the database. We each hoped that the other team would take care of it. Can you guess what happened? A week after the first delivery of the first increment, a senior vice president decided to see how his favorite customer was using the new sales devices. He fired up his brand-new system and inquired about this large customer. The system replied, "No data found." One way to describe his reaction would be "excited" (but not in the positive sense).

It wasn't very many hours before the entire senior staff was gathered in an emergency meeting to decide what to do about database errors. We found that there was only one bad data cell in the database, so the error message should have read, "Some data missing." More important, we had missed that *how the system reacts when detecting bad internal data* is really a part of its external requirements.

We redesigned the system to do the best it could with partial data and to pass along both its best available results and the message that some data was missing.

The lesson we learned was to consider internal errors, such as discovering missing data.

### About Your Brainstormed List

Your brainstorming list will contain more ideas than you will finally use, which is all right. The point of the exercise is to try to capture all the situations that the system will ever encounter in this use case. You will reduce the list later.

At this point your list is probably still incomplete. You are likely to think of a new failure condition while writing the extension scenarios or when adding a new validation step somewhere inside the use case. Don't worry about this. Do the best you can during this brainstorming stage and add to the list over time.

## *Rationalize the Extensions List*

The purpose of the rationalizing activity is to make the extensions list as short as possible. The ideal extension conditions list shows *all* and *only* the situations the system must handle. Recall that a long requirements document is always hard to read and that redundant descriptions are hard to maintain. By merging extension conditions, you shorten your writing and your readers' reading.

After brainstorming, you should have a short and simple main success scenario and a long list of conditions to consider. Go through the list carefully, weeding out the ones the system need not handle and merging those that have the same net effect on the system. Use these two criteria:

- ◆ The system must be able to detect the condition.
- ◆ The system must handle detection of the condition.

Try making undetectable conditions detectable before deleting them. Eliminate the condition Customer forgot ATM card because there is no equivalent condition the system can detect. Convert the undetectable condition Customer forgot PIN code to Time-out entering PIN code, which the system can detect.

Next, merge equivalent conditions. You might have written: Card is scratched; Card reader is malfunctioning; Card is not even an ATM card. From a requirements point of view, the ATM's behavior is the same: Return the card and notify the customer. Therefore, try to merge these conditions. If you can't find a meaningful single phrasing for all of them, just make a compound condition: Card unreadable or non-ATM card.

## Rollup Failures

As part of merging conditions that produce the same net effect, merge failures from lower-level use cases that all have the same net effect on a higher-level use case. This *rolling up* of lower-level failures is one of the ways we avoid an explosion of extension conditions at the higher levels.

Consider, as an example, that you are working on our PAF package and writing the user-goal use case *Update Investment*. Let's suppose that one of the last steps is

**Use Case: Update Investment**

. . .
7. User has PAF <u>save the work</u>.
8. . . .

This reference calls the use case *Save Work*, which contains conditions of the following sort:

**Use Case: Save Work**

. . .
**Extensions:**
3a. File already exists (user doesn't want to overwrite): . . .
3b. Directory not found: . . .
4a. Out of disk space: . . .
4b. File write-protected: . . .
. . . and so on . . .

*Save Work* ends with success or failure, putting the execution back at the end of step 7 of *Update Investment*. On success, execution continues with step 8. But what if the save fails? What should we write for extension 7a? The reader of *Update Investment* doesn't care *why* the save failed—all failures have the same net effect—so in *Update Investment,* write just the one extension describing what happens.

**Use Case: Update Investment**

. . .
7. User has PAF <u>save the work</u>.
8. . . . .
**Extensions:**
7a. Save fails:
    7a1. . . .whatever should happen next . . .

The best part about this rolling up of failures is that even at the highest-level use case, failures are reported in a vocabulary appropriate for the level. Even busy executives can take the time to read them because the failure reporting in a very high level use case is at a similarly high level.

## 8.3 EXTENSION HANDLING

In the simplest case, a basic sequence of steps deals with the condition. In the general case, though, the extension is a miniature use case. The trigger is the extension condition; the goal is either to complete the use case goal or to recover from whatever failure was encountered. The body is a set of action steps, and possibly extensions to them. The extension can end with delivery or abandonment of its goal, just as in a use case. This similarity is not accidental, and it proves very handy in streamlining a complicated extension.

Start writing the handling of a condition with the action step that follows the condition being detected. You needn't repeat that the condition was detected. Continue the story in exactly the same way as when writing the main success scenario, following all the guidelines for goal level, verb style, and sentences discussed earlier. Keep writing until you reach a place where the main scenario can be rejoined or the use case fails.

Typically, the scenario fragment ends in one of the following four ways:

The step that branched to the extension has been fixed and replaced. At the end of the extension handling, the situation is as though the step had succeeded.

3. User activates web site URL.

4. . . . .

**Extensions:**

3a. No URL available:
    3a1. User <u>searches for web site</u>.

3b. . . . .

The system gives the actor another chance. At the end of the extension handling, the story is back at the beginning of the same step. Notice in the following example that the system will revalidate the password:

3. User enters password.

4. System validates password.

5. . . . .

**Extensions:**

4a. Invalid password:
    4a1. System notifies user, requests password again.
    4a2. User reenters password.

4b. . . . .

The use case ends because of total failure.

3. User enters password.

4. System validates password.

5. . . . .

**Extensions:**

. . .

4c. Invalid password entered too many times:
    4c1. System notifies user, terminates user session.

5a. . . . .

The behavior follows a completely different path to success.

3. User does . . .

4. User does . . .

5. . . . .

**Extensions:**

3a. User runs personal macro to complete processing:
    3a1. Use case ends.

In the first two cases, it is not necessary to say what happens next in the extension, because it is obvious to the reader that the step will restart or continue. In the last two cases, it is generally not necessary to say more than Fail or Use case ends because the steps show the system setting the stakeholders' interests in place.

Most extensions do not say where the story goes after the extension. Usually, it is obvious, and writing Go to step N after every extension makes the overall text harder to read. On the rare occasion that it is not obvious that the story jumps to some other part of the main success scenario, the final step may say Go to step N.

Examples of all of these situations can be found in the various writing samples throughout the book.

## Guideline 12: Indent Condition Handling

When using the numbering style I show in this book, indent the action steps that indicate how the condition is handled, and restart the numbering at 1, after the letter. The action steps follow all the style guidelines given earlier.

> **Extensions:**
> 2a. Insufficient funds:
>> 2a1. System notifies customer, asks for a new amount.
>> 2a2. Customer enters new amount.

Just before this book went to press, Volker Schaberg of Software Futures CCH described a simplifying numbering convention: His writers omit the leading number-letter pair, starting directly with a dot and a number. The above example now looks like:

> 2a. Insufficient funds:
>> .1 System notifies customer, asks for a new amount.
>> .2 Customer enters new amount.

The advantage of this convention is that should the numbering change, and step 2 become step 3, renumbering the extension handling steps is a lot simpler.

When using the straight prose (unnumbered) style, either indent or start a new paragraph for the action steps. The Rational Unified Process template has a special heading level for the extension condition, with the action steps being the text under that heading.

## Failures within Failures

Inside the extension-handling scenario fragment, you may face a new branching condition, probably a failure. If you are using the indentation writing style as shown in this book, simply indent again and continue with the condition naming and scenario writing as before.

At some point, your indentation and numbering will become so complex that you will decide to break out the extension into another use case entirely. Most of the people who have written to me agree that this happens at about the third indentation level.

Here is an example, taken from Use Case 22, *Register a Loss,* on page 75.

> 6a. Clerk decides to exit without completing minimum information:
>> 6a1. System warns Clerk it cannot exit and finalize the form without date, name or policy number, or adjuster name provided.
>> 6a1a. Clerk chooses to continue entering loss.
>> 6a1b. Clerk saves as "intermediate" report and exits.
>> 6a1c. Clerk insists on exiting without entering minimum information:
>>> System discards any intermediate saved versions and exits.

In this example, notice that the writer did not put a number on the last line. Faced with numbering it 6a1c1, she decided that the extension was cluttered enough and that a short piece of straight text would be more readable.

In general, the cost of creating a new use case is high enough that people delay breaking out an extension into its own use case for as long as possible. The consensus seems to be that the above example is as far as it makes sense to indent before a break out.

## Creating a New Use Case from an Extension

To break out an extension into a new sub use case, simply decide what the primary actor's goal is, give the use case that name, name it at its new level (probably *subfunction*), open up the template for a new use case, and fill in the details that you pulled out of the calling use case.

Use Case 32, *Manage Reports,* on page 146 illustrates this. It once contained a step that said

> User can Save or Print report at any time.

It had a set of extensions describing the various alternatives and failure situations, but they kept growing: unnamed report, preexisting name (do or don't overwrite), user cancels save in the middle, and so on. Finally, the writers decided to put *Save Report* in its own use case.

In the original use case, you must still deal with the fact that the new sub use case might fail, so your writing is likely to show both success and failure conditions.

From a theoretical and an effort point of view, it is a simple matter to move an extension into its own use case and back again. The use case model permits us to consider this a minor decision. It was no trouble to move the *Save Report* extensions out of *Manage Reports*, and is only a few minutes of work with the text editor to move them back in.

However, the cost of creating a use case is not in the mechanical effort. The new use case must be labeled, tracked, scheduled, tested, and maintained. These are expensive operations for the project team.

Keeping an extension inside the use case generally makes better economic sense. Two situations will drive you to create a new use case for the extension:

◆ *It is used in several places.* Putting it into its own use case means that it can be tracked and maintained in one place. Ideally, this is the only reason for ever creating a use case below sea level.

◆ *It makes the use case hard to read.* I find the limit of readability at around two pages of use case text and three levels of indentation. (My use cases are shorter than most people's, so your page length may be greater.)

## 8.4 EXERCISES

### Extensions

**8.1.** Brainstorm and list the things that can go wrong during operation of an ATM.

**8.2.** Brainstorm and list the things that can go wrong with the first user-goal use case for the PAF Extension Handling system (described in Exercise 4.4 on page 60).

**8.3.** Write the "Withdraw Cash" use case, containing failure handling, using *if* statements. Write it again, this time using scenario extensions. Compare the two.

**8.4.** Find a requirements file written in a different form from the one used with use cases. How does it capture the failure conditions? What do you prefer about each way of working, and can you capitalize on those observations?

**8.5.** Write the full use case using the PAF system, filling out the failure repair steps (PAF is described in Exercise 4.4 on page 60).

# Chapter 9

# Technology and Data Variations

Extensions express that *what* the system does is different, but occasionally you want to express that "there are several different ways this can be done." *What* is happening is the same, but *how* it is done might vary. Almost always this is because there are some technology variations or some differences in the data that must be captured. Write these into the Technology & Data Variations List, not in the Extensions section.

*Example 1:*

Your system must credit a customer for returned goods. You write this action step:

> 7. Repay customer for returned goods.

The customer can be paid by check, by electronic funds transfer, or by a credit against the next purchase. Thus, you add

**Technology & Data Variations List:**
7a. Repay by check, EFTS, or credit against future purchases.

*Example 2:*

You are specifying a new ATM. Technology has advanced to the point that customers can be identified by bank card, eye scan, or fingerprints. You write:

**Main Success Scenario:**
. . .
2. User identifies him/herself, bank, and account #.
. . .

**Technology & Data Variations List:**
2a. Use magnetic bank card, eye scan, or fingerprints.

These points of variation are not extensions to *this* use case. Each unfolds into its own extension in some lower level use case, which you might never write. Each variation has a noticeable impact on your cost and work plan, so you need to capture and track them. You mark the possibilities using the technology and data variations list.

The technology and data variations list contains no action steps. If you put conditions and action steps there, you are using this section incorrectly.

The technology and data variations list is seen in Use Case 13, *Serialize Access to a Resource,* on page 46.

If you are determined to use UML use case diagrams, create an empty, generic base use case for the basic step, and a specializing use case for each variation. The empty generic base use case names the *what* but not any *how*. Each specialized use case defines its own steps to explain *how* it is done. The UML notation is explained in Appendix A. Figure 9.1 shows an example.

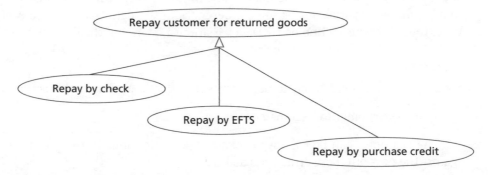

***Figure 9.1*** *Technology variations using specialization in UML*

# Chapter 10

# *Linking Use Cases*

## 10.1  SUB USE CASES

An action step can be a simple step or the name of another use case. Writing

> **User saves the report**

with no emphasis or annotation indicates a simple, atomic step. Writing either of these steps:

> User <u>saves the report</u>
> User ***saves the report*** (UC 35 Save a Report)

indicates a use case called *Save a Report*. This is so natural that it scarcely needs more explanation. Even casual use case readers understand the idea, once they are told that an <u>underlined</u> (usually from hyperlinking) or ***italicized*** action indicates that another use case is being called, one that expands the action mentioned.[*] It is extremely pleasant writing use cases this way, rolling up or unrolling the action as needed. Moreover, it is the easiest way of connecting use cases. It takes little time to learn and little space to describe.

---

[*] In UML vocabulary, another use case is being *included*. I find that beginning writers and casual readers are much happier saying that one use case refers to or calls another. Which term you use is up to you.

## *10.2  EXTENSION USE CASES*

On occasion, you need a different linkage between use cases, one closely matching the *extension* mechanism. Consider this example:

> You are designing a new word processing program called *Wapp*. The user's main activity is typing. However, she might suddenly decide to change the zoom factor or the font size, run the spell checker, or do any of a dozen different of things not directly connected to typing. In fact, you want the typing activity to remain ignorant of anything else that might happen to the document.
>
> Even more importantly, you want different software development teams to come up with new ideas for services without having them update the base use case for each new service. You want to be able to extend the requirements document without trauma.

The characteristics of such a situation are as follows:

- There is a main activity, which can be interrupted.
- The main activity can be interrupted in a number of ways, and is not in control of the interruptions.

This is different from having a main menu that lists the system services for the user's selection. The main menu is in control of the user's choices, whereas in our example, the main activity is not in control but it is simply interrupted by another activity.

In this instance, you do not want the base use case to explicitly name all the interrupting use cases. Doing so produces a maintenance headache, since every person or team adding a new interrupting use case has to edit the base use case. Every time it is edited, the use case might get corrupted or need to be versioned, reviewed, and so forth.

Use the same mechanism as described for scenario extensions, but create a new use case. The new one is called an *extension use case* and is identical to a scenario extension except that it stands on its own. Just like a scenario extension, it starts with a condition, referencing a situation in the base use case where the condition might occur. Put all that into the Trigger section of the template.

To illustrate, here are some extracts for the word processor *Wapp*. Figure 10.1 shows the *Wapp* situation in UML diagram form. I carefully use a special style of connector, a *hook*, to show a use case extending (or hooking into) another. See Appendix A for details.

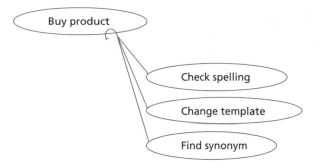

**Figure 10.1** *UML diagram of extension use cases*

**Use Case: Edit a Document**

**Primary Actor:** User
**Scope:** Wapp
**Level:** User goal
**Trigger:** User opens the application.
**Precondition:** None
**Main Success Scenario:**
1. User <u>opens a document to edit</u>.
2. User <u>enters and modifies text</u>.
. . .
. . . User <u>saves document</u> and exits application.

**Use Case: Check Spelling**

**Primary Actor:** User
**Scope:** Wapp
**Level:** Subfunction!
**Precondition:** A document is open.
**Trigger:** Anytime in <u>Edit a Document</u> that the document is open and the user selects to run the spell checker
**Main Success Scenario:**
. . .etc.. . .

**Use Case: Find Synonym**

---

**Primary Actor:** User
**Scope:** Wapp
**Level:** Subfunction!
**Precondition:** A document is open.
**Trigger:** Anytime in <u>Edit a Document</u> that the cursor is in a word and the user selects to run the thesaurus
**Main Success Scenario:**
...etc....

**Use Case: Change Document Template**

---

**Primary Actor:** User
**Scope:** Wapp
**Level:** Subfunction!
**Precondition:** A document is open.
**Trigger:** Anytime in <u>Edit a Document</u> that the document is open and the user selects this function
**Main Success Scenario:**
. . .etc.. . .

## When to Use Extension Use Cases

Create extension use cases only when you need to, because they are harder for people to understand and maintain. Two situations call for their use.

The most common situation is when there are many asynchronous or interrupting services the user might use, which should not disturb the base use case. Often, these services will be developed by different teams and show up with shrink-wrapped software such as word processors.

The other situation is when you are writing additions to a locked requirements document. As Susan Lilly of S.R.A. wrote me,

> You're working on a project with an iterative process and multiple drops. You have baselined requirements for one drop. In a subsequent drop, you *extend* a baselined use case with new or additional functionality. You do *not* touch the baselined use case.

If the base use case is not locked, the extension is fragile. Changing the base use case can damage the condition mentioned in the extending use case, so be wary about using extension use cases is such situations. Exercise 10.2 gives you a chance to experiment with extension use cases of this sort.

Alan Williams wrote in with a useful principle to help with the decision of whether a use case should call a sub use case or the second use case should extend the base one:

> If the trigger involves things for which the base use case is responsible—that is, the base use case knows when/where/why the second use case should be followed—then the base use case *includes /calls/references* the other.
>
> If the trigger involves things for which the second use case is responsible—that is, the second use case knows when/where/why it should be followed—the second use case *extends* the base use case.

Note that when the base use case *calls* a second use case, the base use case names the other, saying when and where it executes. The referenced use case does not contain the name of the base use case. When the second use case *extends* a base use case, the base use case does not name or, indeed, know anything about the extending (interrupting) use case. The extending use case names the use case it interrupts and determines the circumstances under which it executes.

## 10.3 EXERCISES

### Use Case Linkage

**10.1.** Find a condition in a user-goal use case for the PAF system (described in Excercise 4.4) that requires a sub use case to be broken out. Write that sub use case and link to it from your user-goal use case attending to both its success and its failure.

**10.2.** Consider the ATM situation in which you are not at your home bank but are a guest at another bank. Write the sub use case for a bank-to-bank withdrawal request, and link it with your previous use case(s) about withdrawing money. Do this in two ways: as a sub use case that your base use case references and as an extension use case. Discuss with a colleague which you prefer and why.

# Chapter 11

# *Use Case Formats*

## 11.1 FORMATS TO CHOOSE FROM

### *Fully Dressed*

Most of the examples in this book are in my preferred style, which is fully dressed:

- One column of text (not a table)
- Numbered steps
- No *if* statements
- A numbering convention in the extensions section that involves combinations of digits and letters (e.g., 2a, 2a1, 2a2, and so on).

The alternate forms that compete best with this are the casual form, the two-column style, and the Rational Unified Process template, all described in the following sections. However, when I show a team the same use case in multiple styles, they almost always select the one-column, numbered-step version, and so I continue to use and recommend it. Here is the basic template, which project teams around the world have put into Lotus Notes, DOORS, Word, Access, and various other text tools.

### Use Case 24  🗊 Fully Dressed Use Case Template <name>

<the name should be the goal as a short active verb phrase>
**Context of Use:** <a longer statement of the goal, if needed, its normal occurrence conditions>
**Scope:** <design scope, what system is being considered black-box under design>
**Level:** <one of: summary, user-goal, subfunction>

**Primary Actor:** <a role name for the primary actor or description>
**Stakeholders and Interests:** <list of stakeholders and key interests in the use case>
**Precondition:** <what we expect is already the state of the world>
**Minimal Guarantees:** <how the interests are protected under all exits>
**Success Guarantees:** <the state of the world if goal succeeds>
**Trigger:** <what starts the use case, may be time event>
**Main Success Scenario:**
<put here the steps of the scenario from trigger to goal delivery and any cleanup after>
<step #> <action description>
**Extensions:**
<put here there extensions, one at a time, each referring to the step of the main scenario>
<step altered> <condition>: <action or sub use case>
<step altered> <condition>: <action or sub use case>
**Technology & Data Variations List:**
<put here the variations that will cause eventual bifurcation in the scenario>
<step or variation # > <list of variations>
<step or variation # > <list of variations>
**Related Information:**
<whatever your project needs for additional information>

## Casual

Contrast the fully dressed form with the following, an example of a casual use case taken from a draft manuscript by Grady Booch. I have added the primary actor, scope, and level to make a fully formed example. Notice that the extensions are still present in the second paragraph.

## Use Case 25    Actually Login (Casual Version)

**Primary Actor:** User
**Scope:** Application
**Level:** Subfunction
Upon presenting themselves, the user is asked to enter a username and password. The system verifies that a submitter exists for that username and that the password corresponds to that submitter. The user is then given access to all the other submitter commands.

If the username corresponds to a submitter that is marked as an administrator, then the user is given access to all the submitter and administrator commands. If the username does not exist, or if the password does not match the username, then the user is rejected.

## One-Column Table

Some people like to put the scenario steps in a table. I feel that the lines on the table obscure the actual writing, but people often choose the table style. Table 11.1 illustrates the template.

**Table 11.1.** *One-Column Table Format of a Use Case*

| USE CASE # | <the name is the goal as a short active verb phrase> | |
|---|---|---|
| Context of Use | <a longer statement of the context of use if needed> | |
| Scope | <what system is being considered black box under design> | |
| Level | <one of summary, primary task, subfunction> | |
| Primary Actor | <a role name for the primary actor, or a description> | |
| Stakeholder and Interests | Stakeholder | Interest |
| | <stakeholder name> | <put here the interest of the stakeholder> |
| | <stakeholder name> | <put here the interest of the stakeholder> |
| Preconditions | <what we expect is already the state of the world> | |
| Minimal Guarantees | <the interests as protected on any exit> | |
| Success Guarantees | <the interests as satisfied on a successful ending> | |
| Trigger | <the action upon the system that starts the use case> | |
| Description | Step | Action |
| | 1 | <put here the steps of the scenario from trigger to goal delivery and any cleanup after> |
| | 2 | <...> |
| | 3 | |
| Extensions | Step | Branching Action |
| | 1a | <condition causing branching> : <action or name of sub use case> |
| Technology and Data Variations | | |
| | 1 | <list of variations> |

## Two-Column Table

Rebecca Wirfs-Brock invented the idea of a *conversation*, whose distinguishing characteristic is the use of two columns, with the primary actor's actions in the left column and the system's actions in the right column. Conversations are most often written in preparation for designing the user interface, so they may contain more detail on the user's movements.

You can write a use case using the two-column table form. The result is clear but often quite long, even exceeding three pages (see, for example Use Case 36, *Research a Solution—Before*, on page 194). Usually, by the time we revise the text to fit into 3 to 9 steps at appropriate goal levels, the writing is so simple and clear that people no longer find the need for the columns.

Constantine and Lockwood adopt the conversation format when capturing user interface requirements in their *essential use cases*, as described in *Software for Use* (1999). The difference is that in an *essential use case,* all of the user movements (*interface detail*) are omitted, so the result is very short, exactly as described.

A difficulty with using the two-column format to capture behavioral requirements is that there is no place to write about the supporting actors. One could add a third column for them, but I have never heard it suggested nor seen it done. This is because *conversations* and *essential use cases* are aimed at user interface requirements rather than overall system behavioral requirements.

Taking all of this into account, many people still find the two-column form attractive. Experiment with it if you like, and read what Wirfs-Brock, and Constantine and Lockwood are doing with it. Table 11.2 is a scenario fragment in two-column style.

**Table 11.2.** *Two-Column Table*

| Customer | System |
| --- | --- |
| Enters order number | |
| | Detects that the order number matches the winning number of the month. |
| | Registers the user and order number as this month's winner. |
| | Sends an e-mail to the sales manager. |
| | Congratulates the customer and gives her instructions on how to collect the prize. |
| Exits the system | |

## *RUP Style*

The Rational Unified Process (RUP) uses a template fairly similar to the fully dressed template. The numbering of steps is optional. Extensions are given their own heading sections and called *alternate flows*. Everything in this book works nicely with this template, which, although a bit cluttered with heading numbers, is attractive and easy to follow. Here it is in its basic form:

**1. Use Case Name**
   **1.1. Brief Description**
      . . . text . . .
   **1.2. Actors**
      . . . text . . .
   **1.3. Triggers**
      . . text . . .
**2. Flow of Events**
   **2.1. Basic Flow**
      . . . text . . .
   **2.2. Alternative Flows**
      2.2.1. Condition 1
         . . . text . . .
      2.2.2. Condition 2
         . . . text . . .
      2.2.3. . . .
**3. Special Requirements**
   **3.1. Platform**
      . . . text . . .
   **3.2.** . . .
**4. Preconditions**
   . . . text . . .
**5. Postconditions**
   . . . text . . .
**6. Extension Points**
   . . . text . . .

Rational Software Corporation sent me the following use case to use as an example. Normally, it would be accompanied in the tool set by a use case diagram and other work artifacts. I find the use case quite self-explanatory, and I think you will, too. Note that both simple paragraphs and numbered steps are used as the writer felt best suited the presentation. I added the two graphical icons to the title to be consistent with the examples in this book, but I did not add any fields to the template itself.

Use Case 32, *Manage Reports,* on page 146 also uses the RUP template.

## Use Case 26    Register for Courses

1. **Use Case Name:** Register for Courses
    1.1. **Brief Description**

    This use case allows a Student to register for course offerings in the current semester. The Student can also modify or delete course selections if changes are made within the add/drop period at the beginning of the semester. The Course Catalog System provides a list of all the course offerings for the current semester.

    The main actor of this use case is the Student. The Course Catalog System is an actor within the use case.

2. **Flow of Events:**

    The use case begins when the Student selects the "maintain schedule" activity from the Main Form. [*Refer to user-interface prototype for screen layout and fields.*]

    2.1. **Basic Flow**
        2.1.1.  Create a Schedule
            2.1.1.1.  The Student selects "create schedule."
            2.1.1.2.  The system displays a blank schedule form. [*Refer to user-interface prototype for screen layout and to the domain model for required fields*]
            2.1.1.3.  The system retrieves a list of available course offerings from the Course Catalog System. [*How is this selected and displayed? Text? Drop-down lists?*]
            2.1.1.4.  The Student selects 4 primary course offerings and 2 alternate course offerings from the list of available offerings. Once the selections are complete the Student selects "submit." [*Define "primary course offerings" and "alternative course offerings" in project glossary. Must exactly 4 and 2 selections be made? Or "up to 4. . .," etc.*]
            2.1.1.5.  The Add Course Offering subflow is performed at this step for each selected course offering.
            2.1.1.6.  The System saves the schedule. [*When is the master schedule updated? Immediately? Nightly (batch)?*]

    2.2. **Alternative Flows**
        2.2.1.  Modify a Schedule
            2.2.1.1.  The Student selects "modify schedule."
            2.2.1.2.  The system retrieves and displays the Student's current schedule (e.g., the schedule for the current semester). [*Is this only available for the current semester?*]
            2.2.1.3.  The system retrieves a list of all the course offerings available for the current semester from the Course Catalog System. The system displays the list to the Student.
            2.2.1.4.  The Student can then modify the course selections by deleting and adding new courses. The Student selects the

courses to add from the list of available courses. The Student also selects any course offerings to delete from the existing schedule. Once the edits are complete the Student selects "submit."

2.2.1.5. The Add Course Offering subflow is performed at this step for each selected course offering.

2.2.1.6. The system saves the schedule.

2.2.2. Delete a Schedule

2.2.2.1. The Student selects the Delete Schedule activity.

2.2.2.2. The system retrieves and displays the Student's current schedule.

2.2.2.3. The Student selects "delete."

2.2.2.4. The system prompts the Student to verify the deletion.

2.2.2.5. The Student verifies the deletion.

2.2.2.6. The system deletes the schedule. *[At what point are the student slots freed up?]*

2.2.3. Save a Schedule

At any point, the Student may choose to save a schedule without submitting it by selecting "save." The current schedule is saved, but the student is not added to any of the selected course offerings. The course offerings are marked as "selected" in the schedule.

2.2.4. Add Course Offering

The system verifies that the Student has the necessary prerequisites and that the course offering is open. The system then adds the Student to the selected course offering. The course offering is marked as "enrolled in" in the schedule.

2.2.5. Unfulfilled Prerequisites or Course Full

If in the Add Course subflow the system determines that the Student has not satisfied the necessary prerequisites or that the selected course offering is full, an error message is displayed. The Student can either select a different course offering or cancel the operation, at which point the use case is restarted.

2.2.6. No Schedule Found

If in the Modify a Schedule or Delete a Schedule subflows the system is unable to retrieve the Student's schedule, an error message is displayed. The Student acknowledges the error and the use case is restarted.

2.2.7. Course Catalog System Unavailable

If the system is unable to communicate with the Course Catalog System after a specified number of tries, the system will display an error message to the Student. The Student acknowledges the error message and the use case terminates.

2.2.8.   Course Registration Closed

If, when the student selects "maintain schedule," registration for the current semester has been closed, a message is displayed to the Student and the use case terminates. Students cannot register for courses after registration for the current semester has been closed.

3. **Special Requirements**

No special requirements have been specified for this use case at this time.

4. **Preconditions**

4.1.   Login

Before this use case begins the Student has logged onto the system.

5. **Postconditions**

There are no postconditions associated with this use case.

6. **Extension Points**

There are no extension points associated with this use case.

## *If-Statement Style*

Programmers inevitably want to write *if* statements in the text. After all, they say, it is easier to write this:

If the order matches the winning number, then <all the winning number business>, otherwise tell the customer that it is not a winning number.

than it is to learn how to write extensions.

If there were only one *if* statement in the use case, I would agree. Indeed, there is nothing in the use case model that precludes if . . . then . . . else. However, once there are even two *if* statements, the writing becomes much harder to understand, and there is almost certainly a third, a fourth, and a fifth. There is probably even an *if* statement inside an *if* statement.

When people insist on writing with *if* statements, I invite them to do so and to report back on their experience. Everyone who has done so has concluded within a short time that the *if* statements made the use case hard to read, and has gone back to the extensions style. Therefore, my strong stylistic suggestion is "Don't write *if* statements in your scenario."

## *Occam Style*

If you are determined to construct a formal writing model for use cases, look first to the Occam language, invented by Tony Hoare. With Occam you can annotate the alternate, parallel, and optional sequencing you will need more easily than with any other language I know. I don't know how Occam handles exceptions, which are necessary for the extension style of writing.

In Occam you write

**ALT**
   Alternative 1
   Alternative 2
   **TLA** (this ends the alternatives)
**PAR**
   Parallel action 1
   Parallel action 2
   **RAP** (this ends the parallel choices)
**OPT**
   Optional action
   **TPO**

If you do decide to create or use a formal language for use cases, make Use Case 22, *Register a Loss,* on page 75 your first test case as it has parallel, asynchronous, exceptional, and coprocessing activities. I think it shows how well natural language deals with these activities in a way that is still quite easy to understand.

## *Diagram Style*

A use case details the actions and interactions of actors achieving a goal. A number of diagram notations can express these things: sequence charts, collaboration diagrams, activity diagrams, and Petri nets. If you use one of these notations, you can still use most of the ideas in this book to inform your writing and drawing.

Graphical notations suffer from two usability problems. First, end users and business executives are not likely to be familiar with them and have little patience to learn. The use of graphical notations cuts you off from valuable readers.

Second, the diagrams do not show all that you need to write. The few CASE tools I have seen that implement use cases through interaction diagrams force the writer to hide the text of the steps behind a pop-up dialog box attached to the interaction arrows. This make the use case impractical to scan—the reader has to double-click on each arrow to see what is hidden behind it. In the "bake offs" I have held, use case writers and readers uniformly choose no tool support and simple word processing documents over CASE tool support in diagram form.

The next section discusses one particular diagramming style that is not suitable to use cases.

### The UML Use Case Diagram

The UML use case diagram, consisting of ellipses, arrows, and stick figures, is *not* a notation for capturing use cases. The ellipses and arrows show the packaging and decomposition of use cases, not their content.

Recall that a use case names a goal. It consists of scenarios, which consist of action steps, each of which is phrased as a goal and so can be unfolded to become its own use case. It is possible to make the use case goal an ellipse, to break out every action step as an ellipse, and to draw an arrow from the use case ellipse to the action step ellipse, labeling it *includes*. And it is possible to continue with this decomposition from the highest- to the lowest-level use case, producing a monster diagram that shows the entire decomposition of behavior.

However, the ellipse diagram is missing essential information, such as which actor is doing each step and notes about the step ordering. It is useful as a table of contents and should be saved for that purpose. See Reminder 24: The Great Drawing Hoax on page 227 and Section A.1 in Appendix A, Ellipses and Stick Figures.

The point here is that you should not try to replace the text of the use case with ellipses. One student in a lecture asked me, "When do you start writing text? At the leaf level of the ellipse decomposition?"

The answer is that the use case lives in the text, and all or any drawings are only illustrations to help readers locate the text they need to read.

Many people find the topmost use case diagram (the one showing the external actors and user-goal use cases) useful. It provides a *context diagram*, similar to context diagrams that people have been drawing for years. The value of use case diagrams drops rapidly from there. I discuss this more in Appendix A.

## 11.2  FORCES AFFECTING USE CASE WRITING STYLES

At the 1998 OOPSLA conference, 12 experienced use case writers and teachers gathered to discuss common points of confusion or difficulty with use cases and the forces that drive people to write them differently. Paul Bramble, the workshop organizer, put together the following categorization of the items collected. If you feel overwhelmed by all the different situations in which use cases are used, feel comforted by the fact that we were, too.

You may find that some combination of the issues listed below obliges you to work differently than you had expected. Be patient, be tolerant, and write use cases to suit your purpose. Given all these forces, we are lucky to find a consistent answer to the question: "How does one write readable use cases?"

## Countervailing Forces: Business Setting, Social Interaction, Conflicting Cultures

You want to introduce use cases, but run into the following situation/argument (I won't try to fix the argument, but you may enjoy recognizing that you are not alone):

We've always done it this other way.

With multiple cultures, you may find

There is prejudice across teams.

There are different work cultures, and people in them simply "do things differently."

The people writing the use cases use a different vocabulary than the people who read them.

### Level of Understanding

Understanding is different at different times and places and among different people. You might choose to shift the recommended writing style based on:

How much you know now
- About the domain
- About use cases in general

Where in the life cycle you know it.

Whether you need to establish content, or cost.

Whether you need the breadth view or the depth view now.
- The presence of clandestine analysis or creeping analysis
- People tend to stress the things they know
- Scheduling versus depth of knowledge versus domain knowledge

### Stakeholder Needs

What Viewpoint you are after:

The customer is a reader, the use case consumer, happy with a high-level description.

The corporate/IT person is a writer, or an implementer, interested in a detailed description.

Several groups may be present wanting to represent multiple viewpoints concerning use cases across several service groups, or differing on whether to produce a complete model or an incomplete model.

Are there different readers involved? If so, who are they?

### Experience versus Formality

*Experience:* Every team includes people new to use cases, but they soon become "experienced" writers. Experienced people know some short cuts; new people want clear directions and consistent instructions.

*Formality:* Perhaps the leader, or perhaps departmental methodology, dictates a formal (or informal) writing style, despite any experience or lack thereof.

### Coverage

Breadth of coverage depends on the team's composition, their writing skill, their intercommunication, and their need to cover the whole problem versus their need to communicate information to readers.

Coverage may vary based on

The subject matter experts (they may focus narrowly)

The number of writers

The number of readers

The number of implementers

Whether or not the business people know what they want

The decision to work along a common model

The geographic dispersion of the group

## Consistency

The need for consistency of content can conflict with uncertainty or inconsistancy in customer requirements:

Requirements volatility

Consistency of format

## Complexity

Use Case complexity involves the following factors:

Desire for Completeness

Describing the full problem domain

Multiple viewpoints

Simplifying the view of a system

Simplicity of expression

Detailed expression

Narrow versus broad view

Problem complexity

The desire to add technical details (especially when the problem is difficult)

The following factors influence system complexity:

Analysis paralysis (the complexity of the system overwhelms the analyst)

Number of actor profiles

Number of function points

Kind of system

Simplicity of the user system

Realtime system

Embedded system (it must be error resistant)

## Conflict

The need is to resolve customer conflict, but ambiguity masks that conflict.

## Completeness

Completeness can be hampered by the following factors:

Requirements are incomplete for the engineering.

The writers don't have access to users (users are not your customers).

## Goals versus Tasks—What to Accomplish versus How to Accomplish It

Users often specify requirements rather than usage.

Context can conflict with usage.

Activities and tasks describe what is happening in a system, not why it is happening.

## Resources

Time is required to write good use cases, but project time is critical. Management must buy in to a writing project.

## Other Factors

Other factors that affect use case writing are:

Tool Requirements/support

An unknown objective

The need to partition the requirements for subsequent analysis

Unconstrained design versus level of design to do.

Clean versus understandable design

Abstract versus concrete use cases

Traceability

Corporate agility

Whew! That was quite the list. Even though most of the book applies to all situations, you might use this list to decide whether to use more or less formality, whether to do less now and more later, how much to write or how to stage the writing, and how much breadth or how much precision to use before getting some depth.

## 11.3  STANDARDS FOR FIVE PROJECT TYPES

You are on the project. You and the others have read this book, so you know the ideas. The question now is "What standards are *we* going to adopt?" The answer depends on who you are, what your skills are, and what your objective is at this moment. Compare your answer to the list of forces just given.

In this section, I nominate writing standards for five particular situations. You will notice that the basic choice in each is between casual and fully dressed. The five situations are

1. Eliciting requirements, even if use cases will not be used at all in the final requirements document.
2. Modeling the business process.
3. Drafting or sizing system requirements.
4. Writing functional requirements on a short, high-pressure project.
5. Writing detailed functional requirements at the start of an increment, on a longer or larger project.

You should find it practical to use these standards *as is*. After some consideration, you may decide to tune them to your corporate needs or the needs of the moment or according to the principles given in the book.

In the following examples, I use the example of a company, MyCo, about to develop a new system, Acura, to replace an old system, BSSO. I do this to remind you not to write the words *corporation* and *system* but their actual names instead.

## *For Requirements Elicitation*

### Use Case 27    ▱ Elicitation Template—Oble a New Biscum 〰

**Scope:** Acura

**Level:** Sea level

**Context:** The quibquig needs to oble a new biscum once a dorstyp gets nagled. (text about the goal in operational context)

**Primary Actor:** A quibquig (or whoever the primary actor is)

**Stakeholders and Interests:** Qubquig, MyCo, . . . (whomever and whatever is appropriate).

**Preconditions:** What must be true before this use case can be triggered

**Triggers:** The quibquig selects the obling function (whatever it may be).

**Main Success Scenario:**

. . . A paragraph of stuffstuff describing the quibquig successfully obling a biscum with Acura . . . actors do this, that, and the other.

. . . Another paragraph of stuffstuff describing conditions and alternate paths in trying to oble the biscum or failing . . . actors do this, that, and the other.

**Frequency of Occurrence:** Yay many times a day

**Open Issues:** . . . a good thing to fill in at this point . . .

Use this template when your ultimate purpose is to *discover* the requirements (reread Steve Adolph's account, "Discovering" Requirements in New Territory on page 12). Bear in mind that your requirements may be written in a form other than a use case. The game thus is to move quickly through the use cases, drafting them in a lively work session.

The template is casual. Keep the stakeholders and interests in the template to remind everyone about their requirements, but don't include system guarantees.

Your use cases will generally be black boxes ▱, and most of them will be at the user-goal level 〰. You may generate higher-level use cases for context, but you shouldn't go below sea level very often.

## *For Business Process Modeling*

### Use Case 28 ⌂ Business Process Template—Symp a Carstromming ✎

**Scope:** MyCo operations
**Level:** Summary
**Context:** Text about the goal in operational context
**Primary Actor:** Whoever the primary actor is
**Stakeholders and Interests:** Whomever and whatever is appropriate
**Minimal Guarantees:** Whatever they are
**Success Guarantees:** Whatever they are
**Preconditions:** What must be true before this use case can be triggered
**Triggers:** Whatever it may be
**Main Success Scenario:**
1. . . . action steps . . .
2. . . .
**Extensions:**
1a. . . . Extension conditions:
    1a1. . . . action steps . . .
**Frequency of Occurrence:** Whatever
**Open Issues:** . . . a good thing to fill in at this point . . .

This template is for redesigning the business or the process to handle new software. The people reading these use cases will be senior line staff, department managers, and senior executives, so keep them easy to read and reduce the emphasis on data details. Number the steps to make the sequencing stand out. Be sure to describe failure handling in the extensions, as that handling reveals important business rules.

The top-level, outermost use cases will be the black-box variety ⌂, showing the company interacting with external partners. These are used either as specifications against which the business process will be measured or to set the context for the white-box use cases. White-box use cases ⌂ working with systems such as *MyCo Operations* show the organization in action, with people and departments working together to deliver the organization's responses. You will use goal levels from cloud to sea level. I selected a kite-level summary goal for the example in the template.

## *For Sizing the Requirements*

### Use Case 29     ▱ Sizing Template—Burble the Tramling ⌒⌒

---

**Scope:** Acura

**Level:** Blue

**Context:** Put here preconditions or conditions of normal usage.

**Primary Actor:** Whomever

. . . Put here a few sentences describing the actors successfully freeing the necessary fadnap in the main success scenario . . .

. . . Put here a few sentences mentioning some of the alternate paths and the handling . . .

**Frequency of Occurrence:** How often

**Open Issues:** . . . always a good idea to mark . . .

This template is for when you are drafting the system requirements to estimate system size and shape. Later, you may detail the requirements further, making them fully dressed. You might choose to design directly from the casual use cases if your project fits the profile (see the section, The Use Case Briefs, on page 37, and Reminder 19: Know the Cost of Mistakes on page 223).

The template is casual, as befits early work at medium precision, and the system under discussion can be a system or the business. The goals may be at any level, including subfunctions, since project effort depends largely on the complexity of the subfunction use cases. In the preceding example, I used Acura and user goal. See also Use Case 25, *Actually Login (Casual Version),* on page 120.

## *For a Short, High-Pressure Project*

### Use Case 30    ☐ High-Pressure Template: Kree a Ranfath ⌇⌇

**Scope:** Acura
**Level:** User goal
**Context:**
**Primary Actor:**
**Stakeholders and Interests:**
**Minimal and Success Guarantees:**
**Preconditions:**
**Triggers:**
**Main Success Scenario:**
. . . A paragraph of text describing the actors achieving success in the main success scenario . . .
**Extensions:**
. . . A paragraph of text mentioning *all* the alternate paths and the handling . . .
**Frequency of Occurrence:**
**Open Issues:** . . .

Use this template when you need written requirements but the project is short and under heavy time pressure. For time and economic reasons, you want to avoid the overhead of numbers and a full template; therefore, use the casual form. Still, you must capture preconditions, guarantees, and extensions. I assume that you will work carefully on improving project internal communications, as described in Reminder 19: Know the Cost of Mistakes on page 223.

## *For Detailed Functional Requirements*

**Use Case 31**   ⬠ **Use Case Name—Nathorize a Permion** 〜〜

> **Scope:** Acura
> **Level:** User goal
> **Context of Use:**
> **Primary Actor:**
> **Stakeholders and Interests:**
> **Minimal Guarantees:**
> **Success Guarantees:**
> **Preconditions:**
> **Triggers:**
> **Main Success Scenario:**
> 1. . . .
> 2. . . .
> **Extensions:**
> 1a. . . .
>    1a1. . . .
> **Frequency of Occurrence:**
> **Open Issues:** . . .

Use this template when your purpose is to collect behavioral requirements using all of the features of fully dressed use cases. This might be for a larger or critical cost project, a fixed-price bid, a geographically distributed team, at the start of an increment when it is time to expand and examine the sizing use cases drafted earlier, or because it is your culture to do so.

The system under design may be anything, as may the actors and goals. Again, I used Acura and user-goal level in the sample template.

## 11.4 CONCLUSION

All of the different formats for a use case express approximately the same basic information. The recommendations and guidelines of this book apply to each. Don't fuss too much about which format you should use on your project, but select one that both writers and readers can be comfortable with.

## 11.5 EXERCISE

### If Statements

**11.1.** Rewrite the following use case, getting rid of the *if* statements and using goal phrases at the appropriate levels and alternate scenarios or extensions.

#### Perform clean spark plugs service

**Conditions:** Plugs are dirty or customer asks for service.

1. Open hood.
2. Locate spark plugs.
3. Cover fender with protective materials.
4. Remove plugs.
5. If plugs are cracked or worn out, replace them.
6. Clean the plugs.
7. Clean gap in each plug.
8. Adjust gap as necessary.
9. Test the plug.
10. Replace the plugs.
11. Connect ignition wires to appropriate plugs.
12. Check engine performance.
13. If ok, go to step 15.
14. If not ok, take designated steps.
15. Clean tools and equipment.
16. Clean any grease from car.
17. Complete required paper work.

**Outcome:** Engine runs smoothly.

# Part 2

## Frequently Discussed Topics

# Chapter 12

# *When Are We Done?*

You are "done" when:

- You have named *all the primary actors and all the user goals* with respect to the system.

- You have captured *all trigger conditions* to the system either as use case triggers or as extension conditions.

- You have written all the user-goal use cases, along with the *summary and sub-function use cases* needed to support them.

- Each use case is written clearly enough that
  - The sponsors *agree* that they will be able to tell whether or not it is actually delivered.
  - The users *agree* that it is what they want or can accept as the system's behavior.
  - The developers *agree* that they can actually develop that functionality.

- The sponsors *agree* that the use case set covers all they want (for now).

**ALL THE PRIMARY ACTORS AND THEIR USER GOALS.** This delimits what the system must accomplish. Since there is no other source of this information to compare the list of primary actors and user goals against, but only the minds of the people who have to accept the system, you cannot know that you are done with it. You can only suspect that you are done, so it is worthwhile going over the list in brainstorming mode several times.

**ALL TRIGGER CONDITIONS.** These represent the fine-tuning of the boundary. The system will have to react to all of them. In the use cases, some of the triggering events will show up as use case triggers, for example, User puts card into slot, Customer calls to add or remove a clause to or from his insurance policy, or User selects to install software upgrade. Others are taken care of in the scenario extensions: User hits cancel button, System detects power drop, and so forth.

One way to reexamine the set of system triggers is to identify all the elements that have a life cycle and then review these lifecycles. Look for all events that cause something to change its state in its life cycle.

**SUMMARY AND SUBFUNCTION USE CASES.** The summary use cases create the context for the user-goal use cases. They answer the often asked question, "But how do all these (user-goal) use cases fit together?" I like to make sure that every use case sits inside a higher-level one, up to a single root. That root use case is only a table of contents without much story line, but new readers find it useful to have a single starting point from which they can start accessing every use case in the system.

Subfunction use cases support  user-goal use cases. They are needed only if called from several other use cases or to isolate a complicated piece of behavior.

**AGREEMENT ON THE USE CASES.** The use cases are done only when both the sponsors and the usage experts can read and agree with them and say that they are all they want, *and* the developers can read them and agree that they can build a system to these specifications. That is a difficult challenge. It is *the* challenge of requirements writing.

## On Being Done

The phrase *"being done"* gives the impression that you should write all the use cases, beginning to end, before starting on design tasks. Be aware that this is not the case. See Section 17.1, Use Cases in Project Organization, on page 167 for a discussion of developing a project plan with partial release of use cases. Also see *Surviving Object-Oriented Projects* (Cockburn, 1998) for a longer description of incremental development and the article "VW-Staging" (*http://members.aol.com/acockburn/papers/vw-stage.htm*) for a short, dedicated discussion of incremental and iterative development.

Different project teams use different strategies, depending on their situation. Some draft all the use cases right away, perhaps to prepare a bid for a fixed-price contract. They should know that their use cases will need fine-tuning over the course of the project. Some teams only draft the actors and user goals, delaying use case elaboration until the appropriate increment. Others create the use cases for each six to nine months of work, deferring all other requirements discussion until that work is almost finished. Still others write use cases just before starting on a round of work. Each of these strategies has its place and its advocates.

# Chapter 13

# Scaling Up to Many Use Cases

There are two ways to deal with a large number of use cases: Say less about each one or separate them into clusters. You should use both techniques.

### Say Less about Each One (Low-Precision Representation)

The use case name alone is useful—that's why it counts as the first level of precision. The collection of use case names is an excellent working medium for manipulating the full set of use cases, particularly for estimating, planning, and tracking. Put the list of names in a spreadsheet and use the spreadsheet's capabilities to sort, order, and summarize the various qualities of interest about each use case. Section 1.5, Manage Your Energy, on page 16, and Section 17.1, Use Cases in Project Organization, on page 167 discuss this approach.

The second level of precision is the use case brief, a two- to three-sentence summary of the use case. This, too, can be put into spreadsheet or table form and reviewed. (See Table 3.3, Sample Use Case Briefs, on page 38.) It is useful as an overview of the system and for organizing the work.

Saying less about each use case is valuable when you want to scan the full use case set at one time. There will be times, though, when you need to collect them into separate clusters.

### Create Clusters of Use Cases

If you are working from text-based tools such as Lotus Notes or spreadsheets and word processors, you can form *use case clusters* using ordinary labeling techniques. If you are using UML tools, you will call them *packages*. Three common and effective clustering techniques are described in the following paragraphs.

**BY ACTOR.** The most obvious way to cluster use cases is by primary actor. However, perhaps at around 80 or 100 use cases, this approach loses effectiveness. At that point, you will have too many per primary actor or too many primary actors, or too much overlap of primary actors to use cases.

**BY SUMMARY USE CASE.** Some use cases naturally cluster by their lifecycle or, on larger projects, by their place in the lifecycle. These related use cases show up in a summary use case. If you do not write summary use cases, you may still want to cluster the use cases to create, update, and delete certain kinds of information that naturally cluster. On one project, one system maintained a mock checkbook for customers. We referred to all of the checkbook-altering use cases as "the checkbook use cases." This cluster was developed by the same development team, and its members progressed together in a way that was easy for the project managers to handle.

**BY DEVELOPMENT TEAM AND RELEASE.** Clustering use cases by which team will develop the design and release number simplifies the work tracking. It becomes natural to ask questions like "Is the user profile cluster going to make it on time?" Clustering by team holds even for larger projects.

**BY SUBJECT AREA.** If a project has over 100 use cases, people will automatically separate them by subject area in their speaking. It is usually quite easy to name natural subject areas. One project used customer information, promotions, invoicing, and advertising. Another used booking, routing, tracking, delivery, and billing. Often there are subprojects within the different subject areas. Each subject area might contain 20 to 100 use cases.

Although tracking 240 use cases is difficult, tracking 15 to 20 clusters is quite reasonable. On a large project, I would cluster first by *subject area* to get 3 to 6 clusters of 20 to 100 use cases each, and then by *release and development team*. Depending on the number of use cases in these clusters, I would summarize work progress using clusters of related or summary use cases.

# Chapter 14

# CRUD and Parameterized Use Cases

## 14.1 CRUD USE CASES

So far there is no consensus on how to organize all those little use cases of the sort *Create a Frizzle, Retrieve a Frizzle, Update a Frizzle,* and *Delete a Frizzle*. These are known as CRUD use cases, from the Create, Retrieve, Update, and Delete operations on databases. The question is, are they all part of one bigger use case, *Manage Frizzles*, or are they separate?

In principle, they are separate because each is a separate goal, possibly carried out by a different person with a different security level. However, they clutter up the use case set and can triple the number of items to track.

Opinion is split on the best way to deal with CRUD use cases. Susan Lilly of S.R.A. advocates keeping them separate in order to track which primary actors have security access to the different functions. I tend to start with just one, *Manage Frizzles,* to get the advantage of less clutter. If the writing gets complex, I break out that one part, as described in the subsection Creating a New Use Case from an Extension on page 109. I track user access to system data and functions using separate worksheets. Neither way is wrong, and I have not seen enough evidence to form a rule one way or the other.

The following is a use case written by John Colaizzi and Allen Maxwell of Empower IT.[*] They started writing both ways, but then decided to merge the use cases into the summary-level *Manage* use case and eventually broke out the *Save* sub use case to deal with the complexity. Their use cases show how they fit their personal writing style into a given template. Starting with the Rational Unified Process template, they numbered the steps and extensions.

---

[*] Used with permission from the authors.

## Use Case 32   ▭ Manage Reports ∿

### 1. Brief Description

This Use Case describes and directs operations for Creating, Saving, Deleting, Printing, Exiting, and Displaying Reports. This particular use case is at a very low level of precision and utilizes other use cases to meet its goal(s). These other use cases can be found in the documents listed in the "Special Requirements" Section.

### 1.1. Actors

User (Primary).

File System: typical PC file system or network file system with access by user. (Secondary)

### 1.2. Triggers

User selects operations explicitly using the Explorer interface.

### 1.3. Flow of Events

#### 1.3.1. Basic Flow—Open, Edit, Print, Save, and Exit report

a. User selects Report by clicking report in Explorer and selects open (open also triggered by double-clicking on report in the Explorer).

b. System displays report to screen.

c. User sets report layout, etc., using use case <u>Specify Report Specs</u>. System displays altered report.

d. Steps c and d repeat until user is satisfied.

e. User Exits report using use case <u>Exit Report</u>.

f. User can Save or Print report at any time after step c using use case <u>Save Report</u> or the Print Report Alternative Flow listed below.

#### 1.3.2. Alternative Flows

##### 1.3.2.1. Create New Report

a. User selects "Create New Report" from Explorer by right clicking and selecting option from pop-up menu.

System creates new report with default name and sets report status for name as "unset," status as "modified."

b. Use case flow continues with Basic Flow at step b.

##### 1.3.2.2. Delete Report

a. User selects Report by clicking report in Explorer and selects Delete.

b. System opens report (or makes it current if it is already open) and requests validation from user for deleting report.

c. Report is closed and resources cleaned up.

d. System removes report entry from report list and report data is removed from storage medium.

1.3.2.3. Print Report

    a. User selects Report by clicking report in Explorer and selects Print, OR user selects print option of current report (a report being edited/displayed in Basic Flow of this use case).

    b. User selects printer to send report to and printing options specific to printer (print dialog, etc., controlled by operating system), OR user selects to Print Report to File . . .

    c. System loads report and formats. System sends report job to operating system or prints report to designated report file. System closes report.

1.3.2.4. Copy Report

    a. User selects Report by clicking report in Explorer and selects Copy.

    b. System prompts for new report name and validates that name doesn't exist yet.

    c. System repeats b until user enters a valid (nonexistent) name, opts to save over existing report, or cancels copy operation altogether.

    d. System saves report with designated name as a new report.

    e. If copy is replacing an existing report, existing report is removed.

1.3.2.5. Rename Report

    a. User selects Report by clicking report in Explorer and selects Rename.

    b. User enters new name, system validates that name is valid (not the same as it was previously, doesn't exist already, valid characters, etc.)

    c. System repeats step b until valid name accepted or user cancels use case operation with "cancel" selection.

    d. System updates Report List with new name for Selected Report.

**1.3.3. Special Requirements**

1.3.3.1. Platform

The platform type must be known for control of the report display operations and other UI considerations.

**1.3.4. Preconditions**

A data element exists on the machine and has been selected as the current element.

### 1.3.5. Postconditions

#### 1.3.5.1. Success Postcondition(s) [note: this is the Success Guarantee]

System waiting for user interaction. Report may be loaded and displayed, or user may have exited (closed) the report. All changes have been saved as requested by user, hard copy has been produced as requested, and report list has been properly updated as needed.

#### 1.3.5.2. Failure Postcondition(s) [note: this is the Minimal Guarantee]

System waiting for user. The following lists some state possibilities:

Report may be loaded:

Report list still valid.

### 1.3.6. Extension Points

None

## Use Case 33    Save Report

### 1. Brief Description

This Use Case describes the Save Report process. This use case is called from the use case <u>Manage Reports</u> and from the use case <u>Exit Report</u>.

### 1.1. Actors

User (Primary)

File System: Typical PC file system or network file system with access by user. (Secondary)

### 1.2. Triggers

User selects operations through tasks in the <u>Manage Reports</u> use case or <u>Exit Report</u> use case (which is included in <u>Manage Reports</u> use case) to call this use case.

### 1.3. Flow of Events

#### 1.3.1. Basic Flow—Save New Report

a. Use case begins when user selects Save Report.

b. System detects that report name status is "not set" and prompts for new report name. User chooses report name; system validates that the report name doesn't exist in Report List yet. Adds entry to Report List.

c. User cancels save operation . . . Use case ends.

d. System updates Report List with Report information. System creates unique report file name if not already set, and saves report specs to file system.

e. Report is set as "unmodified" and name status set to "set."

f. Use Case ends with report displayed.

### 1.3.2. Alternative Flows

1.3.2.1. Alternative Subflow—Report name exists—overwrite

    a. System finds name in list, prompts user for overwrite. User elects to overwrite. System uses existing report filename and Report List entry. Use case continues with step d of Basic Flow.

1.3.2.2. Alternative Subflow—Report name exists—cancel

    a. System finds name in list, prompts user for overwrite. User elects to cancel. Use case ends with report displayed.

1.3.2.3. Alternative Flow—Save Report As . . .

    a. User selects Save Report As . . .

    b. User enters new report name, system checks for existence of name in Report List. Name does not exist yet. System finds name in list, prompts user for overwrite. User elects NOT to overwrite. Use case continues at step b.

    c. Use case continues with step d of Basic Flow.

1.3.2.4. Alternative Subflow—Report name exists—overwrite

    a. System finds name in list, prompts user for overwrite. User elects to overwrite. System uses existing report filename and Report List entry. Use case continues with step d of Basic Flow.

1.3.2.5. Alternative Subflow—Report name exists—cancel

    a. System finds name in list, prompts user for overwrite. User elects to cancel. Use case ends with report displayed.

1.3.2.6. Alternative Flow—Save Existing Report

    a. User Selects Save Report for Current Report (where Current Report has been saved before and exists in the Report List).

    b. System locates entry in Report List, updates List information as needed, saves report specs to report file.

    c. Report is set as "unmodified."

    d. Use Case ends with report displayed.

### 1.3.3. Special Requirements

None

### 1.3.4. Preconditions

A data element exists on the machine and has been selected as the "Current element."

A report is currently displayed and set as the "Current Report."

Report status is "modified."

### 1.3.5. Postconditions

1.3.5.1. Success Postcondition(s) [note: this is the Success Guarantee]

    System waiting for user interaction. Report loaded and displayed. Report List is updated with report name, etc., as required by specific Save operation. Report status is "un-modified." Report Name Status is "Set."

1.3.5.2 Failure Postcondition(s) [note: this is the Minimal Guarantee]

System waiting for user.

Report loaded and displayed.

Report status is "modified." Report name status same as at start of use case.

Report list still valid (Report list cleaned up when save fails as necessary).

1.3.6. **Extension Points**

None

## 14.2 PARAMETERIZED USE CASES

We are occasionally faced with writing a series of use cases that are almost the same. The most common examples are *Find a Customer, Find a Product, Find a Promotion,* and the like. Probably just one development team will create the generic searching mechanism, and other teams will make use of it.

Writing a half-dozen similar *casual* use cases is not much of a problem. However, writing six similar fully-dressed use cases is a chore, and it won't take the writers long to want a short cut. I'll describe that short cut using as an example Use Case 23, *Find a Whatever (Problem Statement),* on page 78.

With that use case we first observed that

- ◆ Naming a goal in a step is very like a subroutine call in programming.
- ◆ Use cases will be read by people, not computers.

Next we noted that finding a thing, whatever it might be, must use basically the same logic:

1. User specifies the thing to be found.
2. System searches, brings up a list of possible matches.
3. User selects, perhaps resorts the list, perhaps changes search
4. System finds the thing (or doesn't).

What differs from use to use is

- ◆ The name of the thing to be found
- ◆ The searchable qualities (search fields) of the thing to be found
- ◆ What to display about the thing to be found (the display values, in sequence)
- ◆ How to sort the choices (the sort criteria)

We created a parameterized use case, one that works with a nickname for each of those items. We chose to call the use case *Find a Whatever*. We decided that with a little bit of coaching, the reader could safely recognize that the phrase clerk <u>finds a customer</u> means call *Find a Whatever* looking for a customer. Readers are surprisingly intelligent and will make this jump with little trouble.

We did the same for all the nicknames in the parameterized sub use case: search fields, display values, and sort criteria. We just had to decide where the writer would specify the details.

For the data values, we defined three levels of precision. The first was the phrase mentioned in the use case text, the *data nickname*, such as *Customer Profile*. The second was the *field lists* associated with the data nickname, naming all the information collected under it, for example, *Name, Address, Day Phone, Night Phone*, and so on. The third level of precision was a precise field definition listing field lengths, validation criteria, and the like.

Only the first level of precision was put into the use case. The data descriptions and the search and sort criteria were all put on a separate page that was hyperlinked into the use case step.

The result was an action step that looks like this:

Clerk <u>finds a customer</u> using <u>customer search details</u>.

The page *Customer search details* specified the search fields, the display fields in sequence, and the sort criteria. The reader of the use case would click on the underlined phrase to see it. This entire mechanism was easily and quickly understood by readers, writers, and implementers.

*Find a Whatever* now starts to look like this:

1. The user identifies the <u>searchable qualities</u> of the whatever.
2. The system finds all matching whatevers and displays their <u>display values</u> in a list.
3. The user can resort them according to the <u>sort criteria</u>.
4. The user selects the one of interest.

With this neat trick, the calling use cases remain uncluttered by the gory (and lower-level) details of searching, sorting, resorting, and the like. The common searching behavior is localized and written only once. Consistency across finders is ensured, and the people who really need to know the details for programming purposes can find them. Indeed, the implementation team was delighted to be given just *one* specification for their search mechanism, so they didn't have to wonder if all the searches were really the same.

Those are enough hints. Now finish Exercise 5.4 at the end of Chapter 5. Pay particular attention to the guarantees and extensions because both are important to the callers.

# Chapter 15

# *Business Process Modeling*

Everything in this book applies to business processes as well as to software systems design. Any system, including a business, that offers a set of services to outside actors while protecting the interests of the other stakeholders can be described with use cases. The readability of textual use cases is particularly helpful in business modeling.

Examples of business use cases in this book are

- Use Case 2, *Get Paid for Car Accident,* on page 5.
- Use Case 5, *Buy Something (Fully Dressed Version),* on page 9.
- Use Case 18, *Operate an Insurance Policy,* on page 65.
- Use Case 19, *Handle a Claim (Business),* on page 70.
- Use Case 20, *Evaluate Work Comp Claim,* on page 72.

## 15.1 MODELING VERSUS DESIGNING

The statement "We are using use cases for business process reengineering" may mean any of the following:

"We use them to document the old process before we redesign it."

"We use them to create outer behavioral requirements for the design to meet."

"We use them to document the new process after it is redesigned."

All of these are valid and interesting. I ask you to understand which one you intend.

I carefully say business process *modeling* or *documentation* instead of business process *reengineering* or *design* when talking about use cases. A use case only documents a process, it doesn't reengineer or redesign it. In creating the design, the designers take a leap of invention. The use cases do not tell them how to do that. Each level of documentation serves as a behavioral requirement that the next level of design must meet (indeed, we say "this design *meets* these behavioral requirements").

Introducing new technology often changes the business's processes. You can work to realign them from the core business toward technology, from the new process to the technology, or from the technology directly (deriving the process concurrently). Any of these methods can work.

## Work from the Core Business

In this top-down way of working, you start by carefully identifying the organization's core business, as described in *Reengineering the Corporation* (Hammer, 1984). At the end of the exercise you will know

The *stakeholders* in the organization's behavior

The *external primary actors* whose goals you propose that the organization satisfy

The *triggering events* that the organization must respond to

The *services* the business offers, with the success outcomes for the stakeholders

Notice that without saying *how* your organization will work, you now have the information that sets boundary conditions for its behavior. Not accidently, this is also the bounding information for a use case: stakeholders and interests, primary actors with goals, success guarantees.

The context for the business process design can be documented using business black-box use cases with the company or organization as the system under design (Figure 15.1).

At this point, you invent new groupings of your resources and new processes to make the best use of current technology. These days, computer systems serve as active memories and active communication conduits for the organization. *Reengineering the Corporation* gives many examples of how different acts of invention lead to different business designs and their relative effectiveness. The outcome is a new corporate or organizational design (Figure 15.2).

The result of the process re-invention is then documented using white-box use cases, showing people and departments (and perhaps computers) interacting to deliver the organization's externally visible behavior.

The fully developed white-box use cases must show the organization's handling of all failure and exceptional conditions, just as any complete set of use cases or any

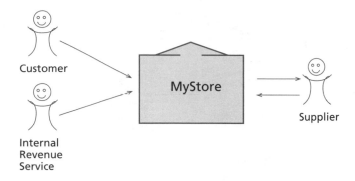

**Figure 15.1**  *Core business black box*

**Figure 15.2**  *New business design in white box*

complete business process model must. You may choose to name the technology in the use cases or not as suits your purpose.

## Work from Business Process to Technology

With this intermediate starting point, you are not questioning the organization's core purpose but rather defining the new business that the new technology will fit into. You probably have already nominated some new technology—perhaps a new set of software applications or mobile devices. You want to set boundary conditions for the technologists' invention.

You will write white-box business use cases that document the proposed new business processes *without* mentioning the new technology (Figure 15.3). Mentioning the

**Figure 15.3** *New business design in white box (again)*

new technology in this situation is as inappropriate as describing a user interface in a system use case. See, for example, Use Case 21, *Handle a Claim (Systems),* on page 73.

In principle, the computer can be replaced in the descriptions by baskets of paper shipped from person to person. Your team's task will be to see how active conduits such as full-size computers or a mob of palm computers and radios can improve the process.

The designers now know what process their invention must support. After inventing, they will write black-box *system* use cases that show the new system fitting into the technology-free white-box business use cases. These system use cases become the requirements for the system design, as shown in Figure 15.4.

While this looks wonderful on paper, it costs a lot in money and time. Since technology moves so fast and creates such pressure, often there is no time to work this way. Many times I have found that *usage experts,* people in the business who are experts

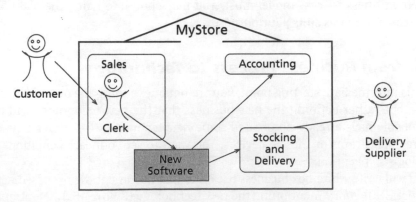

**Figure 15.4** *New business process in black-box system use cases*

in their working areas, can do the new business process modeling in their heads, allowing you to save time and money. That allows you to work in the third way, described next.

### *Work from Technology to Business Process*

First, collect some experienced usage experts who are probably eager to improve their groups' technology and work habits. Make sure you have two representatives for each part of the business that your system will affect.

In your negotiations with them, the technology experts will nominate system capabilities that can improve the processes. Be prepared. They will nominate more than your development team can deliver (that's all right—technologists need to be stretched!).

Have these usage experts write system black-box use cases for the system they imagine. These use cases will not mention the user interface. They will describe what the system will *do* to support the primary actors in their business goals as effectively as possible. Their extensions sections will involve all sorts of critical or seldomly discussed business rules. The usage experts may have to talk to their colleagues to clarify fine points of system behavior. As part of the writing process, they will, of course, write a few summary-level and business use cases showing context and the linkage of goals over time.

In other words, a light business process documentation will be generated as a normal part of the system requirements exercise. The usage experts will have done the new process modeling in their heads, while arguing about how the actors and the new system should behave under various circumstances. I have found this to be an effective way of working.

- Use Case 3, *Register Arrival of a Box,* on page 6, illustrates how system behavior documentation can end up describing a fragment of the business process, complete with exceptional conditions.
- Use Case 21, *Handle a Claim (Systems),* on page 73, is a summary (kite-level) use case that shows the business process context for the system.

## 15.2 *LINKING BUSINESS AND SYSTEM USE CASES*

A business use case has the same appearance as a system use case, so all the training in use case writing and reviewing can be applied to both. The ever-unfolding story starts in the business use cases and unfolds into the system use cases. That is the synergy that business and system use cases offer.

The bad news is that writers and readers will accidentally mix them, likely putting system behavior into the business use cases and business operations into the system use cases. That might be useful if done deliberately, but often the writers and readers don't realize they are doing so. A reader expecting a system use case will criticize a business use case for being too high level, not noticing that it is not intended to provide system behavior detail. A writer of a business use case might accidentally include many details of system behavior, with the result that the business executives lose interest while reading these overly detailed documents.

To help reduce the confusion, *always* write the scope and level in the use case template. Train your writers to write them, and train your readers to read them at the start of every reading. Use graphic icons if you can. Use slightly different templates for the two and number them with entirely different numbers (one group started the business use cases at 1,000 and the system use cases at 1). Concoct something *immediate* and *visual*. Then you can take advantage of the synergy available without getting people lost.

The other bad news is that it is rarely worth the effort to completely and properly link business and the system use cases. Usually, the people writing the business use cases describe the business process down to, but not including, the use of the system. They run out of time, money, energy, and motivation before writing how the new system is used in the daily life of the business people. The people writing the system use cases sometimes add a sentence or two of business process for context, but they have no motivation to rewrite the business use cases to include the new system's functionality.

The result is that there is a gap between business and system use cases. Rusty Walters of FirePond comments on this:

> I have yet to experience to my satisfaction a full-fledged story of business use cases that unfold into system use cases. In my experience, it is quite common to have three levels of business use cases. A few black-box, cloud-level business uses cases to get started. These quickly turn into white-box, cloud-level business use cases that unfold, meaning that they name a white-box, kite-level business use case.
>
> However, I have not seen a clean connection from the business use case to system use cases.

This is not good for those looking for an automatic way to derive system requirements from business processes. I don't think that automatic derivation is possible, as I described in Section 15.1, Modeling versus Designing.

Some people find this troubling. I don't. Most of the people I deal with in organizations are quite capable of making the mental leap to link the lowest *business* use case with the kite- or sea-level *system* use cases, once they know to do that. Furthermore, I have yet to see that writing that final set of use cases, which completely links the business to the system use cases, is worth the time and money it costs to do so. The two efforts run from separate budgets, and each activity appropriately ends when its goal is satisfied.

Reexamine the use cases starting with Use Case 19, *Handle a Claim (Business)*, on page 70. The system use cases are indeed mentioned in the business ones, but they were written specifically to provide context for the system requirements group, not as the start of a separate business process reengineering activity.

Rusty Walters of FirePond tells of his experiences with business process use cases in this account.

---

◆ **Rusty Walters: Business Modeling and System Requirements**

Having the benefit of reading your book early, I've been able to rationalize problem areas with previous attempts, and utilize my newfound knowledge.

**My Pre-Book Experiences**

Prior to reading the book, I helped document functional requirements for several applications in a product suite.

For one application, we developed *system* use cases at summary, user, and subfunctional levels. We concentrated totally on system functionality. We were pleased with the outcome of the use case model, as it read quite well. We found no need to develop any business use cases to show context; the system summary-level use cases were all that we needed.

On another application within the suite the story was quite different, even though the same group was responsible for this use case model as for the previous one. Looking back, I now can see the crux of the problem was different people on the team approaching the problem from different perspectives. I was working from business process to technology. Some other people were working from technology to

business process. Needless to say, the design scope for each use case wasn't clear between the two groups.

The business-process-to-technology group never got to writing the system use cases, and the technology-to-business-process group never got to writing the business use cases. Instead, they sort of hit each other in a head-on collision, with each group trying to use the other group's use cases directly. Not having the insight or the necessary understanding at the time to label the use cases correctly for scope and level, the use case model became quite a mess. In the end, the team was never really happy with the use case model; they knew it didn't "smell" right, but they didn't know what exactly was wrong.

**My Post-Book Experience**

Working from the core business seems to cause the least confusion, as I discovered in a group whose purpose was to understand and document their processes.

It was clear to everyone that we were gathered to talk about their processes and the way they work within the business, and not about software/

hardware systems. The areas of confusion that did come up were related to *business* versus *department* scope.

We started with business, very summary (cloud) *black*-box use cases—this was very clear to everyone, even though the group quite often wanted to dive down into lower-level steps. We quickly moved into writing very summary (cloud) *white*-box use cases, as you describe. When we decided to talk about the next-lower-level use cases, confusion arose quickly about the design scope—were we talking about the business or about a particular department? This also went hand-in-hand with what constituted success for the use case. In one particular case, we ended up removing the last two steps after we realized those steps were really done in the calling use case and were not properly part of the current one. Currently the group has no intention of ever unfolding the business use cases into system use case requirements.

It was much easier to understand the problem areas after the meeting, although it was difficult to notice and correct the course during the meeting. In documenting the outcome, I used the design scope context diagrams, labeling the design scope and level of each use case with graphic icons as you suggested. As simple as the graphics may seem, they have quite an impact on reading the use cases and help greatly in keeping them straight in everyone's mind.

# Chapter 16

# *The Missing Requirements*

It is all very well to give the advice, "Write the *intent* of the actor, just use a *nickname* for the data that is passed," as in Customer supplies name and address. However, it is clear to every programmer that this is not sufficient information for development. The programmer and the user interface designer need to know exactly what is meant by address, which fields the address contains, the lengths of the fields, and the validation rules for addresses, zip codes, phone numbers, and the like. All of this information belongs in the requirements somewhere—but not in the use case.

Use cases are only "Chapter 3" of the requirements document—the behavioral requirements. They do not contain performance requirements, business rules, user interface design, data descriptions, finite state machine behavior, priority, and probably some other information.

"Well, where are those requirements?" the system developers cry. We can say that the use cases shouldn't contain them, but they have to be documented somewhere.

Some of the information can, in fact, be attached to each use case as associated information. This might include

- Use case priority
- Expected frequency of occurrence
- Performance needs
- Delivery date
- Secondary actors
- Business rules (possibly)
- Open issues

Different projects adjust this list to contain whatever they consider important.

In many cases, a simple spreadsheet or table captures the information well. Many people use a spreadsheet at the start of the project to get an overview of the use case information. With the use case name in the leftmost column, they fill in the other columns as follows:

- Primary actor
- Trigger
- Delivery priority
- Estimated complexity
- Probable release
- Performance requirement
- State of completion, and
- Whatever else is needed

That still leaves out the section the programmers need just as much as they need the behavioral requirements—the data requirements, including field checks to perform.

## 16.1 PRECISION IN DATA REQUIREMENTS

Collecting data requirements is subject to the same directive to manage energy with "precision" as is every other work product (Section 1.5, Manage Your Energy). I find it useful to divide the data requirements into three levels of precision:

- Information nicknames
- Field lists or data descriptions
- Field details and checks

**INFORMATION NICKNAMES.** We write Clerk collects customer information or Clerk collects customer's name, address, and phone number. We expect to expand on the individual descriptions of *name*, *address*, and *phone number* in some other place.

The nicknames are appropriate within a use case. To write more would slow down the requirements gathering and make the use cases much longer and harder to read and more brittle (that is, sensitive to changes in the data requirements). Also, it is likely that many use cases will reference the same information nicknames.

For these reasons, break out the details of the data requirements from the use case, and link from the use case to the relevant *field list*. This can be done with a hyperlink in many tools or with a requirements number in tools that support the crosslinking of numbered elements.

**FIELD LISTS.** At some point, the requirements writers will have to negotiate over what each information nickname means. Does customer's name consist of two parts—first and last names—or three parts (or more)? What exactly is needed for address? Addresses around the world have many different formats. This is the appropriate place for the writers to expand the data descriptions to the second level of precision. It might be done gently in parallel with writing the use cases, or it might be done afterward, perhaps working alongside the user interface designer.

There are many strategies for dealing with the second level of precision. I'll name two and you can consult *Software for Use* (Constantine and Lockwood, 1999) and *GUIs with Glue* (Hohmann, in press) for others, or you may have experience in this area yourself.

♦ The first strategy is to have a separate entry in your tool for each nicknamed item. Under customer name, identify three fields: first name, middle name, last name. That's all. Over time, you will add more precision to this entry, with field details and checks, until it contains all the details about those fields, as described in the next item, *Field details and field checks*.

♦ The second strategy is to notice that you wrote name, address, and phone number together in a single use case step. That you did so means that it is significant to you that these three parcels of information are entered and displayed together. This is useful for the user interface designer, who may design a subscreen, or field cluster, to support the fact that these three parcels show up together in different places. Therefore, you create a single entry in your tool for "name, address, and phone number." There you list what fields are required for name, what fields are required for phone number, and what fields are required for address, but you don't expand those lists further.

The difference between the two strategies is that in the second you put clusters of nicknamed information on each field list page. When you expand to more precision, you don't expand in that entry but create a separate entry for each field.

Whichever strategy you choose, you can expect the information at the second level of precision to change as the project moves forward and as the team learns more about the specifics of the data. You may also have different people defining the second and third levels of precision for the data. It will probably be handy to keep the second level of data precision separate from the use case itself.

**FIELD DETAILS AND FIELD CHECKS.** What the programmers and database designers really need an answer to are the questions "How many characters long can the customer's name be?" and "What restrictions are there on date of loss?" These are field types, field lengths, and field checks.

Some project teams put these items into a requirements chapter called Data Requirements or External Data Formats. Some, who use a hyperlinked medium or database, put them into separate entries classified under Field Definitions, and others put user interface data details directly into the user interface requirements and design document.

Whatever you decide, note that

- You need to expand the field details and checks to the third level of precision.
- The use case is not the place to do that expansion.
- The use case should link to that expansion.
- The field details are likely to change over time, independently from the use case details.

## 16.2 CROSS-LINKING FROM USE CASES TO OTHER REQUIREMENTS

Data formats are not part of the use case, but the use case names the need for the data, and so we can hyperlink from the use case to the data descriptions. Complex business rules do not fit well into the use case narrative, but, again, we can link to entries containing them. This sort of hub-and-spoke linking makes the use cases the center of the requirements document, even for many of the nonfunctional requirements, as illustrated in Figure 16.1.

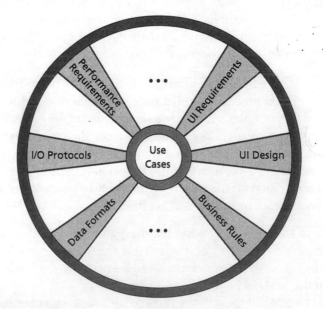

**Figure 16.1** *Recap of Figure 1.1, "Hub-and-Spoke" model of requirements*

Just be careful not to force into use cases those requirements that don't fit the use case form. Use cases are best suited to the capture of interactions between actors.

Occasionally, I hear someone complain that it is hard to describe the requirements for a tape merge operation or a compiler with use cases. I wholeheartedly agree. Those are best described using algebraic or tabular forms.

Only a fraction of the requirements set is suited to the use case form. It just so happens that the interaction part is central and connects many other requirements.

# Chapter 17

# Use Cases in the Overall Process

## 17.1 USE CASES IN PROJECT ORGANIZATION

Use cases give the management team a handle on usable function being delivered to users. The title of each use case names a goal that a primary actor will find supported by the system. The body of each use case announces what the system will require and provide.

### Organize by Use Case Titles

During early project planning, create a table with the use case and primary actor names in the left two columns. In the third column, have the business sponsors put a priority or value on the business of each use case. In the fourth column, have the development team estimate the complexity or difficulty of delivering that function. This is a natural evolution of the actor-goal list (see the subsection The Actor-Goal List on page 36).

In a nice variation on this theme, Kent Beck, in his "Planning Game" (*Extreme Programming Explained: Embrace Change,* 1999), has developers estimate the development cost while the business sponsors decide the priority of each use case. The business sponsors have the opportunity to change the priorities after seeing the work estimates, but may not change the estimates. In light of this idea, you may wish to fill the columns of your planning table in two passes.

Add any other columns to the planning table, as you wish, to capture the development priority of the use case, the release it will first show up in, or even the team that will develop it (see Table 17.1).

You can view and manipulate this table with ease over the course of the project.

***Table 17.1.*** *Sample Planning Table*

| Actor | Task-level Goal | Business Need | Technical Difficulty | Priority | UC # |
|---|---|---|---|---|---|
| Any | Check on requests | Top | Large job in general case | 1 | 2 |
| Authorizor | Change authorizations | High | Simple | 2 | 3 |
| Buyer | Change vendor contacts | Medium | Simple | 3 | 4 |
| Requestor | Initiate an request | Top | Medium | 1 | 5 |
| | Change a request | Top | Simple | 1 | 6 |
| | Cancel a request | Low | Simple | 4 | 7 |
| | Mark request delivered | Low | Simple | 4 | 8 |
| | Refuse delivered goods | Low | Unknown | 4 | 9 |
| Approver | Complete request for submission | High | Complex | 2 | 10 |
| Buyer | Complete request for ordering | Top | Complex | 1 | 11 |
| | Initiate PO with vendor | Top | Complex | 1 | 12 |
| | Alert of nondelivery | Low | Medium | 4 | 13 |
| Authorizer | Validate Approver's signature | Medium | Hard | 3 | 14 |
| Receiver | Register delivery | Top | Medium | 1 | 15 |

Over time, you will complete the estimates for each use case, assign them to teams, and track the work per use case per release.

On the next page is a short, true story about using the planning table to gauge, estimate, prioritize, and reduce the possible working set of use cases. The benefits of working this way are these:

♦ The use case list clearly shows the system's value to the business.

♦ The list of names provides a structure for working with development priority and timeframe.

## Handle Use Cases Crossing Releases

It would be soothing to say that a tidy set of complete use cases maps to each release, except that it doesn't.

A use case such as *Order Product* calls out all sorts of special handling, which will be delivered over time. A typical staging strategy is

- Deliver the simple case in release 1.
- Add high-risk handling in release 2.
- Put preferred customer handling in release 3.

Either you write one use case and deliver a fraction of it in each release, or you write three use cases. Each way will work, and each way will hurt.

Some teams choose to split the use cases into units that are delivered *completely* on releases. They write *Order Product (Base Case)* followed by *Order Product (High-Risk Handling)* and *Order Product (Preferred Customer Addition)*. They either repeat the use case body, adding the new elements in italics, or they write the second use case as an extension use case on the first and the third unit as an extension use case on the second. Splitting the use cases simplifies tracking; however, there are then three times as many use cases to track, and writing the add-on use cases can become tricky.

Others (me, for instance) like the use cases to be as readable as possible and can live with the fact that they will be released portions at a time. They highlight (in yellow or italics) the parts that will be released first and refer to "the highlighted portions of Use Case 5." This is the way I have seen most projects go, and it works passably well. Even so, it is not as tidy as we might like.

A possible middle-road strategy is to start by writing the full, multi-release use case. Then, at the start of an increment, write a version of it, isolating just the functionality you plan to deliver in that increment. On the next increment, write the parts of the use case that have already been delivered in plain text and the parts that are new in the upcoming release **in bold text**. With this strategy, the number of use cases still multiplies but in a more controlled way. If there are 80 use cases to start with, the team's sensation is of managing 80 plus however many are being delivered in the specific increment. The use case set expands but in a localized and controlled fashion.

You will have to choose which way to work, knowing that each has drawbacks.

Note that all approaches presuppose that the organization is using incremental staging and delivery of the system, with increments of up to about four months. Incremental development has become a standard recommendation in modern software projects and is discussed in detail in *Surviving Object Oriented Projects* (1998) and in the article "VW Staging" (http://members.aol.com/acockburn/papers/vwstage.htm).

## Deliver Complete Scenarios

◆ **A Short, True Story about Integration**

The test and integration manager of a very large project asked me about the hazards of incremental development. It turned out that the writing team was developing and delivering the application in sets of "features" rather than by use case. His team could not test the pieces given to him, since there was no "story" that they supported but just a heap of mechanisms. The project leaders eventually rebuilt the project plan so that each increment's work produced a usable story line.

It often happens that not all of a use case is delivered at one time. Even so, each delivery must contain a full scenario. The use case says what the user wants to accomplish, and enumerates the many scenarios involved in that. The software you deliver must contain some of those scenarios *top to bottom* or your application will not be delivering usable function.

Planning and design must coincide to produce collections of functions usable by the end user. Those are complete scenarios from the use cases. Functional testers will test for use case compatibility. Deployment can only be in fully usable use case threads.

This seems trivial, but overlooking it can hurt, as the preceding story illustrates.

## 17.2  USE CASES TO TASK OR FEATURE LISTS

Development teams with good communications work out their design tasks from the use cases. This is good, because otherwise a small project management nightmare awaits them in mapping the use cases to the design tasks and in keeping the mapping current.

The following email from a colleague illustrates this.

Two of us visited [the client] the last two weeks to relay the requirements and to establish a working relationship with the developers. We had been focusing on the use cases and felt they were 90%–95% precise enough for design and development, so we were confident. There was a scope document created with the intent of describing what features or feature sets were in or out, very similar to the sample scope section you made available. This document was originally very small, short and sweet, but we kept getting requests for a "traditional" requirements document. So we had someone expand it a little bit but tried to keep the level of detail to a minimum.

Low and behold, in our first meeting with the developers, they wanted to review the "requirements." The "requirements" to them were represented in this scope document. We saw how the development team was latching on to this document, and knew it lacked the detail we wanted because we were hoping to focus around the use cases. We spent the next three days developing the newly revised scope document that you will see attached. I like to refer to it as "spoon feeding" the use cases to them. Hoping to make an impact on the development culture and to help the company make a transition to use-case-based requirements, we essentially used the name of each use case as a feature set, and each step within the scenarios as a feature. We were literally copying the steps from the use case documents and pasting them into the scope document underneath their appropriate use case heading.

The problem we faced, and that ultimately caused us to do this double-duty maintenance, is that the exact text from the scenarios doesn't stand on its own very well as a line-item feature. Even though we copied the text from the scenarios, we would constantly reword a little, or add some context around it.

This is the start. The designers want to work from numbered requirements paragraphs, or feature lists, much as just described. In other but similar versions of the story, the "detailed requirements," or numbered paragraph document, was written first. Someone then decided to write use cases from them (this seems a little backwards to me, but that's what happens).

There is a fundamental tension between the flow of the system's behavior as described in use cases and the design tasks an individual designer is given. A designer works on a single line item or feature buried in one use case, or perhaps crosslinked across many. That might be the Undo mechanism, the Transaction Logging mechanism, or the Search Screen Framework. The designers cannot describe their work in use case language because they are not working with the flow of the system. The best they can say is, "I'm working on the Search Screen part of Use Case 5."

At the same time, the sponsors of the software want to see the application in full flow, delivering value to the users. The individual design tasks are not themselves interesting.

It is time-consuming and tiring to keep the use case document and the design task list in sync, requiring the work that my colleague described, repeated many times on the project. I view this as work best avoided. So far, I have not had to break apart the use cases into line items on projects of up to 50 people in size. Perhaps that is because I stress personal communication and cooperation on my projects and have been fortunate with the cultures I have worked in. We have been able to break apart the line items in our heads, or by using a yellow highlighter, and to write the key ones into the task list for scheduling without much overhead.

The other alternative is to generate two documents and work hard to keep them up to date. If you decide to follow this strategy, break the use case text into pieces that can be allocated to single developers or single development teams. Each piece becomes a program feature, mechanism, or design task that will be assigned, tracked, and checked off. The detailed estimate for the software development is the sum of all the design task estimates. Project tracking consists of noting the starts and completions of each.

The following is an example of converting a use case to a work list.

### Use Case 34    Capture Trade-In

**Goal in Context:** The Shopper has a shopping cart containing products and wants to add a trade-in to see how it will affect costs.

**Scope:** Commerce software system

**Level:** Subfunction

**Preconditions:** The shopping cart must contain product(s).

**Success Guarantees:** The trade-in has been valued, added to the shopping cart, and has reduced the cost of the items contained in the shopping cart.

**Minimal Guarantee:** If not finalized, the trade-in is not captured or added to the shopping cart.

**Primary Actor:** Shopper (any arbitrary web surfer)

**Trigger:** Shopper selects to capture a trade-in.

**Main Success Scenario:**

1. Shopper selects to capture a trade-in.

2. System determines the value of trade-in by presenting information to the Shopper and asking a series of questions to determine the value of the trade-in. The series of questions and information presented depend on the answers the Shopper gives along the way. The path of questions and information is predetermined, in order to highlight probable business practices around trade-ins.

3. The system logs the navigation and trade-in information along the way.
4. Shopper reviews the trade-in summary and value, considers it.
5. Shopper adds it to the shopping cart.
6. System adds to the shopping cart the trade-in and the navigation information.
7. System presents a view of the shopping cart with all the products and trade-ins contained in it, as well as re-calculating the total cost taking into consideration the trade-in(s).

Shopper repeats the above steps as many times as desired to capture and value different trade-ins, adding them to the shopping cart as desired.

**Extensions:**

2a. At any time prior to adding the trade-in to the cart, the shopper can go back and modify any previous answer.
5a. Shopper decides not to add the trade-in to the shopping cart: System retains the navigation information for later.
5b. Shopper wants the trade-in to be applied to a specific item in the shopping cart: Shopper specifies a product contained in the shopping cart they wish the trade-in to be applied against.

Table 17.2 is the generated work list.

***Table 17.2.*** *Work List for Capture Trade-In*

| Ref | Feature | Business Need | Version |
|-----|---------|---------------|---------|
| EC10 | **Capture Trade-In** | Must have | 1.0 |
| EC10.1 | Provide the ability for the shopper to enter a trade-in into the shopping cart. | Must have | 1.0 |
| EC10.2 | Provide the ability to present and navigate through generated UI forms (based on templates) to gather the shopper's trade-in information to determine its value. | Must have | 1.0 |
| EC10.3 | Provide the ability to go to an external trade-in system (or site) to determine trade-in value. The shopper's related trade-in information is passed to the external site, and the external site evaluates the trade-in and returns its value and important characteristics. | Must have | 1.0 |
| EC10.4 | Provide the ability for the shopper to be presented a trade-in summary, including its value. | Must have | 1.0 |

*continued*

**Table 17.2.** Work List for Capture Trade-In (Continued)

| Ref | Feature | Business Need | Version |
|---|---|---|---|
| EC10.5 | Provide the ability for the shopper to add or discard the trade-in. Upon adding the trade-in to the shopping cart, the shopper can associate it with an individual product or all products in the shopping cart. | Must have | 1.0 |
| EC10.6 | Provide the ability to recalculate the total cost of the contents of the shopping cart, taking into consideration the trade-in(s). | Must have | 1.0 |
| EC10.7 | Provide the ability to edit an existing trade-in by returning to the trade-in question/answer process for editing. | Must have | 1.0 |
| EC10.8 | Provide the ability to delete an existing trade-in from the shopping cart and recalculate the total cost. | Must have | 1.0 |
| EC10.9 | Provide the ability to log any trade-in information or steps based on preconfigured triggers. | Must have | 1.0 |

## 17.3 USE CASES TO DESIGN

Use cases provide *all and only* black-box behavioral requirements that the design must meet. The requirements are to name everything that the system must do without usurping any freedom the designers should have. It is for the designers to use their craft to produce a "good" design that meets the requirements. Requirements and design are not supposed to meet more than that.

There are several things to say about transitioning from use cases to design, some good and some bad. The bad is that

- The design doesn't cluster by use case.
- Blindly following the use case structure leads to functional decomposition designs (this is really of concern to object-oriented and component design teams).

The good is that

- Some design techniques can take advantage of all the scenarios.
- Use cases name the concepts needed in domain modeling.

Let's look at the bad first.

**DESIGN DOESN'T CLUSTER BY USE CASE.** The design tasks do not map themselves tidily to use case units. A design task results in a business object or a behavioral mechanism that will be used in several use cases. A use case scheduled for a later release is likely to contain important information for a design task carried out in an earlier release. That means that the designers will have to change their designs in the later release, when they encounter that information.

There are three ways to handle this. The first is to have the designers scan all the use cases for key information that might apply to their design task. This can clearly be done only on smaller projects. If you can manage it, however, you will be ahead.

The second approach is to scan all the use cases looking for *high-risk* items, key functions that are likely to have a strong effect on the design. The team creates a design to fit these key functions, hoping that the remaining functions will not disturb the design too much.

The third alternative, which is my preference, is to recognize that the software will change over its lifetime and relax. The team designs each release as well as is practical. They recognize that sometime in the next year new requirements that will cause a change are likely to surface.

This alternative may cause some of your team discomfort, particularly those coming from a database design culture. In many of those environments, it is expensive to add new fields to a table and reoptimize the database; economics dictate that the designers should first identify all the attributes that will *ever* be referenced. They build and release software that can then be called 20%, 40%, up to 100% complete, with respect to the total set of attributes.

In most modern environments using incremental development, however, adding an attribute to a class or table is a minor operation, cheap enough that developers define only those parts of a class or entity that are needed immediately. The consequence is that the classes and components are only ever "complete with respect to a given set of functions." As new functions are delivered, the notion of "complete" changes.

### ◆ A Short, True Story

This matter came to a head on one project, when one team lead complained that he had not been allowed to "complete" the classes past the 20% completion mark, even though the delivered application did everything the customer wanted! It took us a long time to sort out that he was speaking from the database design culture but working on a project using the incremental development culture.

Be prepared for this discussion. Unless there are extremely strong economic penalties, I suggest that your team work to the model of "completeness with respect to a named function set."

**USE CASES AND FUNCTIONAL DECOMPOSITION.** If you are using structured decomposition techniques, the functional decomposition in your use cases is probably useful. However, if you are doing object-oriented design, take note of the following.

## A Special Note to Object-Oriented Designers

Sets of use cases forming a functional decomposition or function hierarchy have been demonstrated as being effective in communicating behavioral requirements. The writing is easy to understand, and the behavior rolls up neatly into higher and higher levels. It makes life easier on the people who have to agree on *what* the system must *do*.

Such functional decomposition may be good for requirements, but that does not mean it is good for software design. Co-encapsulating data and behavior has shown itself to be useful for simplifying maintenance and evolution of software designs. However, there is no evidence that it makes a good structure for gathering or communicating requirements. My experience is that it is *not* as good as the function-based structure. In other words, requirements gathering benefits from functional decomposition *at the same time* that software design benefits from data-plus-behavior componentization.

Designers have to read the use cases, think and discuss for a while, and then come up with useful abstractions. It is their job, not the user's, to do this.

One hazard is that the inexperienced or unwary designer will create classes that mirror the functional decomposition of the requirements document, simply casting each use case as a class/object/component. Experience has proven this to be a poor strategy, and many OO experts explicitly warn against it.

One can probably defend casting a user-goal use case into its own class, since it captures a full transaction, with coherent commit and rollback semantics. It may be a good candidate for encapsulation. However, subfunction use cases rarely have those characteristics. They are usually partial mechanisms, belonging piecewise in different classes.

The opposite hazard lies with OO designers who want to model the domain directly, without worrying about the functions it needs to support. These designers miss out on the contribution of the functional requirements. The use cases tell the domain modeler *which aspects of the domain are interesting to consider*. Without that information, the domain modeler is likely to spend excessive time modeling parts of the domain not relevant to the system at hand. The use cases provide boundary conditions for sound domain modeling. Read more on this in "An Open Letter to Newcomers to OO" (*http://members.aol.com/humansandt/papers/oonewcomers.htm*).

It is clear that in all cases, use cases partition the world along a different organizing scheme than do objects. This means that you will have to think while designing.

Now let's look at the good news.

**DESIGNS MAKE USE OF SCENARIOS.** Use cases serve as handy scenarios when designing the program. They are particularly useful with *Responsibility-Driven Design,*[*] which is based on designing while stepping through scenarios. Use cases also serve well with other design techniques, showing when the design is complete and handling all situations (the extensions).

**USE CASES NAME DOMAIN CONCEPTS.** The use cases fairly shout out the names of the domain objects involved. Consider the use case phrase

> System produces an *invoice*, fills the *invoice line items* with their costs, adds tax and shipping costs, and produces the total. The *invoice footer* states terms of delivery.

It does not take a great leap of imagination to see Invoice, InvoiceLineItem, and InvoiceFooter with the attributes cost, tax, shipping, and total. These are not necessarily your final design items, but they certainly are a good business objects starter set. I have seen project teams go directly from the concepts in the use cases to a draft design. They tighten and refine the design from there.

## 17.4 USE CASES TO UI DESIGN

Larry Constantine and Lucy Lockwood, in *Software for Use,* and Luke Hohmann, in *GUIs with Glue,* have written better than I can about designing the user interface. However, during use case writing, most project teams ask, "How do we transition from UI-free use cases to actual UI design?"

Some of the people on your staff have the assignment, and hopefully the skill, to invent a pleasant-to-use interface. These people will read the use cases and invent a presentation that preserves the use case steps while minimizing the effort required of the user. Their UI design will *satisfy the requirements given by the use cases*. The design will be reviewed by users and programmers for that.

Use case writers often find it helpful to pretend that they are typing into a data-capturing screen, or filling out a paper form, to discover what information has to be entered and whether there are any sequencing constraints on entering it. Make sure that these forms are interpreted just as indications of how the usage experts view their task and not as part of the requirements.

While it is not for the requirements document to describe the UI design, it is useful to *augment* the requirements document with samples of the UI design as it

---

[*] Read the original article by K. Beck and W. Cunningham, "A Laboratory for Object-Oriented Thinking," *ACM SIGPLAN*, or the book by R. Wirfs-Brock, B. Wilkerson, and L. Wiener, *Designing Object-Oriented Software*. Online, visit *http://c2.com/cgi/wiki?CrcCards* or *http:// members.aol.com/humansandt/papers/crc.htm*.

evolves. This design information can add to the readability of the requirements document, since it gives both textual (abstract) and visual (concrete) renditions of the system's behavior.

The UI design has three levels of precision, low, medium, and high:

- The *low-precision* description of the user interface is a screen-navigation diagram, drawn as a finite state machine or statechart. Each state is the name of a screen the user will encounter. The finite state machine shows what user events cause movement from one screen to another.

- The *medium-precision* description is a drawing or a reduced-size snapshot of the screen. Place this at the end of the use case so that readers can both see and read the design being nominated.

- The *high-precision* description lists all the field types, lengths, and validation checks of each screen and does not belong in the requirements document at all.

## 17.5 USE CASES TO TEST CASES

Use cases provide a ready-made functional test description for the system. Most test groups positively salivate at the opportunity to work with use cases. It is often the first time they have been given something so easy to work with. Even better, they are given this test suite right at requirements time! Best of all is when they get to help write the use cases.

In a formal development group, the test team will have to break up the use cases into numbered tests and write a plan that identifies the individual settings that will trigger the different paths. They will then construct all the test cases that set up and exercise those settings. In addition, they will exercise all the different data settings needed to test the various data combinations and will design system performance and load tests. These last two tasks are not derived from the use cases.

All of this should be business as usual for the test team. Tables 17.3 and 17.4 were provided by Pete McBreen (http://www.mcbreen.ab.ca/papers/TestsFromUseCases.html). First comes the use case and then the set of acceptance tests. I leave it for your test team to work from this example and map it to their own work habits.

Notice Pete's use of stakeholders and interests to help identify the test cases and how his test cases contain specific test values.

### Use Case 35  ⬚ Order Goods, Generate Invoice (Testing Example) ∿

**Context:** Customer places order for goods, an invoice is generated and sent out with the ordered items.

**Minimal Guarantees:**

In case of failure, goods will not be allocated to the Customer, Customer account information will remain unchanged, and the transaction attempt will have been logged.

**Success Guarantees:**

Goods will have been allocated to the Customer.

Invoice will have been created (Customer Invoicing Rule applies).

Picking list will have been sent to distribution.

**Main Success Scenario:**

1. Customer selects items and quantities.
2. System allocates required quantities to customer.
3. System obtains authenticated invoicing authorization.
4. Customer specifies shipping destination.
5. System send picking instructions to distribution.

**Extensions:**

2a. Insufficient stock to meet required quantity for item:

  2a1. Customer cancels order.

2b. Out of stock on item:

  2b1. Customer cancels order.

3a. Customer is bad credit risk (link to acceptance test case for this exception).

4a. Invalid shipping destination: ??

At least one test case is needed for every extension listed above. For complete coverage you need more test cases for testing the data values. The main success scenario test case (Tables 17.3 and 17.4) should come first, since it is nice to show how the system works in a high volume situation. Often it can be generated before all of the extension conditions and recovery paths are known.

**Table 17.3.** *Main Success Scenario Tests (Good Credit Risk)*

| | |
|---|---|
| Initial System State/Inputs | Customer Pete, a Good Credit risk, orders one of Item #1 at a price of $10.00. |
| | Quantity on hand for Item #1 is 10. |
| Expected System State/ Outputs | Quantity on hand for Item #1 is 9. |
| | Delivery instructions are generated. |
| | Invoice is generated for Customer Pete for one of Item #1 at a price of $10.00. |
| | Transaction is logged. |

***Table 17.4.*** *Main Success Scenario Tests (Bad Credit Risk)*

| | |
|---|---|
| Initial System State/Inputs | Customer Joe, a Bad Credit risk, orders one of Item #1 at a price of $10.00. |
| | Quantity on hand for Item #1 is 10. |
| Expected System State/Outputs | Quantity on hand for Item #1 is 9. |
| | Delivery instructions specify Cash on Delivery. |
| | Transaction is logged. |

## 17.6  THE ACTUAL WRITING

Your group will have to form and sort out a set of working habits. In the next section, I show a branch-and-join process, which is my preferred way of working. Andy Kraus, then at IBM, describes with wonderful clarity his group's experiences coordinating a large, diverse user group. You should get some useful insights from his report.

### A Branch-and-Join Process

A team does two things better than individuals can: brainstorming and forming consensus (aligning). However, they produce more text when they split up. For that reason, my favorite process is to have people work in a full group when it is necessary to align or brainstorm and to spend the rest of their time working in ones or twos. Here is the process, first in outline and then in more detail.

1. Produce a low-precision view of the system's function:
   - Align on a usage narrative (group).
   - Align on the scope and brainstorm actors and goals (group).
   - Write the narratives (separately).
   - Collect the narratives (group).
2. Produce the high-precision view, the use cases:
   - Brainstorm the use cases to write (group).
   - Align on a use case form (group).
   - Write the use cases (separately).
   - Review the use cases (separately).
   - Review the use cases (group).

## Stage One—Produce a Low-Precision View of the System's Function

Stage one is done in four rounds.

**ROUND 1.1  ALIGN ON A USAGE NARRATIVE STYLE (GROUP).** The team spends time together to learn what a narrative is and looks like (review Section 1.6, Warm Up with a Usage Narrative). Each person writes one, perhaps all on the same story, perhaps not. The group then reads and discusses the writing to generate a common idea of what a decent narrative looks like, its length, and what details it does and doesn't contain. This can take a few hours. At the end of this time, the team has a concrete idea of (some part of) what is being built.

**ROUND 1.2  ALIGN ON THE SCOPE AND BRAINSTORM ACTORS AND GOALS (GROUP).** The team spends as much time as needed to work out the overall purpose, scope, and primary actors of the system. They create a vision statement, an in/out list, a design scope diagram, a list of primary actors and stakeholders, and a list of the most important initial set of user goals. Each of these items involves the others, so discussing one shifts the understanding of the others. In this way, the items are all built at the same time. If the team thinks they know what they are going to build, this can take several hours to a day. If they don't know yet, it can take several days. At the end, there is consensus on what is within the scope of the discussion, what is being built, and who the key primary actors are.

**ROUND 1.3  WRITE THE NARRATIVES (SEPARATELY).** The team splits up to write usage narratives for selected functions of the proposed system. They write individually and then trade with a partner or circulate their writing in a small group. They then send the results to the entire group.

**ROUND 1.4  POOL THE NARRATIVES (GROUP).** The team gets together to discuss the content (not the writing style) of the narratives. They address the question "Is this a sample of what we really want to build?" There may be more discussion about the nature of the system, and there may be another writing cycle, until the members decide that the narrative portrays how they want the system to look.

At this point, the first phase of work is done. The team has a packet that can be distributed to their sponsoring groups. This packet shows a (low-precision) draft view of the new system:

- ◆ A system vision statement
- ◆ A list of what is in and what is out of scope (both function and design scope)
- ◆ A drawing of the system in its environment
- ◆ A list of the key primary actors

- A list of the stakeholders in the system and their main interests
- A list of the most important user goals
- A set of narratives (each less than half a page long)

## Stage Two—Produce the High-Precision View, the Use Cases

Stage two is done in five rounds.

**ROUND 2.1 BRAINSTORM THE USE CASES TO WRITE (GROUP).** This first round produces a more exact list of use cases to write. The team uses facilitated techniques to review, brainstorm, and list *all* the primary actors the system will encounter in its life. Then they brainstorm and list *all* the user goals they can imagine, for all primary actors. They may split into subgroups for this activity.

A useful technique for dealing with large, heterogeneous teams is to split into working groups of three to five people. Usually, there are several domains or interest groups whose knowledge needs to be combined, so the working groups have one person from each domain. Each group contains all the knowledge needed to resolve discussion, and each person can easily be heard. The small group can move more quickly than the full team. Having the team split into several such groups means that they cover more territory in the same time.

If the full list of primary actors and user goals is constructed using subgroups, these subgroups get together again to pool their results. They do a group review to complete and accept the list. At the end of this period, the team has a tentative full set of user goal use cases to write. They are, of course, almost certain to discover new user goals over time.

The team publishes the list of primary actors and user goals. There may be additional discussion at this point about the development priorities to give them, estimates of complexity and development time, and so forth.

**ROUND 2.2 ALIGN ON A USE CASE FORM (GROUP).** This round starts with the team writing a use case as a group (or individually and then bringing the individual versions to the group). They discuss the level and style of writing, the template, the stakeholders and interests, the minimal guarantees, and so on. At the end of this session, they have an initial standard for their writing.

**ROUND 2.3 WRITE THE USE CASES (SEPARATELY).** In this round, the team reorganizes into subgroups by specialty, probably two to four people per subgroup. Use cases are selected for each specialty subgroup.

Over the next days or weeks, the subgroups write use cases, individually or in pairs (I don't find larger writing partnerships to be effective). They circulate them for comment and improve their drafts within their speciality groups until the writing is "correct." Then they write the summary use cases. They will almost certainly split some use cases, create subfunction use cases, add some primary actors and new goals, and so on.

It is useful to have two people associated with each use case, even if one is designated the primary writer. Many questions will surface about the rules of the business, that is, what is really the requirement versus what is merely a holdover from the old days. It helps to have someone to ask about the business rules. The second person can double-check that the GUI has not crept in and that the goals are at the right levels.

**ROUND 2.4 REVIEW THE USE CASES (SEPARATELY).** The writers circulate the drafts, either electronically or on paper. Interestingly, paper has a peculiar advantage. A paper copy collects everyone's comments, so the writer can make one editing pass through the use case, merging all the suggestions. One team said that when they tried online suggestions, they ended up doing much more revising, at one moment editing to fit one person's suggestion, then taking that change out to meet another person's suggestion. In all cases, a peer group should check the level of writing and the business rules inside the use cases.

The writers send the use cases for review to both a system developer and an expert on system use. The technical person ensures that the use case contains enough detail for implementation (excluding the data descriptions and UI design). The usage expert makes sure that all the requirements are true requirements and that the business really works that way.

**ROUND 2.5 REVIEW THE USE CASES (GROUP).** Eventually there is a group review at which software designers, business experts, usage experts, and UI designers are present. What actually happens after the writing teams have created their best draft depends upon the project and its policy and mechanism of review. The writers need to make sure that the steps are understandable, correct, and detailed enough to implement. This may be done by official reviews, unofficial reviews, user reviews, or developer reviews.

A use case reaches its first official baseline once the draft has passed user and technical scrutiny. Start design then, and change the use case only to fix mistakes, not just to change wording.

You will quickly see the difference between drafting a use case and completing it. In completing a use case, the writers must:

◆ Name all the extension conditions.

◆ Think through the business policies connected with failure handling.

◆ Verify that the interests of the stakeholders are protected.

◆ Verify that the use case names all and only actual requirements.

◆ Ensure that each use case is readable by the users or usage experts and clear enough that the developers know what to implement.

## Time Required per Use Case

I find that it takes several hours to draft a use case and days to chase down the extension handling. One team of 10 people produced 140 use case briefs in a week (2.8 use case briefs per person per day) and then spent the next four weeks working on them and adding the other requirements. This added up to two work-weeks per one use case plus its associated requirements. A team on a different project spent an average of three to five work-weeks per use case; the use cases that resulted were of extremely high quality.

## Collecting Use Cases from Large Groups

On occasion, you will find yourself working with a large, diverse, nontechnical group of usage experts. This is very challenging. I excerpt below an illuminating report Andy Kraus wrote on his successful experience facilitating use case sessions with up to 25 people of different specialties. This report appeared in *Object Magazine.*\*

---

◆ **Andy Kraus: Collecting Use Cases from a Large, Diverse Lay Group**

***Don't skimp on conference facilities.*** You'll be living in them for weeks, and you need to "own" them for the duration of your sessions . . . We faced significant logistical problems moving from one conference room to another. Try to stay in one room.

***You can't elicit the right use cases without the right people in the room.*** Better too many people and points of view than not enough . . . The people whose ideas and experience we needed were the real-life analysts, officers, detectives, data entry operators, and supervisors from the twenty-three departments and numerous "ex officio" members. Without knowing in advance what the *real* system actors were, it was impossible for us to predict which users would need to come to which sessions, a real problem when trying to get a piece of so many people's time. We solved the problem by staging a "Use Case Kick-Off" with representatives from all the user areas, at which we jointly determined a tentative schedule for future sessions.

***Large groups are more difficult to facilitate than small ones.*** You'll have to cope as best you can. Above all, be organized. As things actually evolved we found ourselves forced to conduct sessions with groups ranging in size from eight to twenty-five people with all the problems we had been told could derive from working with such large groups. Only by having representation from the diverse membership in the room at the same time could we flush out nuances to the requirements

---

\* From Kraus, A., "Use Case Blue." *Object Magazine,* May 1996 (pp 63–65). SIGS Publications, New York. Reprinted with permission.

caused by the differing philosophies and operating procedures among the members.

***Don't spend more than half of each work day in session with the users.*** Our sessions taught us that we had been too ambitious in our estimates of the amount of material that could be covered in a session and/or our ability to process that material before and after the sessions. It will take you every bit as long to process the raw material gained in the sessions as it did to elicit it. You'll have plenty of housekeeping chores, administrative work, planning, and preparation for the next session to do in that half-day.

***Get management into the boat with you.*** The administrator and the project manager were all present during various parts of the elicitation process.

***Those responsible for architecting the system should be present during use case elicitation.*** The architect brought expertise in the development process . . . An "SME" (subject matter expert) provided the domain expertise to jump-start the process and keep it on track once it was moving.

***You've got a better chance of attaining your goal if you get people who support the application being replaced into the sessions with you.*** A number of participants from the organization and DIS (the Department of Information Services) participated in the sessions. They provided insights into the emerging requirements, particularly with respect to the external interfaces, as well as into the history of the current system.

***There's no substitute for getting the "true" users involved in use case solicitation.*** We were able to secure the participation of actual officers, analysts, investigators, data entry operators, and supervisors for those groups of people, in the sessions.

***Use a scribe.*** The importance of fast, accurate scribes cannot be over emphasized . . . We had several scribes working the early sessions who proved invaluable . . .

***Display the cumulative use case output to facilitate the process.*** The use cases were developed interactively, recorded on flip chart paper by a facilitator and on a word processor by the scribe. The flip charts were then taped to the conference room walls. Unwieldy as it was to deal with use cases on flip charts, we discovered some unexpected benefits from doing so. We were unintentionally sloppy in hanging the use cases out of sequence. As new use cases were developed, this lack of sequencing forced participants to scan the previously developed use case. Such iteration seemed to have the effect of helping people become more familiar with existing use cases, developing new ones that were "like another use case" as well as developing new ones faster.

***A job title may not an actor make.*** It was extremely difficult for our users to accept the notion that an actor *role* could be different from a job title. At the end of a difficult day's discussion, we were able to derive a tentative actor list, but people did not seem comfortable with it. How could we help them be more comfortable?

***The application doesn't care who you are; it cares about the hat you wear.*** Struck by the notion that playing an actor *role* with a computer system is similar to "wearing a hat," we bought a set of baseball caps and embroidered the actor names, one per cap. The next day, when the participants arrived at the session, the caps were arrayed in a row on the facilitator's table at the front of the room. As soon as use case elicitation began, the facilitator took one of the hats, "Query(or)," and put it on his head. The results were very gratifying. We were able to help the users understand that no matter what their job title, when they were using the system they had to wear a certain "hat" (play a certain role).

***Expect to miss some actors in the initial formulation of actors.*** . . . It wasn't until several weeks into the elicitation process that we (facilitators) realized that there appeared to be some use cases missing—dealing with the supervision of users of the system. Despite all our efforts to ensure a broad range of participation, no supervisory personnel had been part of the sessions, and, interestingly enough, the people who worked for them did not conceive of any supervisory use cases.

***"Daily work use cases" can facilitate use case brainstorming.*** [*Usage narratives* by another name] . . . our users seemed to lack a "context" for the use cases, so we decided to have them write (at a very high level) the steps they followed in their daily activities to perform some task, e.g., making a stop. At some point in the making of that step the system would be used, and this is the way we were able to free them to think of "uses of the system." A day spent developing these daily work use cases on day three yielded twenty use cases on day four.

***Don't expect "use cases by the pound."*** Like any creative activity, use case elicitation has its peaks and valleys. Trying to rush people in the creative process is counter-productive.

***Expect to get stuck; react with catalysts.*** "Prompting"—i.e., the use of overheads and handouts with topic and/or issue bullets related to the system uses under discussion—proved to

be an effective catalyst. Intentionally we sometimes introduced controversial topics and viewpoints as discussion generators. We found that people, when confronted by a viewpoint they could not support, would be able to express their own viewpoints more quickly and clearly.

***Eliciting use cases is a social activity.*** Feelings were hurt, ideas were bashed, and participants sided against the facilitator only to defend him later in the same session. A few after- hours mixers served as social lubricants and kept us all friends. Ultimately, we all bonded, having come to respect and support each other in the task of bringing the ideas from the use case sessions to the project's decision makers.

***Standard "descriptors" help facilitate the process.*** . . . Standard descriptors held attributes for the new system divided along certain lines, e.g., People, Places, Locations. The descriptor sets provided a pathway to a consistent presentation of information . . . The sets were named and cataloged, and evolved so that we could use them generically in session discussions as well as in subsequent use case refinement, Similarly, standard system responsibilities, and success and failure scenarios allowed us to focus on the exceptions rather than redundantly copying from one use case to another,

***Build, maintain, and display an assumptions list.*** During certain periods of the work we found it necessary to start sessions with a "reading of the assumptions." That reading tended to minimize arguments over points already considered.

***Be a minimalist.*** Keep your use case template as slim as possible.

# Chapter 18

# Use Case Briefs and Extreme Programming

The ultralight methodology, Extreme Programming (XP), uses an even lighter form of behavioral requirements than the one I show in this book (see *Extreme Programming Explained,* Beck, 1999). In XP, usage and business experts sit with the developers. Since they are right there, the team does not write down detailed requirements for the software but *user stories,* as a sort of promissory note to have a further discussion about the requirements around a small piece of functionality.

An XP user story, in its brevity, may look like either a *use case brief,* as described in Table 3.3, Sample Use Case Briefs, on page 38, or a system *feature,* as described in Table 17.2, Work List for Capture Trade-In, on page 173.

Each XP user story needs to be detailed just enough for both the business and the technical people to understand what it means and estimate how long it will take. It must be a small enough piece of work that the developers can design, code, test, and deploy it in three weeks or less. Once it meets those criteria, it can be as brief and casual as the team can manage. It is often written just on an index card.

When the time comes to start working on a user story, the designer simply takes the card over to the business expert and asks for more explanation. Since the business expert is always available, the conversation continues as needed until the functionality is shipped.

On rare occasions, a small, well-knit development team with full-time users on board will take usage narratives or use case briefs as their requirements. This happens only when the people who own the requirements sit very close to the people who design the system. The designers collaborate directly with the requirements owners during system design. Just as with XP's user stories, this can work *if* the conditions for fulfilling the promissory note are met. In most projects, the conditions are not met, and so it is best to keep the usage narrative as a warm-up exercise at the start of a use case writing session and the use case brief as part of the project overview.

# Chapter 19

# Mistakes Fixed

The most common mistakes in use case writing are leaving out the subjects of sentences, making assumptions about the user interface design, and using goal levels that are too low. Here are some examples of these mistakes. The purpose of this chapter is not to quiz you but to sharpen your visual reflexes.

The first examples are short; the last is a long one from a real project. Practice on the small ones first.

## 19.1 NO SYSTEM

### Before

**Use Case: Withdraw Cash**

**Scope:** ATM
**Level:** User goal
**Primary Actor:** Customer
1. Customer enters card and PIN.
2. Customer enters "Withdrawal" and amount.
3. Customer takes cash, card, and receipt.
4. Customer leaves.

### Working Notes

This use case shows everything the primary actor does, but does not show the system's behavior. It is surprising how often people write this sort of use case, leading the reviewer to respond, "I see that the system doesn't actually have to do anything. We can sure design that in a hurry."

The fix is to name all the actors with their actions.

### After

You should be able to write an ATM use case in your sleep by now.

**Use Case: Withdraw Cash**

**Scope:** ATM
**Level:** User goal
**Primary Actor:** Account holder
1.  Customer runs ATM card through the card reader.
2.  ATM reads the bank ID, account number, encrypted PIN from the card, validates the bank ID and account number with the main banking system.
3.  Customer enters PIN. The ATM validates it against the encrypted PIN read from the card.
4.  Customer selects Fast Cash and withdrawal amount, a multiple of $5.
5.  ATM notifies main banking system of customer account, amount being withdrawn, and receives back acknowledgment plus the new balance.
6.  ATM delivers the cash, card, and a receipt showing the new balance.
7.  ATM logs the transaction.

## 19.2  NO PRIMARY ACTOR

### Before

Here is a fragment of a use case for withdrawing money from an ATM.

**Use Case: Withdraw Cash**

**Scope:** ATM
**Level:** User goal
**Primary Actor:** Customer
1.  Collects ATM card, PIN.
2.  Collects transaction type as "Withdrawal."
3.  Collects amount desired.
4.  Validates that account has sufficient funds.
5.  Dispenses money, receipt, card.
6.  Resets.

### Working Notes

This use case is written strictly from the system's viewpoint. It shows everything that the ATM does, but does not show the primary actor's behavior. This sort of writing is hard to understand, verify, and correct. In some cases, critical information is omitted about the actor's behavior, often having to do with sequencing.

The fix is straightforward: Name every actor and action.

**After**

The same as in Section 19.1.

## 19.3 TOO MANY USER INTERFACE DETAILS

**Before**

**Use Case: Buy Something**

**Scope:** Purchasing application
**Level:** User goal
**Primary Actor:** Customer

1. System presents ID and Password screen.
2. Customer types ID and password into system, clicks OK.
3. System validates user ID and password, displays Personal Information screen.
4. Customer types in first and last names, street address, city, state, zip code, phone number, and clicks "OK."
5. System validates that user is a known user.
6. System presents available product list.
7. Customer clicks on pictures of items to be purchased, types in quantity next to each, clicks on "Done" when finished.
8. System validates with the warehouse storage system that sufficient quantity of the requested product is in stock.

. . . etc.

**Working Notes**

This mistake is perhaps the most common one. The writer describes much too much about the user interface, making this use case not really a requirements document but a user manual. The extra UI detail adds nothing to the story, but clutters the reading and makes the requirements brittle.

The fix is finding a way to describe the intentions of the user without actually nominating a specific solution. This sometimes takes a little creative wording.

**After**

**Use Case: Buy Something**

**Scope:** Purchasing application
**Level:** User goal
**Primary Actor:** Customer

1. Customer accesses system with ID and password.
2. System validates user.
3. Customer provides name, address, telephone number.

4. System validates that Customer is a known Customer.
5. Customer selects products and quantity.
6. System validates with the warehouse storage system that sufficient quantity of the requested product is in stock.
. . . etc.

## 19.4  VERY LOW GOAL LEVELS

### Before

**Use Case: Buy Something**

**Scope:** Purchasing application
**Level:** User goal
**Primary Actor:** Customer/user

1. User accesses system with ID and password.
2. System validates user.
3. User provides name.
4. User provides address.
5. User provides telephone number.
6. User selects product
7. User identifies quantity.
8. System validates that user is a known customer.
9. System opens a connection to warehouse system.
10. System requests current stock levels from warehouse system.
11. Warehouse storage system returns current stock levels.
12. System validates that requested quantity is in stock.
. . . etc.

### Working Notes

It is clear that this is going to be a long and dull use case. We can't criticize the steps on the grounds that they describe the user interface too closely, but we definitely want to shorten the writing and make clearer what is going on.

To shorten the text:

- Merge the data items (steps three through five) using separate steps to collect each one. Asking, "What is the user trying to provide, in general?" gets us, "Personal information," which is a good nickname for all of the pieces of information about the person that will be collected. I find the nickname alone to be too vague, so I'll hint at the field list. That field list will be expanded elsewhere without affecting this use case.

◆ Put all the information going in the same direction into one step (steps three through seven). This is not always the best thing to do. Sometimes providing personal information is considerably different from selecting product and quantity, so the writer will place them on separate lines. This is a matter of taste. I like collecting all the information going in one direction. If it looks too cluttered, or if the extensions need them separated, I separate them again.

◆ Look for a slightly higher-level goal (steps eight through eleven). Asking, "Why is the system doing all these things?" gets us, "It is trying to validate with the warehouse storage system that sufficient quantity of the requested product is in stock." That slightly higher level goal captures the requirements as clearly as before and is much shorter.

### After

**Use Case: Buy Something**

**Scope:** Purchasing application
**Level:** User goal
**Primary Actor:** Customer/user
1. User accesses system with ID and password.
2. System validates user.
3. User provides personal information (name, address, telephone number), selects product and quantity.
4. System validates that Customer is a known Customer.
5. System validates with the warehouse storage system that sufficient quantity of the requested product is in stock.
. . . etc.

## 19.5 PURPOSE AND CONTENT NOT ALIGNED

This is a reminder for you to do Exercise 7.4 at the end of Chapter 7, on page 98, which asks you to repair the faulty *LogIn* use case.

If you haven't done it yet, look for these three mistakes:

◆ Its body does not match the intent described in the name and description. In fact, it is at least two use cases rolled together.

◆ It describes user interface details.

◆ It uses programming constructs in the text rather than the language of ordinary people.

If you are determined to avoid the work, turn to Appendix B to see the discussion and resolution.

## 19.6  ADVANCED EXAMPLE OF TOO MUCH UI

FirePond Corporation kindly allowed me to use the following *before* and *after* example. The *before* version covered eight pages, six of which were used for the main success scenario and alternatives. The *after* version is a third as long, holding the same basic information but without constraining the user interface.

Read the main success scenario carefully, and ask yourself how you might make this long use case more palatable without sacrificing content. Notice, particularly, the UI design that shows up in the text. You should look at some of the extensions, but it is not important that you read all of them closely. I removed some of them, but left enough bulk so that you can appreciate the difficulty of working with such a long use case. How would *you* shorten it?

A note about the title of the use case. In the language of information technology marketing, it is considered insufficient to say that a shopper "selects a product." Faced with a complex product set, the shopper "researches a solution" to his "situation." I might like to retitle this use case *Select a Product*, but it is not my place to do so. The title *Research a Solution* is considered correct in the world in which it was written and will be read, so it stays.

Thanks to Dave Scott and Russell Walters of FirePond Corporation.

### Before

### Use Case 36   ☐ Research a Solution—Before  〰

**Scope:** Our web system
**Level:** User goal
**Primary Actor:** Shopper—a consumer or agent wanting to research products she may purchase
**Main Success Scenario:**

| Actor Action | System Response |
|---|---|
| 1. This use case begins when the Shopper visits the e-commerce web site. | 2. System may receive information about the type of Shopper visiting the web site. |
|  | 3. System will require establishing the identity of the Shopper, <u>Initiate establish identity</u>. If the system doesn't establish the identity here, it must be established prior to saving a solution. |
|  | 4. The system will provide the Shopper with the following options: Create a new solution, Recall a saved solution. |
| 5. Shopper selects *Create A New Solution*. | 6. System will present the first question to begin determining the Shopper's needs and interests. |

| | |
|---|---|
| 7. Shopper can repeat adding Product Selections to shopping cart:<br>8. While questions exist to determine needs and interest:<br>9. Shopper will answer questions. | 10. System will prompt with a varying number and type of questions based on previous answers to determine the Shopper's needs and interests along with presenting pertinent information such as production information, features & benefits, and comparison information. |
| 11. Shopper answers last question. | 12. At the last question about needs and interest, the system will present product line recommendations and pertinent information such as production information, features & benefits, comparison information, and pricing. |
| 13. Shopper will select a product line. | 14. System will present the first question to begin determining the product model needs. |
| 15. While questions exist to determine Product Model recommendations:<br>16. Shopper will answer questions. | 17. System will prompt with questions that vary based on previous answers to determine the Shopper's needs and interests related to product models, along with pertinent information such as production information, features & benefits, comparison information, and pricing. |
| 18. Shopper answers last question. | 19. At the last question about product model needs, the system will present product model recommendations and pertinent information such as production information, features & benefits, comparison information, and pricing. |
| 20. Shopper will select a product model. | 21. System will determine standard product model options, and then present the first question about determining major product options. |
| 22. While questions exist to determine Product Option recommendations:<br>23. Shopper will answer questions. | 24. System will prompt with questions that vary based on previous answers to determine the Shopper's needs and interests related to major product options, along with pertinent information such as production information, features & benefits, comparison information, and pricing. |
| 25. Shopper answers last question. | 26. At the last question about major product option desires, the system will present the selected model and selected options for Shopper validation. |

| | |
|---|---|
| 27. Shopper reviews their product selection, determines they like it, and chooses to add the product selection to their shopping cart. | 28. System will add product selection and storyboard information (navigation and answers) to the shopping cart. |
| | 29. The system presents a view of the shopping cart and all of the product selections within it. |
| 30. End of repeating steps of adding to shopping cart. | 31. |
| 32. Shopper will request a personalized proposal on the items in their shopping cart. | 33. System will present the first question to begin determining what content should be used in the proposal. |
| 34. While questions exist to determine proposal content:<br>35. Shopper will answer questions. | 36. System will prompt with questions that vary based on previous answers to determine the proposal content, along with pertinent information such as production information, features & benefits, comparison information, and pricing. |
| 37. Shopper answers the last question. | 38. At the last question about proposal content, the system will generate and present the proposal. |
| 39. Shopper will review the proposal and choose to print it. | 40. System will print the proposal. |
| 41. Shopper will request to save their solution. | 42. If the Shopper identity hasn't been established yet, <u>Initiate Establish Identity</u>. |
| | 43. System will prompt the user for solution identification information. |
| 44. Shopper will enter solution identification information and save the solution. | 45. System will save the solution and associate with the Shopper. |

**Extensions:**

*a. At any point during the Research Solution process, if the Shopper hasn't had any activity by a predetermined time-out period, the system will prompt the Shopper about no activity and request whether they want to continue. If the Shopper doesn't respond to the continue request within a reasonable amount of time (30 seconds) the use case ends; otherwise, the Shopper will continue through the process.

*b. At any point during the question/answer sequences, the Shopper can select any question to go back to, modify their answer, and continue through the sequence.

*c. At any point after a product recommendation has been presented, the Shopper can view performance calculation information as it pertains to their needs. The system will perform the calculation and present the information. The Shopper will continue with the Research Solution process from where they left off.

*d. At any point during the question/answer sequences, the system may interface with a Parts Inventory System to retrieve part(s) availability and/or a Process & Planning System to retrieve the build schedule. The parts availability and schedule information can be utilized to filter what product selection information is shown, or be used to show availability to the Shopper during the research solution process. <u>Initiate Retrieve Part Availability</u> and <u>Retrieve Build Schedule</u> use cases.

*e. At any point during the question/answer sequences, the system is presenting pertinent information, of which industry-related links are a part. The Shopper selects the related link. The system may pass product-related information or other solution information to this link to drive to the best location or to present the appropriate content. The Shopper, when finished at the industry web site, will return to the point at which they left, possibly returning product requirements that the system will validate. <u>Initiate View Product Information</u>.

*f. At any point during the research process, the Shopper may request to be contacted: <u>Initialize Request For Contact</u> use case.

*g. At any point during the question/answer sequences, the system may have established capture market data trigger points, in which the system will capture navigational, product selection, and questions & answers to be utilized for market analysis externally from this system.

*h. At any predetermined point in the research process, the system may generate a lead providing the solution information captured up to that point. <u>Initialize Generate Lead</u> use case.

*i. At any point the Shopper can choose to exit the e-commerce application:

If a new solution has been created or the current one has been changed since last saved, the system will prompt the Shopper if they want to save the solution. <u>Initiate Save Solution</u>.

*j. At any point after a new solution has been created or the current one has been changed, the Shopper can request to save the solution. <u>Initiate Save Solution</u>.

1a. A Shopper has been visiting a related-product vendor's web site and has established product requirements. The vendor's web site allows launching to this e-commerce system to further research a solution:

    1a1. Shopper launches to e-commerce system with product requirements and possibly identification information.

    1a2. System receives the product requirements and potentially user identification.

    1a3. System will validate where the Shopper is in the research process and establish a starting point of questions to continue with the research process.

    1a4. Based on established starting point, we may continue at step 5, 12, or 18.

3a. Shopper wants to work with a previously saved solution:

    3a1. Shopper selects to recall a solution.

    3a2. System presents a list of saved solutions for this Shopper.

    3a3. Shopper selects the solution they wish to recall.

3a4.  System recalls the selected solution.

3a5.  Continue at step 26.

23a.  Shopper wants to change some of the recommended options:

{create a Select Options use case because there are alternatives to the normal flow: System maybe set up to show all options, even incompatible ones; if the Shopper selects an incompatible one, the system will present a message and possibly how to get the product configured so the option is compatible.}

. . . while Shopper needs to change options:

23a1.  Shopper selects an option they want to change.

23a2.  System presents the compatible options available.

23a3.  Shopper selects desired option.

26a.  Shopper wants to change quantity of product selections in shopping cart:

26a1.  Shopper selects a product selection in the shopping cart and modifies the quantity.

26a2.  System will recalculate the price, taking into consideration discounts, taxes, fees, and special pricing calculations based on the Shopper and their related Shopper information, along with their answers to questions.

26b.  Shopper wants to add a product trade-in to the shopping cart:

26b1.  *see section Trade-In.*

26c.  Shopper wants to recall a saved solution:

26c1.  System presents a list of saved solutions for this Shopper.

26c2.  Shopper selects the solution they wish to recall.

26c3.  System recalls the selected solution.

26c4.  Continue at step 26.

26d.  Shopper wants to finance products in the shopping cart with available finance plans:

26d1.  Shopper chooses to finance products in the shopping cart.

26d2.  System will present a series of questions that are dependent on previous answers to determine finance plan recommendations.

System interfaces with Finance System to obtain credit rating approval. <u>Initiate Obtain Finance Rating</u>.

26d3.  Shopper will select a finance plan.

26d4.  System will present a series of questions based on previous answers to determine details of the selected finance plan.

26d5.  Shopper will view financial plan details and chooses to go with the plan.

26d6.  System will place the finance plan order with the Finance System. <u>Initiate Place Finance Order</u>.

## Working Notes

The writers selected the two-column format to separate the actors' actions. They did not visualize any user interface design other than the question-and-answer model, so they described questions and answers in the use case.

My first action was to get rid of the columns and create a simple story in one-column format. I wanted to see the storyline easily and without turning pages.

Looking at the result, I hunted for assumptions about the user interface design and for goals that could be raised a level. The key is in the phrase System will prompt with a varying number and type of questions based on previous answers. While this does not mention anything so obvious as mouse clicks, it does assume a user interface based on the user typing answers to questions. I wanted to imagine a completely different user interface to see how that might affect the writing, so I conjured up a design in which there would be no typing at all. The user would only click on pictures. I was then able to capture the user's intent and remove UI dependency. As you will see, this also enormously shortened the writing.

I rechecked the goal level in each statement, to see if perhaps the goal of the step was too low level and could be raised.

One of the open questions at the start of this work was whether the one-column format would still show the system's responsibility clearly to the designers. Rusty's evaluation was that it would. In fact, he was happier because

- It was shorter and easier to read.
- All the real requirements were still there, clearly marked.
- The design was less constrained.

## After

### Use Case 37   ▢ **Research Possible Solutions—After** 〰

**Scope:** Web software system
**Level:** User goal
**Preconditions:** None
**Minimal Guarantee:** No action, no purchases
**Success Guarantee:** Shopper has zero or more product(s) ready to purchase, the system has a log of the product selection(s) and navigation moves, and characteristics of the shopper are noted.
**Primary Actor:** Shopper (any arbitrary web surfer)
**Trigger:** Shopper selects to research a solution.
**Main Success Scenario:**

1. Shopper initiates the search for a new solution.
2. The **system** helps the shopper select a product line, model, and model options, presenting information to the shopper and asking a series of questions to determine the shopper's needs and interests. The series of questions and the screens presented depend on the answers the shopper gives along the way. The system chooses them according to programmed selection paths, in order to highlight and recommend what will be of probable interest to the shopper. The presented

information contains production information, features, benefits, comparison information, etc.

3. **System** logs the navigation information along the way.
4. Shopper selects a final product configuration.
5. Shopper adds it to the shopping cart.
6. **System** adds to the shopping cart the selected product and the navigation information.
7. **System** presents a view of the shopping cart and all the products in it.

The shopper repeats the above steps, as many times as desired, to navigate to and select different tailored products, adding them to the shopping cart as desired.

**Extensions:**

*a. At any time, the shopper can <u>request contact</u>.

1a. Due to an agreement between this web site owner and the owner of the sending computer, the sending computer may include information about the type of Shopper along with the request:

    1a1. **System** extracts from the web request any and all user and navigation information, adds it to the logged information, and starts from some advanced point in the question/answer series.

        1a1a. Information coming from the other site is invalid or incomprehensible:

            **System** does the best it can, logs all the incoming information, continues as it can.

1b. Shopper wants to continue a previous, saved, partial solution:

    1b1. Shopper <u>establishes identity</u> and saved solution.

    1b2. The **system** recalls the solution and returns the shopper to where shopper left the system upon saving the solution.

2a. Shopper chooses to bypass any or all of the question series:

    2a1. Shopper is presented and selects from product recommendations based upon limited (or no) personal characteristics.

    2a2. **System** logs that choice.

2b. *At any time prior to adding the product to the cart*, the shopper can go back and modify any previous answer for new product recommendations and/or product selection.

2c. *At any time prior to adding the product to the cart*, the shopper can ask to view an available test/performance calculation (e.g., can this configuration tow a trailer with this weight):

    **System** carries out the calculation and presents the answer.

2d. Shopper passes a point that the web site owner has predetermined to generate sales leads (dynamic business rule):

    **System** <u>generates sales lead</u>.

2e. System has been set up to require the Shopper to identify himself:

    Shopper <u>establishes identity</u>.

2f. **System** is set up to interact with known other systems (parts inventory, process & planning) that will affect product availability and selection:

    2f1. **System** interacts with known other systems (parts inventory, process & planning) to get the needed information. (<u>Retrieve Part Availability, Retrieve Build Schedule</u>).

    2f2. **System** uses the results to filter or show availability of product and/or options(parts).

2g. Shopper was presented and selects a link to an industry-related web site: Shopper <u>views other web site</u>.

2h. **System** is set up to interact with known Customer Information System:

    2h1. **System** <u>retrieves customer information</u> from Customer Information System.

    2h2. **System** uses results to start from some advanced point in the question/answer series.

2i. Shopper wants to know finance credit rating because it will influence the product selection process: Shopper <u>obtains finance credit rating</u>.

2j. Shopper indicates he has purchased product before and the **system** is set up to interact with a known Financial Accounting System:

    2j1. **System** <u>retrieves billing history</u>.

    2j2. **System** utilizes the shopper's billing history to influence the product selection process.

2k. Shopper decides to change some of the recommended options: **System** allows the shopper to change as many options as he wishes, presenting valid ones along the way and warning of incompatibilities of others.

5a. Shopper decides not to add the product to the shopping cart: **System** retains the navigation information for later.

7a. Shopper wants to change the contents of the shopping cart: **System** permits shopper to change quantities, remove items, or go back to an earlier point in the selection process.

7b. Shopper asks to save the contents of the shopping cart:

    7b1. **System** prompts the shopper for name and ID to save it under, and saves it.

        7b1a. Shopper's identity has not been determined: Shopper <u>establishes identity</u>.

7c. Shopper has a trade-in to offer: **System** <u>captures trade-In</u>.

7d. Shopper decides to finance items in shopping cart: Shopper <u>obtains finance Plan</u>.

7e. Shopper leaves the E-Commerce System when shopping cart has not been saved:

    7e1. **System** prompts the shopper for name and id to save it under, and saves it.

        7e1.a. Shopper decides to exit without saving: **System** logs navigational information and ends the shopper's session.

7f. Shopper selects an item in shopping cart and wishes to see availability of matching product (new or used) from inventory:

   7f1. Shopper requests to <u>locate matching product from inventory</u>.

   7f2. Shopper exchanges item in shopping cart with matching product from inventory.

      6f2a. Shopper doesn't want the matching inventory item:

         **System** leaves the original shopping cart item the shopper was interested in, matching against inventory alone.

   7f3. **System** ensures there is one item in shopping cart configured to inventory item.

**Calling Use Cases:** <u>Shop over the Web, Sell Related Product</u>

**Open Issues:**

Extension 2c. What questions are legal? What other systems are hooked in? What are the requirements for the interfaces?

# Part 3

## Reminders for the Busy

# Chapter 20

# Reminders for Each Use Case

### Reminder 1:  A Use Case Is a Prose Essay

Recall from the preface, "Writing use cases is fundamentally an exercise in prose essays, with all the difficulties in articulating *good* that comes with prose writing in general."
Russell Walters of FirePond Corporation wrote:

> I think the above statement clearly nails the problem. This is the most misunderstood problem, and probably the biggest enlightenment for the practicing use case writer. However, I'm not sure the practitioner can come to this enlightenment on her own, well, at least until this book is published. I did not understand this as the fundamental problem, and I had been working with the concept of use cases for four years, until I had the opportunity to work alongside you. And even then, it wasn't until I had a chance to analyze and review the before and after versions of the use case you assisted with re-writing [Use Case 36 on page 194] when the light bulb came on. Four-plus years is a long time to wait for this enlightenment! So, if there is only one thing the readers of this book walk away understanding, I hope it is the realization of the fundamental problem with writing effective use cases. (Used with permission.)

Use this reminder to help keep your eyes on the text, not the diagrams, and to be aware of the writing styles you will encounter.

### Reminder 2:  Make the Use Case Easy to Read

You want your requirements document short, clear, and easy to read.
I sometimes feel like an eighth-grade English teacher walking around, saying,

> Use an active verb in the present tense. Don't use the passive voice, use the active voice. Where's the subject of the sentence? Say what is really a requirement; don't mention it if it is not a requirement.

Those are the things that make your requirements document short, clear, and easy to read. Here are a few habits to acquire to make your use cases short, clear, and easy to read:

1. Keep matters short and to the point. Long use cases make for long requirements, which few people enjoy reading.

2. Start from the top and create a coherent story line. At the top will be a strategic use case. The user goal and eventually subfunction-level use cases branch off from here.

3. Name the use cases with short verb phrases that announce the goal to be achieved.

4. Start from the trigger and continue until the goal is delivered or abandoned and the system has done any bookkeeping it needs to with respect to the transaction.

5. Write full sentences with active verb phrases that describe the subgoals being completed.

6. Make sure the actor and the actor's intent are visible in each step.

7. Make the failure conditions stand out and their recovery actions are readable. Let it be clear what happens next, preferably without having to name step numbers.

8. Put alternative behaviors in the extensions rather than in *if* statements in the main body.

9. Create extension use cases only under very selected circumstances.

## Reminder 3: Just One Sentence Form

There is only one form of sentence used in writing action steps in the use case:

- A sentence in the present tense,
- with an active verb in the active voice,
- describing an actor successfully achieving a goal that moves the process forward.

Here are examples:

Customer enters card and PIN.
System validates that customer is authorized and has sufficient funds.
PAF intercepts responses from the web site and updates the user's portfolio.
Clerk <u>Finds a Loss</u> using search details for 'loss.'"

Use this sentence form in business use cases, system use cases, and summary, user, and subfunction use cases, with either the fully dressed or casual template. It is the same in the main success scenario and in the extension scenario fragments. Master this sentence style.

It is useful for the condition part of an extension to have a different grammatical form so it doesn't get confused with the action steps. Use a sentence fragment (or possibly a full sentence), preferably (but not always) in the past tense. End the condition with a colon (:) instead of a period.

> Time-out waiting for PIN entry:
>
> Bad password:
>
> File not found:
>
> User exited in the middle:
>
> Data submitted is not complete:

## Reminder 4: "Include" Sub Use Cases

What you would do quite naturally, if no one told you to do otherwise, would be to write a step that calls out the name of a lower-level goal or use case, as in

> Clerk <u>finds a loss</u> using search details for "loss."

In UML terms, the calling use case just included the sub use case. This is so much the most obvious thing to do that it would not even deserve mention if there weren't writers and teachers encouraging people to use the UML *extends* and *specializes* relations (see Appendix A).

As a first rule of thumb, always use the *includes* relation between use cases. People who follow this rule report that they and their readers have less confusion with their writing than people who mix *includes* with *extends* and *specializes*. See the subsection When to Use Extension Use Cases on page 116.

## Reminder 5: Who Has the Ball?

Sometimes people write in the passive voice or from the point of view of the system itself, looking out at the world. This produces sentences like Credit limit gets entered. This sentence doesn't mention who is doing the entering.

Write from the point of view of a bird up above, watching and recording the scene. Or write in the form of a play, announcing which actor is about to act. Or pretend for a moment that you are describing a soccer game, in which actor 1 has the ball, dribbles it and then kicks it to actor 2; actor 2 passes it to actor 3; and so on.

Let the first or second word in the sentence be the name of the actor who owns the action. Whatever happens, make sure it is always clear who has the ball.

## Reminder 6:  Get the Goal Level Right

- ◆ Review Section 5.5, Finding the Right Goal Level, for the full discussion.
- ◆ Make sure that the use case is correctly labeled with its goal level: summary, user, or subfunction.
- ◆ Periodically review to make sure you know where "sea level" is for your goals and how far below (or above) sea level the steps are. Recall the tests for a sea-level goal:
  - – It is done by one person, in one place, at one time (2 to 20 minutes).
  - – The actor can go away happily as soon as it is completed.
  - – The actor (if an employee) can ask for a raise after doing many of these.
- ◆ Recall that most use cases have three to nine steps in the main success scenario and that the goal level of a step is typically just below the goal level of the use case. If you have more than nine steps, look for steps to merge in the following places:
  - – Where the same actor has the ball for several steps in a row.
  - – Where the user's movements are described. These are typically user interface movements, violating Guideline 5, Show the Actor's Intent, Not the Movements, on page 92.
  - – Where there is a lot of simple back-and-forth between two actors. Ask if they aren't really trying to accomplish something one level higher with all that back and forth.
- ◆ Ask, "Why is the user/actor doing this action?" The answer you get is the next higher goal level. You may be able to use this goal to merge several steps. Figure 20.1 shows how the goals of the steps fit within the goals of the use cases at different levels.

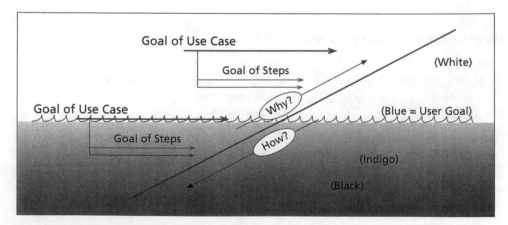

**Figure 20.1**  *Ask "why" to shift levels*

## Reminder 7:  Keep the GUI Out

Verify that the step you just wrote captures the real intent of the actor, not just the movements in manipulating the user interface. This advice applies when you are writing functional requirements, since it is clear that you can write use cases to document the user interface itself.

In a requirements document, describing the user's movements in manipulating the interface has three drawbacks:

- The document is needlessly longer.
- The requirements become brittle, meaning that small changes in the user interface design cause a change in the "requirements" (which weren't requirements after all).
- It steals the work of the UI designer, whom you should trust to do a good job.

Most of the use cases in this book should serve as good examples for you. This extract of Use Case 20, *Evaluate Work Comp Claim,* on page 72, is one.

1. Adjuster reviews and evaluates the reports, . . .
2. Adjuster rates the disability using . . .
3. Adjuster sums the disability owed . . .
4. Adjuster determines the final settlement range.

Here is as an example of what not to do:

1. The system displays the Login screen with fields for username and password.
2. The user enters username and password and clicks OK.
3. The system verifies name and password.
4. The system displays the Main screen, containing function choices.
5. The user selects a function and clicks OK.

It is very easy to slip into describing the user interface movements, so be on your guard.

## Reminder 8:  Two Endings

Every use case has two possible endings, success and failure.

Bear in mind that when an action step calls a sub use case, the called use case can succeed or fail. If the call is in the main success scenario, the failure is handled in an extension. If it is from an extension, describe both success and failure handling in the same extension (see, for example, Use Case 22, *Register a Loss,* on page 75).

You actually have two responsibilities with respect to goal success and failure. The first is to make sure that you deal with the failure of every called use case. The second is to make sure that your use case satisfies the interests of every stakeholder, particularly if the goal fails.

### Reminder 9:  Stakeholders Need Guarantees

A use case does not record only the publicly visible interactions between the primary actor and the system. If it did only that, it would not make acceptable behavioral requirements, but only document the user interface.

The system enforces a contractual agreement between stakeholders. One of these is the primary actor; the others are not there to protect themselves. The use case describes how the system protects all of their interests under different circumstances, with the user driving the scenario. It describes the guarantees the system makes to them.

Take the time to name the stakeholders and their interests in each use case. You should find two to five stakeholders: the primary actor, the owner of the company, perhaps a regulatory agency, and perhaps someone else. Maybe the testing or maintenance staff has an interest in the operation of the use case.

Usually, the stakeholders are the same for most use cases, and usually their interests are very much the same across use cases. It soon takes little effort to list their names and interests. Typically, their interests are these:

- The primary actor's interest is stated in the use case name. It usually is to get something.

- The company's interest is usually to ensure that the primary actor doesn't get away with something for free or that she pays for what she gets.

- The regulatory agency's interest is usually to make sure that the company can demonstrate that it follows guidelines and usually that some sort of log is kept.

- One of the stakeholders typically has an interest in recovering from a failure in the middle of the transaction, that is, more logging.

See that the main success scenario and its extensions address the stakeholders' interests. This takes very little effort. Read the text of the use case, starting with the main success scenario, and see whether those interests are present. You will be surprised by how often one is missing. Very often, the writer has not thought about the fact that a failure can occur in the middle of the main success scenario, leaving no log or recovery information. Check that all failure handling protects all interests of all stakeholders.

Often, a new extension condition reveals a missing validation in the main success scenario. On occasion, there are so many validations being performed that the writer moves the set of checks into a separate writing area, perhaps creating a business rules section.

Pete McBreen, of Roshi, wrote me about the first time his group listed the stakeholders' interests using a system they had already delivered. In that list they discovered all the change requests for the first year of their software's operation. They had successfully built and delivered the system without satisfying certain needs of certain stakeholders. The stakeholders figured this out, of course, and so the change requests came in. What excited this team was that, if they had written down the stakeholders and interests early on, they could have avoided (at least some of) those change requests. As a result, Pete is now a strong advocate of capturing the stakeholders' interests in use cases. Performing this check takes very little time and is very revealing for the time spent.

The guarantees section of the template documents how the use case satisfies these interests. You might skimp on writing the guarantees on a less critical, low-ceremony project on which the team has good personal communications. You will pay more attention to them on more critical projects, where the potential for damage or the cost of misunderstanding is higher. However, in both cases, your team should at least go through the mental exercise of checking both the success and failure exits of the use case.

It is a good strategy to write the guarantees before writing the main success scenario, because then you will think of the necessary validations on the first pass instead of discovering them later and having to go back and change the text.

Section 2.2, Contract between Stakeholders with Interests, and Section 6.2, Minimal Guarantees, have more details on these topics.

## Reminder 10: Preconditions

The preconditions of the use case declare the valid operating conditions of the use case. The preconditions must be things that the system can ensure will be true. You document the preconditions because you will not check them again in the use case.

There are two common situations that give you preconditions. The most common is that the user is logged on and validated. The other is when a second use case picks up the thread of activity partway through a first use case, expecting the first use case to have set up a particular condition that the second can rely upon. An example of this is that the user selects or partially selects a product in the first use case, and the second one uses knowledge of that selection in its processing.

Whenever I see a precondition, I know there is a higher-level use case in which the precondition was established.

## Reminder 11: Pass/Fail Tests for One Use Case

Simple pass/fail tests let us know when we have filled in a part of the use case correctly. Table 20.1 on the next page lists the few I have found. All of them should produce a "yes" answer.

**Table 20.1.**   *Pass/Fail Tests for One Use Case*

| Field | Question |
| --- | --- |
| Use Case Title | 1.  Is it an active-verb goal phrase that names the goal of the primary actor? |
|  | 2.  Can the system deliver that goal? |
| Scope and Level | 3.  Are the fields filled in? |
| Scope | 4.  Does the use case treat the system mentioned in Scope as a black box? (The answer must be "Yes" if it is a system requirements document, but may be "No" if the use case is a white-box business use case.) |
|  | 5.  If the system in Scope is the system to be designed, do the designers have to design everything in it and nothing outside it? |
| Level | 6.  Does the use case content match the stated goal level? |
|  | 7.  Is the goal really at the stated goal level? |
| Primary Actor | 8.  Does he/she/it have behavior? |
|  | 9.  Does he/she/it have a goal against the SuD that is a service promise of the SuD? |
| Preconditions | 10.  Are they mandatory, and can they be set in place by the SuD? |
|  | 11.  Is it true that they are never checked in the use case? |
| Stakeholders and Interests | 12.  Are they named and must the system satisfy their interests as stated? (Usage varies by formality and tolerance.) |
| Minimal Guarantees | 13.  Are all the stakeholders' interests protected? |
| Success guarantees. | 14.  Are all the stakeholders' interests satisfied? |
| Main Success Scenario | 15.  Does it have 3–9 steps? |
|  | 16.  Does it run from trigger to delivery of the success guarantee? |
|  | 17.  Does it permit the right variations in sequencing? |

**Table 20.1.** *Pass/Fail Tests for One Use Case (Continued)*

| Field | Question |
| --- | --- |
| Each Step in Any Scenario | 18. Is it phrased as a goal that succeeds? |
| | 19. Does the process move distinctly forward after its successful completion? |
| | 20. Is it clear which actor is operating the goal—who is "kicking the ball"? |
| | 21. Is the intent of the actor clear? |
| | 22. Is the goal level of the step lower than the goal level of the overall use case? Is it, preferably, just a bit below the use case goal level? |
| | 23. Are you sure the step does not describe the user interface design of the system? |
| | 24. Is it clear what information is being passed in the step? |
| | 25. Does it "validate," as opposed to "check" a condition? |
| Extension Condition | 26. Can and must the system both detect and handle it? |
| | 27. Is it what the system actually needs? |
| Technology and Data Variations List | 28. Are you sure this is not an ordinary behavioral extension to the Main Success Scenario? |
| Overall Use Case Content | 29. To the sponsors and users: "Is this what you want?" |
| | 30. To the sponsors and users: "Will you be able to tell, upon delivery, whether you got this?" |
| | 31. To the developers: "Can you implement this?" |

# Chapter 21

# *Reminders for the Use Case Set*

### Reminder 12:  An Ever-Unfolding Story

For a development project, there is one use case at the top of the stack, called something like *Use the ZZZ System*. This use case is little more than a table of contents for the actors and their highest-level goals. It serves as a starting point for anyone looking at the system for the first time. It is optional, since it doesn't have much of a story line, but most people like to see just one starting place for their reading.

This topmost use case calls out the *outermost use cases*, which show the summary goals of the outermost primary actors of the system. For a corporate information system, there is typically an external customer, the marketing department or the IT or security department. These use cases show the interrelationships of the sea-level use cases that define the system. For most readers, the "story" starts with one of them.

The outermost use cases unfold into user-goal or sea-level use cases. In the user-goal use cases, the design scope is the system being designed. The steps show the actors and the system interacting to deliver the user's immediate goal.

A step in a sea-level use case unfolds into an underwater (indigo or subfunction) use case if the sub use case is complicated or is used in several places. Subfunction use cases are expensive to maintain, so only use them when you have to. Usually, you will have to create subfunction use cases for *Find a Customer, Find a Product*, and so on. On occasion, a step in one indigo use case unfolds to a deeper indigo use case.

The value of viewing the use case set as an ever-unfolding story is that it becomes a "minor" operation to move a complicated section of writing into its own use case or to fold a simple sub use case back into its calling use case. Each action step can, in principle, be unfolded to become a use case in its own right. See Section 10.1, Sub Use Cases.

### *Reminder 13: Both Corporate Scope and System Scope*

Design scope can cause confusion. People have different ideas of where the exact boundaries of the system are. In particular, be very clear whether you are writing a business use case or a system use case.

A business use case is one in which the design scope is business operations. It is about an actor outside the organization achieving a goal with respect to the organization. The business use case often contains no mention of technology, since it is concerned with how the business operates.

A system use case is one in which the design scope is the computer system to be designed. It is about an actor achieving a goal with the computer system; it is about technology.

The business use case is often written in white-box form, describing the interactions between the people and departments in the company, while the system use case is almost always written in black-box form. This is usually appropriate because the purpose of most business use cases is to describe the present or future design of the company while that of the system use case is to create requirements for a new design. The business use case describes the inside of the business; the system use case describes the outside of the computer system.

If you are designing a computer system, you should have both business and system use cases in your collection. The business use case describes the context of the system's function, the place of the system in the business.

To reduce confusion, always label the scope of the use case. Consider creating a graphic icon to illustrate whether it is a business or system use case (see the subsection Using Graphical Icons to Highlight the Design Scope on page 40). Consider placing a picture of the system inside its containing system within the use case itself (see Use Case 8, *Enter and Update Requests (Joint System),* on page 43).

### *Reminder 14:  Core Values and Variations*

Although people keep inventing new use case formats, experienced writers are coming to a consensus on core format values. Two papers in the 1999 TOOLS USA conference (Firesmith, 1999, and Lilly, 1999) described a top dozen or so mistakes made in use case writing. The mistakes and fixes described in those articles echo the core values.

#### Core Values

**GOAL-BASED.** Use cases are centered around the goals of the primary actors and the subgoals of the various actors, including the SuD, in achieving that goal. Each sentence describes a subgoal being achieved.

**BIRD'S EYE VIEW.** The use case is written as describing the actions as seen by a bird viewing the scene from above, or as a play naming the actors. It is not written from the "inside looking out."

**READABLE.** Ultimately a use case, or any specification, will be read by people. If it is not easily understood, it does not serve its core purpose. You can increase readability by sacrificing some amount of precision and even accuracy, making up for the lack with increased conversation. Once you sacrifice readability, however, your constituents won't read your use cases.

**USABLE FOR SEVERAL PURPOSES.** Use cases are a form of behavioral description that can serve various purposes at various times in a project. For example, they have been used to

- Provide black-box functional requirements.
- Provide requirements for an organization's business process redesign.
- Document an organization's business process (white box).
- Help elicit requirements from users or stakeholders (to be discarded when the team writes the final requirements in some other form).
- Specify the test cases that are to be constructed and run.
- Document the internals of a system (white box).
- Document the behavior of a design or design framework.

**BLACK-BOX REQUIREMENTS.** When used as a functional specification, the SuD is always treated as a black box. Project teams who have tried writing white-box requirements (guessing what the inside of the system will look like) report that the resulting use cases are hard to read, not well received, and brittle, changing as the design proceeds.

**ALTERNATIVE PATHS AFTER MAIN SUCCESS SCENARIO.** The original idea of putting alternative courses after the main success scenario keeps showing up as the way to create the use cases that are the easiest to read. Putting the branching cases inside the main body of the text seems to make the story too hard to read.

**NOT TOO MUCH ENERGY SPENT.** Continued fiddling with the use cases does not increase their value. The first draft of the use case creates perhaps half its value. Adding to the extensions adds value, but after a short while, changing the wording of the sentences no longer improves communication. At that point, your energy should go into other things, such as the external interfaces, the business rules, and so on, which are all part of the rest of the requirements. Of course, the rate of diminishing returns varies with the criticality of the project.

## Suitable Variants

Keeping to the core values, a number of acceptable variants have been discovered.

**NUMBERED STEPS VERSUS SIMPLE PARAGRAPHS.** Some people number steps so they can refer to them in the extensions section. Others write in simple paragraphs and put the alternatives in similar paragraph form. Both approaches seem to work well.

**CASUAL VERSUS FULLY DRESSED.** There are times when it is appropriate to allocate a lot of energy to detailing the functional requirements; at other times, even on the same project, that is a waste of energy. (See Section 1.2, Your Use Case Is Not My Use Case, and Section 1.5, Manage Your Energy.) This is true to such an extent that I don't even recommend just one template any more, but always show both the casual and fully dressed versions. Different writers sometimes prefer one over the other. Each works in its own way. Compare Use Case 25, *Actually Login (Casual Version),* on page 120, with Use Case 5, *Buy Something (Fully Dressed Version), on* page 9.

**PRIOR BUSINESS MODELING WITH OR WITHOUT USE CASES.** Some teams like to document or revise the business process before writing the functional requirements for a system. Of those, some choose use cases to describe the business process and some choose another business process modeling form. From the perspective of the system's functional requirements, it does not seem to make much difference which business process modeling notation is chosen.

**USE CASE DIAGRAMS VERSUS ACTOR-GOAL LISTS.** Some people use actor-goal lists to show the set of use cases being developed; some prefer use case diagrams. The use case diagram, showing the primary actors and their user-goal use cases, can serve the same purpose as that of the actor-goal list.

**WHITE-BOX USE CASES VERSUS COLLABORATION DIAGRAMS.** There is near equivalence between white-box use cases and UML collaboration diagrams. You can think of use cases as textual collaboration diagrams. The difference is that a collaboration diagram does not describe the components' internal actions, which the use case might.

## Unsuitable Variants

**"IF" STATEMENTS INSIDE THE MAIN SUCCESS SCENARIO.** If there were only one branching of behavior in a use case, it would be simpler to put that branching within the main text. However, use cases have many branches, and people lose the thread of the story. Individuals who have used *if* statements report that they soon change to the form of the main success scenario followed by extensions.

**SEQUENCE DIAGRAMS AS REPLACEMENTS FOR USE CASE TEXT.** Some software development tools claim to support use cases because they supply sequence diagrams. Sequence diagrams also show interactions between actors, but

- They do not capture internal actions (needed to show how the system protects the interests of the stakeholders).
- They are much harder to read (they are a specialized notation, and they take up a lot more space).
- It is nearly impossible to fit the needed amount of text on the arrows between actors.
- Most tools force the writer to hide the text behind a pop-up dialog box, making the story line hard to follow.
- Most tools force the writer to write each alternate path independently, starting over from the beginning of the use case each time. This duplication of effort is tiring, error prone, and hard on the reader, who has to detect what difference of behavior is presented in each variation.

Sequence diagrams are not a good form for expressing use cases. People who insist on them do so to get the tool benefit of automated services: cross-referencing, back-and-forth hyperlinks, and the ability to change names globally. While these services are nice (and lacking in the textual tools currently available), most writers and readers agree that they are not sufficient reward for the sacrificed ease of writing and reading.

**GUIs IN THE FUNCTIONAL SPECS.** There is a small art to writing the requirements so that the user interface is not specified along with the needed function. This art is not hard to learn and is worth learning. The consensus is strong against describing the user interface in the use cases. See Section 19.6, Advanced Example of Too Much UI, and *Designing Software for Use* (Constantine and Lockwood, 1999).

## Reminder 15: Quality Questions across the Use Case Set

I have only three quality questions for the full use case set:

- Do the use cases form a story that unfolds from the highest- to the lowest-level goal?
- Is there a context-setting, highest-level use case at the outermost design scope possible for each primary actor?
- (To the sponsors and users) "Is this everything that needs to be developed?"

# Chapter 22

# Reminders for Working on the Use Cases

### Reminder 16: It's Just Chapter 3 (Where's Chapter 4?)

Use cases are only a small part of the total requirements-gathering effort, perhaps "Chapter 3" of the requirements document. They are a central part of that effort, acting as a core or hub that links data definitions, business rules, user interface design, the business domain model, and so on. However, they are not all of the requirements, only the behavioral ones.

This has to be stated over and over, because such an aura has grown around use cases that some teams try to fit into them every piece of the requirements somehow.

### Reminder 17: Work Breadth First

Work breadth first, not depth, from lower to higher precision. Work expands with precision (see Figure 22.1), so this will help you manage your energy. (See Section 1.5, Manage Your Energy.) Work in this order:

1. *Primary actors.* Collect all the primary actors as the first step in getting your arms around the entire system, if only briefly. Most systems are so large that you will soon lose track of everything, so it is nice to have the whole system in one place even for a short time. Brainstorm these actors to help you get the most goals on the first round.

2. *Goals.* Listing all the goals of all the primary actors is perhaps the last chance you will have to capture the entire system in one view. Spend enough time and energy to get this list as complete and correct as you can. The next steps will involve more people and much more work. Review the list with users, sponsors, and developers so that they can all agree on the priority and understand the system being deployed.

| Actor | Goal | Success Action | Failure Condition | Recovery Action |
|---|---|---|---|---|
| | | | | Recovery Action |
| | | | | Recovery Action |
| | | | Failure Condition | Recovery Action |
| | | | | Recovery Action |
| | | | | Recovery Action |
| | | Success Action | Failure Condition | Recovery Action |
| | | | | Recovery Action |
| | | | | Recovery Action |
| | | | Failure Condition | Recovery Action |
| | | | | Recovery Action |
| | | | | Recovery Action |
| | Goal | Success Action | Failure Condition | Recovery Action |
| | | | | Recovery Action |
| | | | | Recovery Action |
| | | | Failure Condition | Recovery Action |
| | | | | Recovery Action |
| | | | | Recovery Action |
| | | Success Action | Failure Condition | Recovery Action |
| | | | | Recovery Action |
| | | | | Recovery Action |
| | | | Failure Condition | Recovery Action |
| | | | | Recovery Action |
| | | | | Recovery Action |

**Figure 22.1**   *Work expands with precision*

3. *Main success scenario.* The main success scenario is typically short and fairly obvious. It tells the story of what the system delivers. Make sure that the writers show how the system works once, before investigating all the ways it can fail.

4. *Failure/extension conditions.* Capture all the extension conditions before worrying about how to handle them. This is a brainstorming activity, which is quite different from researching and writing the extension-handling steps. The generated list serves as a worksheet for the writers, who can then write in spurts, taking breaks without worrying about losing their place. People who try to fix each condition as they name them typically never complete the failure list. They run out of energy after writing a few failure scenarios.

5. *Recovery steps.* Although built last of all the use case steps, the recovery steps uncover new user goals, new actors, and new failure conditions surprisingly often. Writing them is the hardest part of the use case writing activity because it forces

the writer to confront business policy matters that often go unmentioned. When I discover an obscure business policy, a new actor, or a new use case while writing recovery steps, I feel vindicated for all my effort.

6. *Data fields.* While formally outside the use case writing effort, often the same people have the assignment of expanding data names (such as "customer information") into lists of data fields (see Section 16.1, Precision in Data Requirements).

7. *Data field details and checks.* In some cases, different people write the data field details and checks while the use case writers are reviewing the use cases. Often the IT technical people will write the field details, while IT business analysts or even users write the use cases. This represents the data formats at the final level of precision. Again, these details and checks are outside the use cases proper but have to be written eventually.

## Reminder 18: The 12-Step Recipe

1. Find the boundaries of the system (context diagram, in/out list).
2. Brainstorm and list the primary actors (actor profile table).
3. Brainstorm and list the primary actors' goals against the system (actor-goal list).
4. Write the outermost summary-level use cases covering all of the above.
5. Reconsider and revise the strategic use cases. Add, subtract, and merge goals.
6. Pick a use case to expand or write a narrative to get acquainted with the material.
7. Fill in the stakeholders, interests, preconditions, and guarantees. Double-check them.
8. Write the main success scenario; check it against the interests and the guarantees.
9. Brainstorm and list possible failure conditions and alternate success conditions.
10. Write how the actors and the system should behave in each extension.
11. Break out any sub use case that needs its own space.
12. Start from the top and readjust the use cases. Add, subtract, and merge as appropriate. Double-check for completeness, readability, and failure conditions.

## Reminder 19: Know the Cost of Mistakes

The cost of lowered quality in a use case depends on your system and project. Some projects need next to no quality in the writing of the requirements document because they have such good communication between users and developers:

The Chrysler Comprehensive Compensation project team, in its building of software to pay all of Chrysler's payroll using the "eXtreme Programming" methodology (Beck

1999), never went further than use case briefs. They wrote so little that they called them "stories" rather than use cases and put them on index cards. Each was really a promise for a conversation between a requirements expert and a developer. Significantly, the 14 team members sat in two adjacent rooms, and had excellent in-team communications.

The better the internal communications between your usage experts and developers, the lower the cost of omitting parts of the use case template. People will simply talk to each other and straighten matters out.

If you are working with a distributed development or multi-contractor development group, or one that is very large, or if you are working on life-critical systems, the cost of quality failure is higher. If it is crucial to get the system's functionality correctly written down, you need to pay close attention to the stakeholders and interests, the preconditions, and the minimal guarantees.

Recognize where your project sits along this spectrum. Don't get too worked up over relatively small mistakes on a small, casual project, but be rigorous if the consequences of misunderstanding are great.

### Reminder 20: Blue Jeans Preferred

Odd though it may sound, you will typically do less damage if you write too little rather than too much. When in doubt, write less text, using higher-level goals, with less precision, and in plain story form. Then you will have a short, readable document, which means that people will bother to read it and then ask questions. From those questions, you can discover what information is missing.

The opposite strategy fails: If you write a hundred or so low-level use cases in great detail, few or no people will bother to read them, and you will shut down communications on the team instead of opening them up. It is a common fault of programmers to write at too low a goal level, so this mistake happens quite often.

◆ **A Short, True Story**

On a successful 50-person, $15 million project, we wrote only the main success scenario and a few failures in a simple paragraph form. This worked because we had excellent communications. Each requirements writer was teamed with two to three designer-programmers. They sat next to each other or visited many times each day.

Actually, enhancing the quality of in-team communications helps every project. The teaming strategy described in the story is the Holistic Diversity pattern from *Surviving Object-Oriented Projects* (Cockburn, 1998).

### Reminder 21: Handle Failures

One of the great values of use cases is that they name all the extension conditions. On many projects, there is a moment when the programmer has just written

```
If <condition>
    then <do this>
else ..?.
```

He stops to muse on the else. . . "I wonder what the system is supposed to do here? The requirements don't say anything about this odd condition, and I don't have anyone to ask about it. Oh, well, . . ." He then types something quick into the program:

```
else <do that>
```

The "else" handling was something that should have been in the requirements document. Very often, it involves significant business rules. I often see usage experts huddling together or calling associates to straighten out just what should be done by the system in these situations.

Finding the failure conditions and writing the failure handling often turn up new actors, new goals, and new business rules. Often, these are subtle and require some research, or they change the complexity of the system.

If you are only used to writing the success scenario, try capturing the failures and failure handling on your next use cases. You are likely to be surprised and heartened by what you uncover.

### Reminder 22: Job Titles Sooner *and Later*

Job titles are important at the beginning and at the end of the project, but not in the middle.

At the beginning of the project, you need to collect all the goals the system must satisfy and put them into a readable structure. Focusing on the job titles or societal roles that will be affected by the system allows you to brainstorm effectively and make the best first pass at naming the goals. Once a long list of goals is in hand, the job titles also provide a clustering scheme to make it easier to review and prioritize the nominated goals.

Job titles allow you to characterize the skills and work styles of the different job. This information informs your design of the user interface.

Once people start developing the use cases, discussions will surface about how roles overlap. The role names used for primary actors become more generic (e.g., "Orderer") or more distant from the people who will actually use the system, until they are only placeholders to remind the writers that there really is an actor having a goal.

Once the system is deployed, job titles become important again. The development team must

- Assign permission levels to specific users for updating or perhaps just reading each kind of information.
- Prepare training materials on the new system, based on the skill sets of the people with those job titles and which use cases each group will be using.
- Package the system for deployment, putting clusters of use case implementations together.

### Reminder 23:  Actors Play Roles

"Actor" means either the job title of the person using the system or the role that person is playing during system use (assuming that it is a person). It is not significant which way we use the term, so don't spend too much energy on the distinction.

The important part is the goal, which says what the system is going to do. Just exactly who calls upon that goal will be negotiated and rearranged over the life of the system. When you discover that the store manager also can act as a sales clerk, you can

- Write in the use case that the primary actor is "either Sales Clerk or Store Manager" (UML fans: Draw the arrow from both actors to the ellipse).
- Write "Store Manager might be acting in the role of Sales Clerk while executing this use case" (UML fans: Draw a generalization arrow from Store Manager to Sales Clerk).
- Create an "Orderer" to be the primary actor. Write "Sales Clerk or Store Manager is acting in the role of Orderer when running this use case" (UML fans: Draw generalization arrows from Sales Clerk and Store Manager to Orderer).

None of these is wrong, so you can choose whichever you find communicates to your audience.

Recognize that a person fills many roles, that a person in a job is just a person filling a role, and that a person with a job title acts in many roles even when acting the role of that job title. Recognize that the important part of the use case is not the primary actor's name but the goal. Recognize that it is useful to settle on a convention for your team to use so that they can be consistent in their use of job titles.

Review the subsection Why Primary Actors Are Unimportant (and Important) on page 55 and Reminder 22, Job Titles Sooner and Later, on page 225, to see how actor names shift to role names and map back to actor names.

## *Reminder 24: The Great Drawing Hoax*

For reasons that remain a mystery to me, many people have focused on the stick figures and ellipses in use case writing since Jacobson's first book, *Object-Oriented Software Engineering* (1993) came out, and have neglected to notice that use cases are fundamentally a text form. The strong CASE tool industry, which already had graphical but not text modeling tools, seized upon this focus and presented tools that maximized the amount of drawing in use cases. This was not corrected in the OMG's Unified Modeling Language standard, which was written by people experienced in textual use cases. I suspect that the strong CASE lobby affected OMG's efforts. "UML is merely a tool interchange standard," is how it was explained to me on several occasions. Hence, the text that sits behind each ellipse somehow is not part of the standard and is a local matter for each writer to decide.

Whatever the reasons, we now have a situation in which many people think that the ellipses *are* the use cases, even though they convey very little information. Experienced developers can be quite sarcastic about this. I thank Andy Hunt and Dave Thomas for their lighthearted spoof of the "requirements made easy" view of use cases in Figure 22.2 (from *The Pragmatic Programmer,* 1999).

It is important to recognize that ellipses cannot possibly replace text. The use case diagram is (intentionally) lacking sequencing, data, and receiving actor. It is to be used as

- A table of contents to the use cases.
- A context diagram for the system, showing the actors pursuing their various and overlapping goals, and perhaps the system reaching out to the secondary actors.
- A "big picture," showing how higher-level use cases relate to lower-level use cases.

These are all fine, as described in Reminder 14, Core Values and Variations, on page 216. Just remember that use cases are fundamentally a text form, so use the ellipses to augment, not replace, the text. Figure 22.3 and Table 22.1 show two ways of presenting the context diagram. The table on the next page shows the same actors and goals, with common use cases repeated for clarity.

**Figure 22.2**    *"Mommy, I want to go home."*

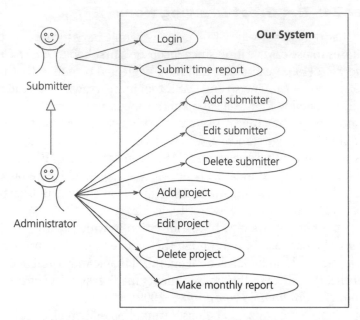

**Figure 22.3**   *Context diagram in ellipse figure form. (Adapted from a draft manuscript by Grady Booch.)*

**Table 22.1.**   *Actor-Goal List for Context Diagram*

| Actor | Goal |
| --- | --- |
| Submitter | Log in |
| | Submit time report |
| Administrator | Log in |
| | Submit time report |
| | Add submitter |
| | Edit submitter |
| | Delete submitter |
| | Add project |
| | Edit project |
| | Delete project |
| | Make monthly report |

## *Reminder 25: The Great Tool Debate*

Sadly, use cases are not well supported by any tools currently on the market. Many companies claim to support them, either in text or in graphics. However, none of their tools contain a metamodel close to that described in Section 2.3, The Graphical Model, and most are quite hard to use. As a result, the use case writer is faced with an awkward choice.

**LOTUS NOTES.** Still my favorite, Lotus Notes has no metamodel of use cases but supports cooperative work, hyperlinking, common template, document history, quick view-and-edit across the use case set, and easily constructed sortable views. These are all significant advantages. Lotus Notes also allows the expanding data descriptions to be kept in the same database but in different views. When you update the template, all use cases in the database are updated. The template is fairly easy to set up and extremely easy to use. I used Lotus Notes to review over 200 use cases on a fixed-cost project bid with the sponsoring customers.

The drawback to Lotus Notes, as to any of the plain-text tools, is that renumbering the steps and extensions while editing a use case soon becomes a nuisance. The hyperlinks eventually become outdated; manually inserted backlinks become outdated very soon. There are no automated backlinks on the hyperlinks, so you can't tell which higher-level use cases invoke the use case you are looking at.

What makes Lotus Notes most attractive to me is its ease of use combined with the way the annotated actor-goal list provides a dynamically generated view of the use case set. Just write a new use case, and the view immediately shows its presence. The view is simultaneously a hyperlinked table of contents, an actor-goal list, and a progress tracking table. I like to view the use cases by priority, release, state of completion, and title, or by primary actor or subject area, level, and title.

**WORD PROCESSORS WITH HYPERLINKS.** With hyperlinking, word processors finally became viable for use cases. Put the use case template into a template file. Put each use case into its own text file using that template, and it becomes easy to create links across use cases. Just don't change the file's name! Writers are familiar with word processors and are comfortable using them to write stories.

Word processors have all the drawbacks of Lotus Notes. More significantly, they provide no way to list all the use cases, sorted by release or status, and click them open. This means that a separate, overview list has to be constructed and maintained, and will soon be out of date. There is no global update mechanism for the template, and so multiple template versions tend to accumulate over time.

**RELATIONAL DATABASES.** I have seen and heard of several attempts to put the model of actors, goals, and steps into a relational database such as Microsoft Access. While this is a natural idea, the resulting tools are awkward to use, sending the use case writers back to their word processors.

**REQUIREMENTS MANAGEMENT TOOLS.** Specialized requirements management tools, such as DOORS or Requisite Pro, are becoming more common. They provide automated forward and backward hyperlinks and are intended for text-based requirements descriptions. On the minus side, none that I know of supports the model of main success scenario and extensions that is at the heart of use cases. The few use cases I have seen from such tools are very lengthy, with a great deal of indenting, numbering, and lines, making them hard to read (remember Reminder 2, Make the Use Case Easy to Read, on page 205, and Reminder 20, Blue Jeans Preferred, on page 224). If you are using such a tool, find a way to make the story shine through.

**CASE TOOLS.** On the plus side, CASE tools support global changes to any entity in its metamodel and automated back links. However, as described earlier, they tend to be built around boxes and arrows, doing poorly with text. Sequence diagrams are not an acceptable substitute for textual use cases, and most CASE tools offer little more than a dialog box for text entry. I have seen writing teams mutiny and revert to word processing rather than use their CASE tools.

That leaves you with a less than pleasant choice to make. Good luck.

## Reminder 26:  Project Planning Using Titles and Briefs

Review Section 17.1, Use Cases in Project Organization, for the pluses and minuses of use cases employed to track project progress and for an example of the actor-goal list as a project-planning framework. Here are the reminders.

**THE USE CASE PLANNING TABLE.** Put the actors and goals in the leftmost two columns of a table, and in the next columns record any of the following as needed: business value, complexity, release, team, completeness, performance requirement, external interfaces, and so on.

Using this table, your team can negotiate over the actual development priority of each use case. They will discuss business need versus technical difficulty, business dependencies, and technical dependencies, and come up with a development sequence.

**DELIVERING PARTIAL USE CASES.** As described in the subsection Handle Use Cases Crossing Releases on page 169, you will quite often decide to deliver only part of a use case in a particular release. Most teams simply use a yellow highlighter or bold text to indicate which portion of a use case that is. You will want to note in the planning table the first release in which the use case shows up and the final release in which the use case will be delivered in its entirety.

# Appendices

# Appendix A

# Use Cases in UML

The Unified Modeling Language defines graphical icons that people are determined to use. It does not address use case content or writing style, but does provide lots of complexity for people to discuss. Spend your energy learning to write clear text instead. If you like diagrams, learn the basics of the relations and then set a few simple standards to keep the drawings clear.

## A.1 ELLIPSES AND STICK FIGURES

When you walk to the whiteboard to draw pictures of people using the system, it is very natural to draw a stick figure for a person, and ellipses or boxes for the use cases they are calling upon. Label the stick figure with the title of the actor and the ellipses with the titles of the use cases. The information is the same as in the actor-goal list, but the presentation is different. The diagrams can be used as a table of contents.

So far, all is all fine and normal.

The trouble starts when you or your readers believe that the diagrams define the system's functional requirements. Some people become infatuated with the diagrams, thinking that they will make a hard job simple (as in Figure 22.1 on page 222). They try to capture as much as possible in the diagram, hoping, perhaps, that text will never have to be written. Here are events that are symptomatic of this situation.

> A person in my course recently unrolled a taped-together diagram several feet on a side, with ellipses and arrows going in all directions, and with *includes, extends,* and *generalizes* relations all mixed around (distinguished, of course, only by the little text label on each arrow). He wanted to know whether his project was using all the relations correctly and was unaware that it was virtually impossible to understand what his system was supposed to do.

Another showed with pride how he had "repaired" the evident defect of diagrams not showing the order in which sub use cases are called. He added yet more arrows to show which sub use case preceded another, using the UML precedes relation. The result, of course, was an immensely complicated drawing that took up more space than the equivalent text and was harder to read. To paraphrase the old saying, he could have put a thousand readable words in the space of his one unreadable drawing.

A drawing is a two-dimensional mnemonic device that serves a cognitive purpose, namely, to highlight relationships. Use them for this purpose, not to replace the text.

With this purpose in hand, let us look at the individual relations in UML.

## A.2  UML'S INCLUDES *RELATION*

A *base* use case *includes* an *included* use case if an action step in the base use case calls out the included use cases's name. This is the normal and obvious relationship between a higher-level and a lower-level use case. The included use case describes a lower-level goal than the base use case.

The verb phrase in an action step is potentially the name of a sub use case. If you never break out that goal into its own use case, it is simply a step. If you do break out that goal into its own use case, then the step *calls* the sub use case, in my vocabulary, or it *includes the behavior of* the included use case, in current UML 1.3 vocabulary. Prior to UML 1.3, it was said to *use* the lower-level use case (that phrase is now out of date).

A dashed arrow goes from the (higher-level) base use case to the included use case, signifying that the base use case "knows about" the included one, as illustrated in Figure A.1.

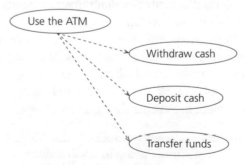

**Figure A.1**  *Drawing Includes*

**Guideline 13:** Draw Higher Goals Higher

*Always* draw higher-level goals higher up on the diagram than lower level goals. This helps reduce goal-level confusion and is intuitive to readers. When you do this, the arrow from a base use case to an included use case will *always* point down.

UML permits you to change the pictorial representation of each of its elements. I find that most people, when drawing by hand, simply draw a *solid* arrow from base to included use case (dashed arrows are tedious). This is fine, and now you can justify it. With a graphics program, you will probably use the arrow style that comes with the program.

It should be evident to most programmers that the *includes* relation is the old subroutine call from programming languages. This is not a problem or a disgrace; rather, it is a natural use of a natural mechanism, which we use both in programming and in our daily lives. On occasion, it is appropriate to parameterize use cases, pass them function arguments, and even have them return values (see Chapter 14, Two Special Use Cases). Keep in mind, though, that the purpose of a use case is to communicate with another person, not with a CASE tool or a compiler.

## A.3 *UML'S* **EXTENDS** *RELATION*

An *extending* or *extension* use case *extends* a base use case by naming the base use case and defining the circumstances under which it interrupts the base use case. The base use case does not name the extending one. This is useful if you want any number of use cases to interrupt the base one without the maintenance nightmare of updating the base use case each time a new, interrupting use case is added. (See Section 10.2, Extension Use Cases.)

Behaviorally, the extending use case specifies some internal condition in the base use case and a triggering condition. Behavior runs through the base use case until the condition occurs, at which point it continues in the extending use case. When the extending use case finishes, the behavior picks up in the base use case where it left off.

Rebecca Wirfs-Brock colorfully refers to the extending use case as a *patch* on the base use case (programmers should relate to the analogy of program patches!). Other programmers see it as a text version of the mock programming instruction, the *come-from* statement.

We use the extension form quite naturally when writing extension conditions within a use case. An *extension use case* is just the extension condition with the handling pulled out and turned into a use case on its own (see Section 10.2, Extension Use Cases). Think of it as a scenario extension that outgrew its use case and was given its own space.

The default UML drawing for *extends* is a dashed arrow (the same as for *includes*) from extending to base use case, with the phrase "<<extends>>" set alongside it. I draw

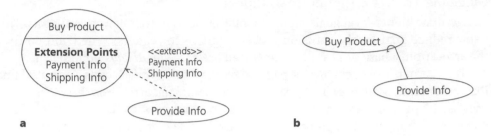

**Figure A.2**   *Drawing Extends*

it with a hook from the extending use case back to the base use case, as shown in Figure A.2, to highlight the difference between *includes* and *extends* relations.

Figure A.2(a) shows the default UML way of drawing *extends* (the example is from *UML Distilled* (Fowler, 1999)). Figure A.2(b) shows the hook connector.

### Guideline 14: Draw Extending Use Cases Lower

An extension use case is generally at a lower level than the use case it extends, so it should be placed lower on the diagram. In the *extends* relation, however, it is the lower use case that knows about the higher use case. Therefore, the arrow or hook should be drawn *up* from the extending to the base use case symbol.

### Guideline 15: Use Different Arrow Shapes

UML deliberately leaves unresolved the style of the arrows connecting use case symbols. Any relation can be drawn with an open-headed arrow and some small text to say what the relation is. The idea is that different tool vendors or project teams might want to customize the arrow style, and the UML standard should not prevent this.

The unfortunate consequence is that people simply use the undifferentiated arrows for all relations, which makes the drawings hard to read. The reader must study the small text to detect which relations are intended, and later on there will be no simple visual clues to help him remember the relations. This, combined with the absence of other drawing conventions, makes many use case diagrams truly incomprehensible.

For that reason, take the trouble to set up different arrow styles for the three relations:

◆ *Includes:* Use the default, open-headed arrow, as it should be the most frequently used one.

◆ *Generalizes:* The standard *generalizes* arrow in UML is the triangle-headed arrow. Use that.

- *Extends:* Create a different shape entirely. I use a hook from the extending to the base use case. Readers find it immediately recognizable, it doesn't conflict with any of the other UML symbols, and it brings its own metaphor of an extending use case having its hooks in the base use case. Whatever you use, make the *extends* connector stand out from the other ones in the diagram.

## Correct Use of Extends

The most common occasion for creating extension use cases (originally discussed in the subsection When to Use Extension Use Cases on page 116) is when there are many asynchronous services the user might activate to interrupt the base use case. Often, they are developed by different teams. These occasions come up in the construction of shrink-wrapped software packages, as illustrated in Figure A.3.

The other common occasion is when you are writing additions to a locked requirements document. In an incrementally staged project, you might lock the requirements after each delivery and then *extend* a locked use case with one that adds function.

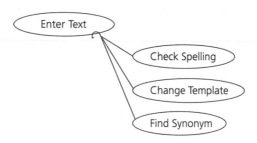

**Figure A.3**   *Three interrupting use cases extending a base use case*

## Extension Points

The reason that *extends* was invented in the first place was the practice of never touching the requirements file of a previous system. In the original telephony systems where use cases were developed, the business often added asynchronous services, and so the *extends* relation was practical. The new team could build on the safely locked requirements document, adding the requirements for a new, asynchronous service in the base use case wherever it was appropriate, without touching a line of the original system requirements.

However, referencing behavior in another use case is problematic. If no line numbers are used, how should we refer to the point at which the extension behavior picks up? And if line numbers are used, what happens if the base use case gets edited and the line numbers change?

Recall that the line numbers are really line labels. As such, they don't have to be numeric or sequential. They are there for readability and so that the extension conditions have a reference point. Usually, however, they *are* sequential numbers, which means that they will change over time.

Extension points were introduced to fix these issues. An *extension point* is a publicly visible label in the base use case that identifies a moment in the use case's behavior by nickname (technically, it can refer to set of places, but let's leave that aside for the moment).

Publicly visible extension points introduce a new problem. The writers of a base use case are charged with knowing where it can get extended. They must go back and modify it whenever someone thinks up a new place to extend it. Recall that the original purpose of *extends* was to avoid having to modify the base use case.

You will have to deal with one of the above problems. I find publicly declared extension points more trouble than they are worth. I prefer describing textually where in the base use case the extending use case picks up, ignoring nicknames, as in the ATM example below.

If you do use extension points, don't show them on the diagram. They take up most of the space in the ellipse, dominating the reader's view and obscuring the much more important goal name (see Figure A.2). The behavior they refer to does not show up on the diagram. They cause yet more clutter.

There is one more thing about extension points. An extension point name is permitted to call out not just *one* place in the base use case where the extending use cases needs to add behavior but as many as you wish. You would want this for, say, an ATM when adding the extension use case *Use ATM of Another Bank*. The extending use case needs to say,

> Before accepting to perform the transaction, the system gets permission from the customer to charge the additional service fee.
>
> . . .
>
> After completing the requested transaction, the system charges the customer's account the additional service fee.

Of course, you could just say that.

## A.4  *UML'S* GENERALIZES *RELATIONS*

A use case may *specialize* a more general one (the general use case *generalizes* the specific one). The (specializing) child should be of a "similar species" to that of the (general) parent. More exactly, UML 1.3 says, "A generalization relationship between use cases implies that the child use case contains all the attributes, sequences of be-havior, and extension points defined in the parent use case, and participates in all the relationships of the parent use case."

### Correct Use of Generalizes

A good test word is *generic*, as in "some kind of." Be alert for when you say, "The user does some kind of this action." When you do, you have a candidate for *generalizes*.

Here is a fragment of the *Use the ATM* use case.

1.  Customer enters card and PIN.
2.  ATM validates customer's account and PIN.
3.  Customer does a transaction, one of:

    Withdraw cash

    Deposit cash

    Transfer money

    Check balance

    Customer does transactions until selecting to quit.
4.  ATM returns card.

What is it the customer does in step 3? The generic answer is "a transaction." There are four *kinds of* transactions the customer can do. *"Generic"* and *"kinds of"* tip us off to the presence of the generic or generalized goal, Do a transaction. In the plain-text version, we don't notice that we are using the *generalizes* relation between use cases; we simply list the kinds of operations or transactions the user can do and keep going. In UML, though, this is the signal to drag out the *generalization* arrow.

Actually, we have two choices. We can ignore the whole *generalizes* business and just *include* the specific operations, as shown in Figure A.4(a). Or we can create a *general* use case for *Do One ATM Transaction* and show the specific operations as spe-cializations of it, as in Figure A.4(b).

Use whichever you prefer. Working in prose, I don't create generalized use cases. There is rarely any text to put into the generic goal, so there is no need to create a new use case page for it. Graphically, however, there is no way to express does one of the following transactions, so you have to find and name the generalizing goal.

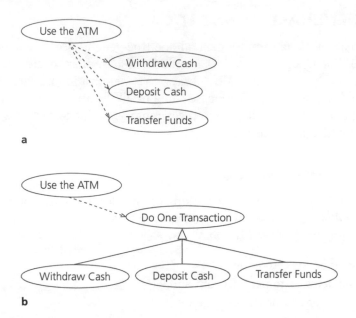

**Figure A.4  Drawing Generalizes.** *A set of included use cases is converted into specializations of a generic action.*

### Guideline 16: Draw General Goals Higher

Always draw the general goal higher on the diagram, and point the triangular arrow-head up into the bottom, not the sides. Figure A.4 illustrates this.

## Hazards of Generalizes

Watch out when combining the specialization of actors with the specialization of use cases. The idiom to avoid is that of a *specialized actor using a specialized use case*. To illustrate, Figure A.5 is trying to express the fairly normal idea that a Sales Clerk can close any deal but that it takes a special kind of sales clerk, a Senior Agent, to close a deal above a certain limit. However, it actually expresses the opposite.

Recall from Section 4.2, The Primary Actor, that the specialized actor can perform every use case the general actor can. Thus, the Sales Clerk is a generalized Senior Agent. To many people, this seems counterintuitive, but it is official and correct.

The other specialization seems quite natural, that closing a big deal is a special case of closing an ordinary deal. However, the UML rule is *A specialized use case can be substituted wherever a general use case is mentioned*. Therefore, the drawing says that an ordinary sales clerk can close a big deal!

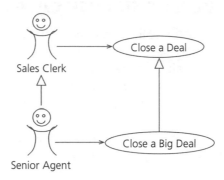

**Figure A.5** *Hazardous generalization—closing a big deal*

The corrected drawing is shown in Figure A.6. You might look at the drawing and ask: Does closing a small deal really *specialize* closing a basic deal, or does it *extend* it? Since working with text use cases will not put anyone in this sort of puzzling and economically wasteful quandary, I leave that question as an exercise to the interested reader.

In general, the problem with the *generalizes* relation is that the professional community has not yet reached an understanding of what it means to subtype and specialize behavior, that is, what properties and options are implied. Since use cases are descriptions of behavior, there can be no standard understanding of what it means to specialize them.

If you do use the *generalizes* relation, my suggestion is to make the generalized use case empty, as in *Do One Transaction* above. Then the specializing use case will supply *all* the behavior, and you will have to worry only about the one trap just described.

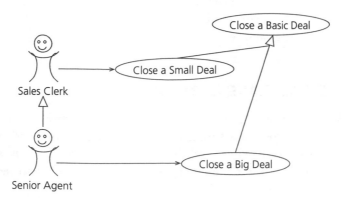

**Figure A.6** *Correctly closing a big deal*

## A.5  SUBORDINATE VERSUS SUB USE CASES

In the extended text section of the UML 1.3 specification, the authors describe two little-known relations between use cases that have no drawing counterpart and are not specified in the object constraint language but simply written into the explanatory text. These are the *subordinate use case* and its inverse, the *superordinate use case*.

The intent of these relations is to let you show how the use cases of a system's *components* work together to deliver the use case of the larger system. In an odd turn, the components themselves are not shown; their use cases just sit in empty space, on their own. It is as though you were to draw an anonymous collaboration diagram, a special sort of functional decomposition, that you are later supposed to explain with a proper collaboration diagram. According to the UML specification,

> A use case specifying one model element is then refined into a set of smaller use cases, each specifying a service of a model element contained in the first one. . . . Note, though, that the structure of the container element is not revealed by the use cases, since they only specify the functionality offered by the elements. The subordinate use cases of a specific superordinate use case cooperate to perform the superordinate one. Their cooperation is specified by collaborations and may be presented in collaboration diagrams.

The purpose of introducing these peculiar relations in the explanatory text of the use case specification is unclear, and I don't propose to explain them. I only bring up the matter because I use the term "sub use case" in this book, and someone will get around to asking, "What is the relation between Cockburn's sub use case and the UML subordinate use case?"

I use the term *sub use case* to refer to a goal at a lower goal level. In general, the higher-level use case will call (*include*) the sub use case. I used to say "subordinate" and "superordinate" for higher- and lower-level use cases, but since UML 1.3 has taken those words, I have shifted vocabulary. My experience is that people do not find anything odd about the terms "calling use case" and "sub use case." They are clear even to the novice writer and reader.

## A.6  DRAWING USE CASE DIAGRAMS

You will find that the use case diagrams will communicate more easily to your readers if you set up and follow a few simple diagramming conventions. Please don't hand your readers a rat's nest of arrows and then expect them to trace out your meaning. Guidelines 13 through 16, for the different use case relations, will help. Two more drawing guidelines can help as well.

**Guideline 17:** User Goals in a Context Diagram

On the main context diagram, do not show any use cases lower than user-goal level. After all, the purpose of the diagram is to provide context and a table of contents for the system being designed. If you decompose use cases in diagram form, put the decompositions on separate pages.

**Guideline 18:** Supporting Actors on the Right

I find it helpful to place *all* the primary actors on the left side of the system box, leaving the right side for the supporting (secondary) actors. This reduces confusion about primary versus secondary actors. Some people never draw supporting actors on their diagrams. This allows them to place primary actors on both sides.

## A.7 WRITE TEXT-BASED USE CASES INSTEAD

If you spend much time studying and worrying about the graphics and the relations, you are expending energy in the wrong place. Put it instead into writing easy-to-read prose. In prose, the relations between use cases are straightforward, and you won't understand why other people are getting tied up in knots about them.

This is a view shared by many use case experts. It is somewhat self-serving to relate the following event, but I wish to emphasize the seriousness of the suggestion. My thanks to Bruce Anderson of IBM's European Object Technology Practice for the comment he made during a panel on use cases at OOPSLA '98, during which a series of questions surfaced around the difference between *includes* and *extends* and the trouble with the exploding number of scenarios and ellipses. Bruce stated that his groups don't run into scenario explosion, and they don't get confused. A questioner asked why everyone else was concerned about "scenario explosion and how to use *extends*" but he wasn't. Bruce's answer was "I just do what Alistair said to do," which is to spend time writing clear text, staying away from *extends*, and not worrying about diagrams.

People who write good text-based use cases simply do not run into the problems encountered by people who fiddle with the stick figures, ellipses, and arrows of UML. The relations come naturally when you write an unfolding story; they become an issue only if you dwell on them. As more consultants gain experience in both text and UML, the more they agree on this.

# Appendix B

# Answers to (Some) Exercises

### Chapter 3, Page 51

**Exercise 3.1**

We could be describing our **neighborhood**, or the set of **electronically connected industries**. On a smaller scale, we could be designing the **bank building and lighting system**. We could be designing a new **bank computer system and ATM**, or just the **ATM**. Or we could be discussing a new **key panel design** or the design for a new **Enter key**. There is no way to tell from this fragment of the story which system is being discussed.

**Exercise 3.2**

Again, we cannot tell from the user story fragment which system we are discussing.

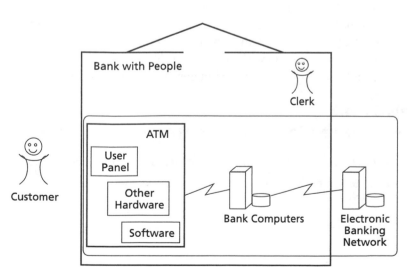

**Figure B.1**  *Design scopes for the ATM.*

## Chapter 4, Page 60

### Exercise 4.2

Recall the pass/fail tests. An actor must be able to execute an *if* statement's worth of behavior. A primary actor has a goal, calling upon a system's promised services.

> **The ATM.** The SuD.
>
> **The customer.** A primary actor and stakeholder.
>
> **The ATM card.** Not an actor. It does not have sufficient behavior (this refers to "dead iron filings" cards; "smart cards" with embedded chips may qualify). The ATM card is really just a data envelope, serving as no more than fast, fixed typing on the customer's part.
>
> **The bank.** Not an actor for our purposes. It is a system containing the ATM.
>
> **The front panel.** Not an actor for our purposes. It is a component of the SuD.
>
> **The bank owner.** A stakeholder, probably not a primary actor.
>
> **The serviceman.** A primary actor.
>
> **The printer.** Not an actor for our purposes. It is a component of the SuD.
>
> **The main bank computer system.** A secondary actor. It might be a primary actor if you can think of a situation in which it initiates a conversation with the ATM.
>
> **The bank teller.** Depends on the job assignments. Who empties and refills the cash? If you said, "Refiller" or "Service staff," perhaps you will never create a use case with the bank teller as primary actor. If you answered, "The bank teller does," the bank teller is a primary actor.
>
> **The bank robber.** Depends on the design scope and your creativity. I could never think of a decent use case for the bank robber that wasn't just an extension condition of a customer's use case, until someone suggested, "Steal the ATM!" That brings up the idea of a movement detector. Depending on how we phrase the goal, we could end up with either the robber having a use case (whose goal never succeeds!) or just more extension conditions in the customer's use case.

### Exercise 4.3

The answers depend on which containing system you choose (see Figure B.1).

> **The ATM.** Not an actor for our purposes. It is a now a component of the SuD.
>
> **The customer.** Still a primary actor and stakeholder.

**The ATM card.** Not an actor, for the same reasons as in Exercise 4.2 (with the same disclaimers).

**The bank.** Look at Figure B.1. If you chose "Bank with people" as the containing system, this is your SuD. If you chose "Electronic Banking Network," this is probably an actor (depending on whether you can justify a service of the Electronic Banking System that it calls upon).

**The front panel.** Not an actor for our purposes. It is a component.

**The bank owner.** Depends on which containing system you chose and what service goals you came up with. It could end up either as a component of the Bank, and hence not a primary actor, or as a primary actor of the Bank, but probably not a primary actor of the Electronic Banking System.

**The serviceman.** A primary actor if a hired outside serviceman, a component if an employee of the bank and you chose the Bank as the SuD.

**The printer.** Not an actor for our purposes. It is a component.

**The main bank computer system.** It is now a component of the containing system (either of them).

**The bank teller.** Either a component (of the Bank) or possibly a primary actor of the Electronic Banking System.

**The bank robber.** Same as for Exercise 4.2.

## Chapter 5, Page 79

### Exercise 5.1

- Summary (white): *Take Someone out for Dinner,* ☁ (this is a somewhat contrived answer in the case of the ATM).
- Summary (white): *Use the ATM,* ⌀.
- User goal (blue): *Get Money from the ATM,* ⚇.
- Subfunction (indigo): *Enter a PIN,* ⊳◦.
- Subfunction (black): *Find the Enter Button,* ⊜.

### Exercise 5.2

| Actor | Goal | Level |
|---|---|---|
| Serviceman | Put ATM in working order | Summary |
| | Run ATM self-test | User goal |
| Bank Clerk | Restock money | User goal |
| | Refill supplies | User goal |
| Customer | Use the ATM | Summary |
| | Withdraw cash | User goal |
| | Deposit money | User goal |
| | Transfer money | User goal |
| | Check balance | User goal |

## Chapter 6, Page 85

### Exercise 6.1

The easiest way to find the minimal guarantee is to ask, "What would make a stakeholder unhappy?" The stakeholders are the customers, the bank, and the banking oversight agency.

The customers will be unhappy if they don't get their cash, but that is not expected in the minimal guarantee. Let's assume that they don't get their cash. In that case they'll be unhappy if they are debited for the transaction. In fact, they'll be unhappy anytime they are debited for more than the cash they receive. They also want a log of all transactions, so they can defend themselves against fraud.

The bank will be unhappy if the customer gets more cash than the amount debited. It also wants a log to protect itself, probably a special kind of log that says how far the transaction got in case of catastrophic failure so it can sort out any errors.

The oversight agency wants to see that guidelines are being followed, so it is mostly interested that a log of all transactions is produced.

As a result, we have a minimal guarantee that the amount debited equals the amount dispensed, with a micro-log of how far the transaction handling got in case of catastrophic failure. Also, each transaction is logged.

### Exercise 6.4

The success guarantee is that the account is debited the amount *dispensed* (not the amount *requested*—check failure conditions!), the card is returned, the machine is reset, and a log is made of the transaction.

## Chapter 7, Page 98

### Exercise 7.1

Here is the interface detail description for withdrawing cash from an ATM. Sending out 100 use cases like this will make for some unhappy readers. See the answer for Exercise 7.2 for an intention description.

1. Customer runs ATM card through the card reader.
2. ATM reads the bank ID and account number.
3. ATM asks customer whether to proceed in Spanish or English.
4. Customer selects English.
5. ATM asks for PIN number and to press Enter.
6. Customer enters PIN number, presses Enter.
7. ATM presents list of activities for the Customer to perform.
8. Customer selects "withdraw cash."
9. ATM asks customer to say how much to withdraw, in multiples of $5, and to press Enter.
10. Customer enters an amount, a multiple of $5, presses Enter.
11. ATM notifies main banking system of customer account, amount being withdrawn.
12. Main banking system accepts the withdrawal, tells ATM new balance.
13. ATM delivers the cash.
14. ATM asks whether customer would like a receipt.
15. Customer replies yes.
16. ATM issues receipt showing new balance.
17. ATM logs the transaction.

### Exercise 7.2

Here is the streamlined version of Fast Cash, showing the actors' intents.

1. Customer runs ATM card through the card reader.
2. ATM reads the bank ID and account number from the card, validates them with the main computer.
3. Customer enters PIN. ATM validates PIN.
4. Customer selects FASTCASH and withdrawal amount, a multiple of $5.
5. ATM notifies main banking system of customer account, amount being withdrawn, and receives acknowledgement plus the new balance.
6. ATM delivers the cash, card, and a receipt showing the new balance.
7. ATM logs the transaction.

## Exercise 7.4

The sample contains three kinds of mistakes. The first thing to catch is that the use case is not about logging in regardless of what the use case name and description say. It is about using the order-processing system. The real use case here is a summary use case at kite level. The first six steps are about logging in, but that is at a different goal level entirely and should be separated out. Once we do that, we notice that the user logs into this system but never logs out!

While the user does not select Exit loop, end if, and end loop are programmer constructs that will not make sense to the users reviewing the use case. The continual *if* statements clutter the writing. The steps describe the user interface design. All of these should be fixed.

The use case starts when . . . and The use case ends when . . . are stylistic conventions suggested by some teachers. There is nothing particularly wrong with them. They are simply ornamentation, which I don't find necessary. Most people naturally assume that the use case starts with step 1 and ends when the writing stops.

The other style to note is the phrasing, User . . . then Use Place Order. The "use" in that phrase refers to the *includes* relation of UML (formerly called the *uses* relation!). I find it clutters rather than clears the writing, and so I prefer User . . . <u>places the order</u>. You will probably follow whatever convention your project team sets up for referring to other use cases.

In the end, we find two use cases to pull apart: the kite use case, *Use the Order Processing System*, and the subfunction, *Log In*. *Log In* you can derive on your own. Note that the links to other use cases are underlined.

## Use Case 38   &#9633; **Use the Order Processing System**   &#8494;

**Main Success Scenario:**
1. User <u>logs in</u>.
2. System presents the available functions. User selects and does one of:
     <u>Place Order</u>
     <u>Cancel Order</u>
     <u>Get Status</u>
     <u>Send Catalog</u>
     <u>Register Complaint</u>
     <u>Run Sales Report</u>
3. This repeats until the user selects to exit.
4. System logs user out when user selects to exit.

## *Chapter 8, Page 110*

### Exercise 8.1

Here is a sampling of failure conditions. Typically, my classes produce a list twice this long. Notice that all conditions are detectable and must be handled. How did you do?

> Card reader broken or card scratched.
> Card for an ineligible bank.
> Incorrect PIN.
> Customer does not enter PIN in time.
> ATM is down.
> Host computer is down, or network is down.
> Insufficient money in account.
> Customer does not enter amount in time.
> Not a multiple of $5.
> Amount requested is too large.
> Network or host goes down during transaction.
> Insufficient cash in dispenser.
> Cash jams during dispensing.
> Receipt paper runs out or jams.
> Customer does not take the money from the dispenser.

### Exercise 8.5

### Use Case 39 　▱ **Buy Stocks Over the Web** ∿

**Primary Actor:** Purchaser/User
**Scope:** PAF
**Level:** User goal
**Precondition:** User already has PAF open.
**Minimal Guarantees:** Sufficient log information exists that PAF can detect that something went wrong and can ask the user to provide the details.
**Success Guarantees:** Remote web site has acknowledged the purchase; PAF logs and the user's portfolio are updated.
**Main Success Scenario:**
1. User selects to buy stocks over the web.
2. PAF gets name of web site to use (E*Trade, Schwab, etc.)
3. PAF opens web connection to the site, retaining control.
4. User browses and buys stock from the web site.
5. PAF intercepts responses from the web site and updates the user's portfolio.
6. PAF shows the user the new portfolio standing.

**Extensions:**

2a. User wants a web site PAF does not support:

    2a1. System gets new suggestion from user, with option to cancel use case.

3a. Web failure of any sort during setup:

    3a1. System reports failure to user with advice; backs up to previous step.

    3a2. User either backs out of this use case or tries again.

4a. Computer crashes or is switched off during purchase transaction:

    4a1. (what do we do here?)

4b. Web site does not acknowledge purchase, but puts it on delay:

    4b1. PAF logs the delay; sets a timer to ask the user about the outcome.

    4b2. (see <u>Update Questioned Purchase</u>)

5a. Web site does not return the needed information from the purchase:

    5a1. PAF logs the lack of information, has the <u>user update questioned purchase</u>.

5b. Disk crash or disk full during portfolio update operation:

    5b1. On restart, PAF detects the log inconsistency and asks the user to <u>update questioned purchase</u>.

## Chapter 11, Page 138

### Exercise 11.1

### Use Case 40   ⌂ Perform Clean Spark Plugs Service ⋈

**Precondition:** Car taken to garage, engine runs.
**Minimal Guarantee:** Customer notified of larger problem; car not fixed.
**Success Guarantee:** Engine runs smoothly.
**Main Success Scenario:**

1. Open hood and cover fender with protective materials.
2. Remove spark plugs.
3. Wipe grease off spark plugs.
4. Clean and adjust gaps.
5. Test and verify plugs work.
6. Replace plugs.
7. Connect ignition wires to appropriate plugs.
8. Test and verify that engine runs smoothly.
9. Clean tools, equipment.
10. Remove protective materials from fenders; clean any grease from car.

**Extensions:**

4a. Plug is cracked or worn out: Replace it with a new plug.

8a. Engine still does not run smoothly:

    8a1. <u>Diagnose rough engine</u> (UC 23).

    8a2. <u>Notify customer of larger problem with car</u> (UC 41).

# Appendix C

# Glossary

## Main Terms

**ACTOR.** Something with behavior (able to execute an *if* statement). It might be a mechanical system, computer system, person, organization, or some combination of these.

An *external actor* is an actor outside the system under discussion.

A *stakeholder* is an external actor entitled to have its interests protected by the system, and satisfying whose interests requires the system to take specific actions. Different use cases can have different stakeholders.

A *primary actor* is a stakeholder who requests that the system deliver a goal. Typically but not always, the primary actor initiates the interaction with the system. The primary actor may have an intermediary initiate the interaction or may have the interaction triggered automatically on some event.

A *supporting* or *secondary* actor is a system against which the SuD has a goal.

An *offstage,* or *tertiary,* actor is a stakeholder who is not the primary actor.

An *internal actor* is either the system under discussion (SuD), a subsystem of the SuD, or an active component of the SuD.

**INTERACTION.** A message, a sequence of interactions, or a set of interaction sequences.

**SCENARIO.** A scenario is a sequence of actions and interactions that occurs under certain conditions, expressed without *if*s or branching.

A *concrete scenario* is a scenario in which all the specifics are named: the actor names and the values involved. It is equivalent to describing a story in the past tense, with all details included.

A *usage narrative*, or just *narrative*, is a concrete scenario that reveals the motivations and intentions of various actors. It is used as a warm-up activity to reading or writing use cases.

In requirements writing, scenarios are sometimes written using placeholder terms like "customer" and "address" for actors and data values. When it is necessary that these be distinguished from *concrete scenarios,* they can be called *general scenarios*.

A *path through a use case* and a *course of a use case* are synonyms for *general scenario*.

The *main success scenario* is the one scenario written in full, from trigger to completion, and includes goal delivery and any bookkeeping that happens after.  It is a typical and illustrative success scenario, even though it may not be the only success path.

An *alternate course* is any other scenario or scenario fragment written as an extension to the main success scenario.

An *action step* is the unit of writing in a scenario. Typically one sentence, it usually describes the behavior of only one actor.

**SCENARIO EXTENSION**. A scenario fragment that starts upon a particular condition in another scenario.

The *extension condition* names the circumstances under which the different behavior occurs.

An *extension use case* is a use case that interrupts another use case, starting upon a particular condition.  The use case that is interrupted is called the *base use case*.

An *extension point* is a tag or nickname for a point in a base use case's behavior at which an extension use case can interrupt it.  An extension point may actually name a set of places in the base use case so that the extension use case can collect all the related extension behaviors that interrupt the base use case for one set of conditions.

A *sub use case* is a use case called out in a step of a scenario. In UML, the calling use case is said to *include* the behavior of the sub use case.

**USE CASE**. A use case expresses the behavioral portion of a contract between the stakeholders of a system. It describes the system's behavior and interactions under various conditions as it responds to a request on behalf of one of the stakeholders, the *primary actor*, showing how the primary actor's goal gets delivered or fails. The use case gathers the scenarios related to the primary actor's goal.

## Use Case Types

**FOCUS.** Whether the focus is on the business or the new system:

The phrase *business use case* is a shortcut indicating that the use case emphasizes the operation of the business rather than the operation of a computer system. It is possible to write a business use case at any goal level, but it can only be at enterprise or organization scope.

The phrase *system use case* is a shortcut indicating that the use case emphasizes the operations of the computer or mechanical system rather than the operation of a business. It is possible to write a system use case at any goal level and at any scope, including enterprise. A system use case written at enterprise scope highlights the effect of the SuD on the behavior of the enterprise.

**FORMALITY.** How much energy, rigor, and formality are used:

A use case *brief* is a one-paragraph synopsis of the use case.

A *casual use case* is written as a simple, prose paragraph. It is likely to be missing project information associated with the use case, and it is likely to be less rigorous in its description than is a fully dressed use case.

A *fully dressed use case* is written with one of the full templates, identifying actors, scope, level, trigger condition, precondition, and the rest of the template header information, plus project annotation information.

**LEVEL.** How high or low the goal is:

A *summary-level use case* is one that takes multiple user-goal sessions to complete, possibly weeks, months, or years. Its sub use cases can be any level of use case. It is marked graphically with a cloud (☁) or a kite (◇). The cloud is for use cases that contain steps at cloud or kite level. The kite is for use cases that contain user-goal steps.

A *user-goal use case* satisfies a particular and immediate goal of value to the primary actor. It is typically performed by one primary actor in one sitting of 2 to 20 minutes (less time if the primary actor is a computer), who can then proceed with other things. Steps are at the user-goal or a lower level. A user-goal use case is marked graphically with waves (〰).

A *subfunction use case* satisfies a partial goal of a user-goal use case or of another subfunction; its steps are lower-level subfunctions. It is marked graphically with a fish (🐟) or a clam (🦪). The clam signifies that the use case is at too low a level and should not be written at all.

**SCOPING.** How large or small the SuD is:

*Enterprise scope* indicates that the SuD is an organization or enterprise. The Scope section of the use case template is filled with the name of the organization, business, or enterprise. The use case is marked graphically with a building in gray (🏠) or white (🏠) depending on whether it is of the black-box or white-box type.

*System scope* indicates that the SuD is a mechanical/ hardware/ software system or application. The Scope section of the use case has the name of the system. The use case is marked graphically with a box in gray (▢) or white (▢) depending on whether the use case is of the black-box or white-box type.

*Subsystem scope* indicates that the SuD in this use case is a portion of an application, perhaps a subsystem or framework. The Scope section of the use case has the name of the subsystem. The use case is marked graphically with a threaded bolt (⬚).

**VISIBILITY.** What entities are visible in the use case:

A *black-box use case* does not mention any components inside the SuD. It is typically used in the system requirements document.

A *white-box use case* mentions the behavior of the components of the SuD in the description. It is typically used in business process modeling.

## Diagrams

**COLLABORATION DIAGRAM.** In UML, this diagram shows the same information as the sequence diagram does but in a different form. The actors are placed around the diagram, and interactions are shown as numbered arrows between actors. Time is shown only by numbering the arrows.

**SEQUENCE DIAGRAM.** In UML, this diagram shows actors across the top, owning columns of space, and interactions as arrows between columns, with time flowing down the page. It is useful for showing one scenario graphically.

**USE CASE DIAGRAM.** In UML, this diagram shows the external actors, the system boundary, the use cases as ellipses, and arrows connecting actors to ellipses or ellipses to ellipses. It is primarily useful as a context diagram and table of contents.

# Appendix D

# *Readings*

## Books Referenced in the Text

Beck, Kent. *Extreme Programming Explained*. Reading, MA: Addison-Wesley, 2000.

Cockburn, Alistair. *Surviving Object-Oriented Projects*. Reading, MA: Addison-Wesley, 1998.

Cockburn, Alistair. *Software Development as a Cooperative Game*. Boston: Addison-Wesley (due 2001).

Constantine, Larry, and Lucy Lockwood. *Software for Use*. Reading, MA: Addison-Wesley, 1999.

Fowler, Martin. *UML Distilled*. Reading, MA: Addison-Wesley, 1999.

Hammer, Michael, and James Champy. *Reengineering the Corporation, Reprint Edition*. New York: HarperBusiness, 1994.

Hohmann, Luke. *GUIs with Glue* (in preparation as of July 2000).

Robertson, Suzanne, and James Robertson. *Mastering the Requirements Process*. Reading, MA: Addison-Wesley, 1999.

Wirfs-Brock, Rebecca, Wilkerson, Brian, and Wiener, Lauren. *Designing Object-Oriented Software*. Upper Saddle River, NJ: Prentice-Hall, 1990.

## Articles Referenced in the Text

Beck, Kent, and Ward Cunningham. "A Laboratory for Object-Oriented Thinking," *ACM SIGPLAN* 24(10):1-7, 1989.

Cockburn, Alistair. "VW-Staging," at *http://members.aol.com/acockburn/papers/vwstage.htm*.

Cockburn, Alistair. "An Open Letter to Newcomers to OO," *http://members.aol.com/humansandt/papers/oonewcomers.htm*.

Cockburn, Alistair. "CRC Cards," at *http://members.aol.com/humansandt/papers/crc.htm*.

Cunningham, Ward. "CRC Cards," at *http://c2.com/cgi/wiki?CrcCards*.

Kraus, Andy, and Michael Dillon. "Use Case Blue," *Object Magazine*, SIGS Publications, May 1996.

Lilly, Susan. "How to Avoid Use Case Pitfalls," *Software Development* 8(1):40–44, 2000.

McBreen, Peter. "Test Cases from Use Cases," at *http://www.mcbreen.ab.ca/papers/TestsFromUseCases.html*.

## Useful Online Resources

The web contains a huge amount of information.  These are just a few starting points.

*http://www.usecases.org*

*http://members.aol.com/acockburn*

*http://www.foruse.com*

*http://www.pols.co.uk/usecasezone/*

# Index

# The Agile Software Development Series

**Surviving Object-Oriented Projects**
Alistair Cockburn
0201498340

**Writing Effective Use Cases**
Alistair Cockburn
0201702258

**Improving Software Organizations**
From Principles to Practice
Lars Mathiassen
Jan Pries-Heje
Ojelanki Ngwenyama
0201758202

**Agile Software Development**
Alistair Cockburn
0201699699

**Agile Software Development Ecosystems**
Jim Highsmith
0201760436

**Patterns for Effective Use Cases**
Steve Adolph
Paul Bramble
With Contributions by Alistair Cockburn and Andy Pols
0201721848

**Configuration Management Principles and Practice**
Anne Mette Jonassen Hass
0321117662

**DSDM**
Business Focused Development
Second Edition
DSDM Consortium
0321112245

**Lean Software Development**
An Agile Toolkit
Mary Poppendieck
Tom Poppendieck
0321150783

**AGILE & ITERATIVE DEVELOPMENT**
A Manager's Guide
Craig Larman
0131111558

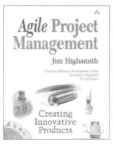
**Agile Project Management**
Jim Highsmith
Creating Innovative Products
0321219775

# Register
# Your Book

at www.awprofessional.com/register

You may be eligible to receive:

- Advance notice of forthcoming editions of the book
- Related book recommendations
- Chapter excerpts and supplements of forthcoming titles
- Information about special contests and promotions throughout the year
- Notices and reminders about author appearances, tradeshows, and online chats with special guests

## Contact us

If you are interested in writing a book or reviewing manuscripts prior to publication, please write to us at:

Editorial Department
Addison-Wesley Professional
75 Arlington Street, Suite 300
Boston, MA 02116 USA
Email: AWPro@aw.com

Visit us on the Web: http://www.awprofessional.com

## Pass/Fail Tests for Use Case Fields

*All of them should produce a "yes" answer.*

| Field | Question |
| --- | --- |
| Use Case Title | 1. Is it an active-verb goal phrase that names the goal of the primary actor? |
| | 2. Can the system deliver that goal? |
| Scope and Level | 3. Are the fields filled in? |
| Scope | 4. Does the use case treat the system mentioned in Scope as a black box? (The answer must be "Yes" if it is a system requirements document, but may be "No" if the use case is a white-box business use case.) |
| | 5. If the system in Scope is the system to be designed, do the designers have to design everything in it and nothing outside it? |
| Level | 6. Does the use case content match the stated goal level? |
| | 7. Is the goal really at the stated goal level? |
| Primary Actor | 8. Does he/she/it have behavior? |
| | 9. Does he/she/it have a goal against the SuD that is a service promise of the SuD? |
| Preconditions | 10. Are they mandatory, and can they be set in place by the SuD? |
| | 11. Is it true that they are never checked in the use case? |
| Stakeholders and Interests | 12. Are they named and must the system satisfy their interests as stated? (Usage varies by formality and tolerance.) |
| Minimal Guarantees | 13. Are all the stakeholders' interests protected? |
| Success Guarantees | 14. Are all the stakeholders' interests satisfied? |
| Main Success Scenario | 15. Does it have 3–9 steps? |
| | 16. Does it run from trigger to delivery of the success guarantee? |
| | 17. Does it permit the right variations in sequencing? |